D1616384

Artificial Life
After *Frankenstein*

Artificial Life
After *Frankenstein*

Eileen Hunt Botting

PENN

UNIVERSITY OF PENNSYLVANIA PRESS

PHILADELPHIA

Published by
University of Pennsylvania Press
Philadelphia, Pennsylvania 19104-4112
www.upenn.edu/pennpress

Printed in the United States of America
on acid-free paper
1 3 5 7 9 10 8 6 4 2

Library of Congress-Cataloging-in-Publication Control Number: 2020015359
ISBN 978-0-8122-5274-3

CONTENTS

Learning to Love the Bomb

Back in the 1980s, it was hard for us American kids to have fun. Even if you were a virgin—like a mock-tragic character in a John Hughes film—you could still catch AIDS. If you didn't "just say no" to drugs, your brain would be fried like an egg cracked into a sizzling hot pan. If you survived into your thirties and got famous, you would probably be assassinated in public like John Lennon or at least need surgery to recover from it, like President Ronald Reagan. You could never forget the threat of nuclear apocalypse, which the communists had built in the shadow of the wall that divided East and West into clear sets of enemy camps.

Without remorse, video had killed the radio star. While Sting mournfully wondered if the Russians love their children too, we teens watching him stateside knew the real, hard truth: the question barely mattered, since the USA would fight back if the USSR took the first strike, even to the point of annihilating the world. We wanted our MTV to be a New Wave antidote to doom, but our chosen medium was not immune to a catastrophic message. The original ID for the channel featured footage of the *Apollo 11* moon landing with the MTV logo optimistically superimposed on the American flag. It played on a nearly endless loop—forty-eight times per day between 1981 and 1986—until NASA's *Challenger* blew up in front of us.

Just seventy-three seconds after takeoff, this spectacular national disaster played on the television sets our teachers had wheeled into their social studies classrooms for a special display of current events. The first American teacher-astronaut, Christa McAuliffe, taught us that no one was safe from the dangers of technological hubris. MTV removed its iconic moon landing ID to protect us—its audience, whose parents paid for subscriptions—but the damage was already done. We had already developed a speculative knack for thinking in terms of worst-case scenarios.

This appetite for destruction may have been a function of the television and music videos we had watched. Before the cable hookup, my parents had a simple two-step rule for determining family-friendly television: it had to be on PBS and finish before 7:30 p.m. Their moral algorithm got me into bed on time, but certainly not to sleep, what with my time spent puzzling through the existential questions of *Doctor Who*. Time travel, reincarnation, octopi-aliens, and the mysterious attractive force of blue British police boxes filtered through my mind in a dreamlike cycle during my elementary school years in suburban Boston.

When I was about twelve, my family moved back to my dad's tiny hometown—way, way up in northern Maine. I quickly fell into a gang of girl-nerds. Perhaps because of the suffocating absence of things to do, we started to obsessively consume science fiction, fantasy, and horror in whatever forms we could find them.[1] This literary enterprise was a challenge to coordinate in our network of villages in Aroostook County, 90 miles past the nearest "Mr. Paperback" bookstore in Bangor, and without the possibility of Amazon home delivery. The Internet had just begun to be imagined in the most cutting-edge science fiction—most famously in the cyberspace of William Gibson's *Neuromancer* (1984).

Up in "The County"—a bleak frontier of forest and fields on the border with Canada—we caught only some crude cinematic glimpses of cybernetics, as in Ridley Scott's 1982 film *Blade Runner*. It starred Han Solo—I mean Harrison Ford—as a bounty hunter in the near future who falls in love with a target android. Our cool English teacher, who had just graduated from Colby, would have known it was based on Philip K. Dick's 1968 philosophical sci-fi satire *Do Androids Dream of Electric Sheep?* We had to settle for finding the disc of *Blade Runner* at the local Qwik Stop, where my parents would pay for a twenty-four-hour rental that included the massive RCA Videodisc player required to watch it. Once home, the slumber party would gather around the TV to collectively memorize the futuristic love story and dark urban aesthetic, as we replayed the disc again and again before it had to be returned.

With a sense of existential urgency only teenagers can possess, my fellow nerds and I circulated books like other kids passed around cigarettes. After school, our gang of girls would huddle behind the walls of the wheelchair ramp to read weighty novels about the end of the world. Snug in our bunker, we inhaled hand-me-down copies of the classics of our local hero Stephen King, who lived in Bangor.

King's best work, *The Stand* (1978), took three full days to read if you did almost nothing else and occasionally snuck a look at it under your desk during class. A whopping 823 pages, the epic presented a pregnant, college-aged woman from coastal Maine who survived a plague made by government scientists. After withstanding the contagion, she helps defeat the Devil himself out West, before returning to the true wilderness of New England, with her heroic lover, to live off the pure fruits of the land and repopulate the Earth. There was a real satisfaction in seeing the good guys and girls win *and* relocate happily to your home state. When you are from Maine, this does not happen much.

Sensing my need for speculative literature more complex than *The Stand*, my Cornell-educated chemistry teacher from upstate New York introduced me to ironic sci-fi in the form of the confessional satires of Kurt Vonnegut and his fictional alter ego, the failed science fiction writer, Kilgore Trout. I felt adult reading books that used alien kidnappings to mitigate the trauma of witnessing the US bombing of Dresden or pictured—in a crude cartoon—the liquid-lye Drano under the sink as the "Breakfast of Champions" for a post-war suburbia. Yet the loneliness and isolation of his characters—including the author, who always depicted himself sleepless, drinking, and writing soliloquys—made me honestly wonder: what could be missing?

The atheist Vonnegut dared to imagine God without omniscience. God was a master artificer who stepped back and laughed at the surprising free choices of his own human creations. Like Dr. Hoenikker in Vonnegut's 1963 novel *Cat's Cradle*, God lacked control over his children. If they wished, they could choose to use the raw materials of the cosmos to construct the instruments of human extinction.

Based on the Nobel Prize–winning chemist and physicist Irving Langmuir of Schenectady, Dr. Hoenikker is "one of the chief creators" of the atomic bomb.[2] He invents ice-nine for the mundane purpose of freezing muddy ground for the swift passage of military troops through the jungle. Seeing its market value in the arms race, his kids steal shards of ice-nine from his kitchen laboratory and sell them to the highest bidders, securing their own financial futures without thought to the risks. When a piece mistakenly falls into the placid waters of the Caribbean, Jonah—a new-age Ishmael—finds himself in the extreme position of being not just the last man on Earth but the last human atop a dead sea of ice.

The theme of human beings as the creative and destructive authors of their own destinies kept appearing in the books I picked up. Pushing back

into the history of American science fiction, to the twilight of the Golden
Age of pulp magazines and the dawn of the New Wave of literary fiction,
I acquired Daniel Keyes's *Flowers for Algernon*. It was first published as a
short story in the *Magazine of Fantasy & Science Fiction* in 1959, then
expanded seven years later into a novel, which won the Nebula award.
This poignant story of a man with an IQ of 68 who voluntarily subjects
himself to surgical experimentation on his brain that turns him, briefly,
into a genius made me break down and cry like a baby. I could not stop
sobbing as Charlie—this artificially enhanced intelligence—mentally de-
teriorated.

Knowing that he would soon lose long-term memory altogether, Charlie scrawls in childish prose his instructions for flowers to be placed on the
grave of his best friend, the mouse Algernon, who had died from the same
neurological experiment. The implication of this ending stuck with me:
the transformation of life through science—and, more broadly, education
itself—does not necessarily constitute improvement. Watching the idiot-
savant Charlie observe himself ascend to the heights of intellect, then
decline to the point where he had lost or virtually forgotten everyone he
had loved, was as close to a real horror story as I had ever encountered. For
a child of the Cold War, this was saying a lot.

I dug deeper into science fiction to try to find the hidden source of
its dark ideas. When my high school friends and I read George Orwell's
post–World War II novels *Animal Farm* (1945) and *Nineteen Eighty-Four*
(1948) in our small, college-track English class, I wanted more. Evading the
censorious small-town librarian, I discovered Aldous Huxley's *Brave New
World* (1932) and Mary Shelley's *Frankenstein* (1818) in the forbidden adult
section of the stacks. The opening pages of Huxley's reproductive dystopia
reminded me dimly of my Catholic parents discussing the first "test-tube"
babies over dinner. Back then, I had silently worried that the babies would
grow too big for the glass tubes. Huxley's bottled fetuses and decanted
children seemed just as preposterous.

Frankenstein, by contrast, affected me much as *Flowers for Algernon* had:
I responded not with skepticism but with pathos. I found Victor Frankenstein's Creature eerily familiar due to the tragicomic—bulky and bolted,
flat-topped and green-tinted—versions of him that I had encountered in
the syndicated midcentury Universal and Hammer monster movies, plus
the Addams Family cartoon series of the 1970s. Although made by a scientist in an extraordinary way, the Creature did not seem unnatural to me.

He resonated more with the geeks and goonies of my favorite adolescent angst films of the 1980s.

The parallels with reality did not escape me. When we were seniors, my high school class of fifty officially voted me "most likely to succeed." At the same time, the scribbled results of a secret poll—passed furtively around school on a crumpled piece of paper—ranked me first on the list of those "most likely to be a virgin." Funny: I heard echoes of my growing desolation in the urgency of the abandoned Creature's voice. "I had never yet seen a being resembling me," he cried, "or who claimed any intercourse with me. What was I?"[3] He may have been an eight-foot monster and I a five-foot-five Mainer, but a strange kinship between us was, undeniably, already there.

Alienated by competition over grades, my studious friends and I had ceased to share books anymore. Rather, we hoarded them as special knowledge for our own private browsing. The summer before senior year, on an extended trip to the University of Maine campus at Orono for the Girls State summer civics course, I drifted away from my classmates with a delegate from another school. Though she was basically a stranger, we instantly bonded: it was so obvious that we were both outsiders. She told me about a computer science lab where we could exchange electronic messages with people at a university in Canada. Without really knowing what we were doing, we created email avatars of ourselves over a direct link to the BITNET network at Yale University and onto the University of Toronto over the Canadian network NETNORTH.[4] Entering the matrix of the nascent Internet, we spent hours chatting virtually with a male graduate student. Thrilled by the illusion of intimacy generated by the shield of digital anonymity, we stopped only when he seemed to be making awkward propositions for us to meet up. The girl and I didn't stay in touch either—ashamed, a bit, by our flirtation with finding an alternate reality.

Soon I left them all behind for my own little utopia. Bowdoin College was just a few hours south of "The County," but it seemed lightyears away to me. During late-night study breaks there, I sat on institutional furniture and stared at the television installed in the common space of the nineteenth-century residence hall. A competitive runner, I dutifully peeled cheese off the warm Domino's pizza delivery, thinking to myself, *Too many calories.* In the silent company of my peers, I observed the Berlin Wall come down and the US bombing of Iraq start up on dorm TVs. Satellites directly transmitted live images of missile-driven destruction into our lounge. CNN newscasters informed us that we were the first generation to see world politics play out like a video game. *But where was the joystick?* I silently wondered. There was no remote control for Gen X to operate the system. A bit numb, I sat and watched the screen, chewing my slice of carbo-heaven.

Political science fiction had become hyperreal.[5]

Mary Shelley and the Genesis of Political Science Fictions

What are the obligations of humanity to the artificial creatures we make? And what are the corresponding rights of those creatures, whether they are learning machines or genetically modified organisms? To respond to these vital questions for our age of genetic engineering and artificial intelligence (AI), we need to delve into the capacious mind and imaginative genius of Mary Wollstonecraft Shelley (1797–1851). Her novels *Frankenstein; or, The Modern Prometheus* (1818) and *The Last Man* (1826) precipitated a modern political strain of science fiction concerned with the ethics of making artificial life and life artificial through science, technology, and other cultural change. By putting Shelley and some classics of modern political science fiction into dialogue with contemporary political science and philosophy, this book explodes three apocalyptic fears at the fore of twenty-first-century political thought on AI and genetic engineering. These are the prevailing myths that artificial forms of life will (1) end the world, (2) destroy nature, or (3) extinguish love.

i. A Threshold for Modern Political Science Fiction

Shelley unleashed a new, or modern, political strain of science fiction with her novels *Frankenstein* and *The Last Man*. "She picked up the novel-as-it-was," the American feminist science fiction writer and critic Joanna Russ argued, "thought 'I can't use this,' and created a new field."[1] This new field, I contend, was *modern political science fiction*. It consists of literary and other artistic works of the imagination with a distinctively futuristic and political orientation. Its stories and allegories draw on facts gleaned through science and history to construct powerful counterfactual narrative premises. By deducing the consequences of these premises, it fabricates alternate political realities. These visionary worlds are foils to the reader's experience of being human in relation to others, including nonhumans. They also predict, sometimes more successfully than the social sciences, the outcomes of real-world cultural and political experiments.

Modern political science fiction speculates with uncanny precision about the consequences of using technology—not solely science but rather any form of artifice—to create, alter, or transform humanity and its experience of the world. It is fiction that often feels all too real for its insights into what is wrong with communities, environments, and other systems and networks of life and intelligence, both as they are known and as they could be made. At the turn of the twenty-first century, the American science fiction writer and editor Frederik Pohl went so far as to say, "Perhaps . . . there is no good science fiction at all, that is not to some degree political."[2] If so, then Shelley's *Frankenstein* and *The Last Man* are a threshold after which modern *political* science fiction takes off in new and philosophically complex directions.[3] This is not to suggest that the best *poliscifi* is necessarily literary fiction modeled after the accepted forms of the English canon. It is rather to submit that most if not all poliscifi—however classified—is valued highly across cultures precisely because it is *political* in its themes.

The narrative premises of Shelley's two most influential novels have seeded the plots of almost every classic of political science fiction since. *Frankenstein* invites readers to speculate the consequences of using science to make a living creature without a family or other community to support it. *The Last Man* presents the history of the ostensibly sole human survivor of a global plague in the year 2100 and how he deals with the prospect of the annihilation of his species. As Russ wrote in a 1975 essay commissioned by the American science fiction editor David G. Hartwell, "Yet, despite the flaws of *Frankenstein* and *The Last Man*, Shelley seized on the two great myths of the industrial age. . . . Every robot, every android, every sentient computer . . . every non-biological person, down to the minuscule, artificially created society in Stanislaw Lem's *Cyberiad* . . . is descended of that 'mighty figure' Shelley dreamed one rainy night in the summer of 1816."[4] Although Russ declined to firmly categorize *The Last Man* as science fiction, since natural science was not an engine of its plot, she concluded that "every novel in which humanity is done in by pollution, plague, overpopulation, alien invasion, or World War II echoes Mary Shelley's creation."[5]

My approach to the question of Shelley's intellectual relationship to later science fiction diverges from Russ and other science fiction criticism on two main fronts. First, *The Last Man* is in fact a major template for modern *political* science fiction because of its social scientific approach to conceptualizing the disaster of the plague as manmade, not purely natural or supernatural, since it arises in the technology-driven destruction of a centuries-long war. *Frankenstein*—as a story of artificially made disaster escalated through both natural science and technology—is the most vital template for this *politically scientific* tradition, including *The Last Man*.

Second, I isolate and philosophically engage three political themes of modern science fiction that resonate profoundly with *Frankenstein* and *The Last Man*. Each of these thematic strands of modern poliscifi tease out the ethical and political implications of humanity's artificial interventions in the course of life and its formation. *Apocalyptic literature* dwells upon the possibility that the failures or lacks of human artifice could cause the end of humanity or the world itself.[6] *Hacker literature* speculates the destruction or reconstruction of nature through artificial intervention in life, autonomy, or intelligence. *Loveless literature* envisions the loss or transfiguration of affect through the application of technology to the making of people and other beings, things, or systems.

Much like Shelley's labyrinthine corpus of writing—which ranges across journals and letters, literary manuscripts, novels, short stories, histories and biographies, poetry, and edited volumes—the artworks of modern political science fiction defy simple categorization. They boldly transgress labels of high and low culture: just as Shelley counted herself "a part of the elect" of English Romantic writers, even while nineteenth-century tabloids scandalized her literary circle as "the League of Incest."[7] With an interdisciplinary nod to its roots in Romanticism, modern political science fiction has taken a range of forms: novels, novellas, short stories, plays, poetry, films, comics, manga, television, performance art, hypertext, puppetry, animation, collage, and multimedia productions, to name merely a few.[8] Extending the ideas of literary historian Arthur B. Evans, we can see political science fiction grown from Shelley as a subgenre of science fiction and "part of a complex network of literary intertextuality, social contexts, and cultural production that stretches back at least to the birth of modern science in the seventeenth century."[9]

The magnitude of *Frankenstein*'s impact in theater, film, literature, and other art is so vast as to be immeasurable. Only to a slightly lesser degree, *The Last Man* has influenced literary, cinematic, and televisual depictions of the end of humanity or the world. For these lasting impressions, Shelley has won almost universal recognition as a leading—if not *the*—mother of science fiction (SF). In 1973, the English science fiction writer and critic Brian Aldiss, OBE, contended that she was no less than "the origin of the species" of SF.[10] In 2000, another leading British scholar and author of science fiction, Adam Roberts, acknowledged *Frankenstein* as "influential" and "important" for "the development of SF" even as he joined Russ and others in dismissing it as "amateurishly constructed and gushingly written."[11]

As a feminist political philosopher approaching Shelley and SF from the seemingly oblique angle of political science, I land somewhere between these warring scholarly perspectives in the worlds of British and American science fiction.[12] Shelley cannot be the genesis of all SF—a genre cosmic in scope, reaching back to ancient mythology and religion and extending to the futuristic exploration of outer space. But she *became* the defining figure of modern political science fiction by reworking its ancient sources, such as the stories of Adam, Eve, Noah, and Prometheus, into two of the most enduring myths or "scripts" of modern life.[13] "Frankenstein"—as a word and a set of images—has evolved into a viral "meme" that signifies the power of scientific or political progress to backfire on its own innovators.[14] Similarly, the concept of "The Last Man" has come to widely represent the central problem of the Anthropocene, or the global crisis in manmade environmental change: will humanity cause its own extinction?

I situate Shelley at the fore of a modern and political strain of SF because of the many-sided concepts of apocalypse, the unnatural, and love at play in *Frankenstein* and *The Last Man*. She should be universally acclaimed as the creative force behind modern political science fiction due to the cross-cutting afterlives of these three concepts in later artworks. More than anyone, Shelley has inspired a legion of writers and other artists to philosophically engage the ethics and politics of making artificial life and life artificial. She modeled how to break down and transform the meanings of apocalypse, nature, and love in the face of widespread and deep-seated fear about the power of technology or artifice to undermine the possibility of humanity, community, or life itself. Her explorations of these themes, along with those of her heirs, have paved the way for a technopolitical philosophy of living with the artifice of humanity in all of its complexity.[15]

Since the late 1990s, the terms "political science fiction" and "political science fictions" have been used to frame the interpretation of SF from various political perspectives, including insights drawn from political science.[16] Literary scholar Donald Hassler and political scientist Clyde Wilcox edited an interdisciplinary collection of essays in this vein. Efficiently titled *Political Science Fiction* (1997), the volume drew out the political content and implications of a range of science fictions from H. G. Wells to *Star Trek*.[17] Wilcox argued, "Science fiction allows political scientists to expand their thinking" by inspiring "thought experiments" that "can stretch the imagination and help us rethink our theories, categories, and hopes."[18]

Responding to Wilcox's challenge, I show how political science and political philosophy might learn to "expand their thinking" on the politics of making artificial life and life artificial by engaging the three prevailing strands of SF born of Shelley. In particular, political science and philosophy might benefit from the unsettling "encounter with difference" presented by the political science fictions she sparked.[19] Ultimately, the narrative premises of Shelley's two greatest novels not only animate the politics of science fiction but also resonate with the conceptualization and criticism of apocalypse, nature, and love in contemporary political science and philosophy.[20] As Wilcox and Hassler maintained in their sequel volume, *New Boundaries of Political Science Fiction* (2008), "The most interesting political thought is what goes 'beyond,' stretching the limits of practical and historical politics in what can be thought about or speculated about in fictions."[21] Reading Shelley's work and SF legacies alongside contemporary political thought enables this creative push "beyond" the historical and philosophical "boundaries" of both politics and political science, especially on pressing questions concerning the making of artificial life and intelligence.

ii. Defining Political Science Fiction

The genre of SF is too big and unwieldy to be reduced to a single stardate. Ancient sacred texts such as the Bible's בְּרֵאשִׁית (beginning or Genesis) and Lucian's second-century epic Ἀληθῆ διηγήματα (*A True Story*) have been plausibly described as forms of SF due to their respective cosmic representations of world building and outer space exploration.[22] Most scholars of science fiction, however, do not push that far back into history to find the roots of the tradition. They instead search the archives of early modernity,

from René Descartes and Francis Bacon to Saint Thomas More and Margaret Cavendish, for more proximate sources amid the rise of a mechanistic
and materialistic Western social imaginary and the utopian literatures it
generated.[23] Like those who follow Aldiss in giving *Frankenstein* special stat-
ure in the development of modern SF, they still find themselves vulnerable
to the charge of anachronism. The term "science fiction" was not widely
used until the 1920s, when the Luxembourgish American editor of the pulp
magazine *Amazing Stories*, Hugo Gernsback, claimed to have coined and
popularized it.[24]

Gary K. Wolfe, the American editor of *Science Fiction Studies*, made a
provocation to the leaders in his field in 2009: should they affix the term
"proto/early" to Shelley and other writers of SF prior to the so-called golden
age of the pulp magazines during the 1940s?[25] After all, weren't the pulps
what had institutionalized the genre through their commercial success and
subsequent critical attention? A roundtable of fourteen scholars responded
to his prompt. Most included pre–"golden age" SF in the genre. Several
(including Aldiss) still wished to give Shelley pride of place. Yet none found
broad agreement on how to define SF and its origins. Jane Donawerth best
articulated a limited consensus: the two novels that "most people recognize
as the beginnings of science fiction"—*Frankenstein* and *The Last Man*—
grew out of the utopian/dystopian literary traditions of the early modern
period.[26] Almost a decade later, Evans began the opening chapter of Roger
Luckhurst's *Science Fiction: A Literary History* (2017) with the disclaimer,
"In much the same way that there exists no single, agreed-upon definition
of SF, there can be no single, agreed-upon history of SF."[27]

Although the definition and history of SF are both contested, critics have
laid out a number of helpful premises for conceptualizing the evolution of
political science fictions after *Frankenstein*. Following the esteemed Croatian
science fiction editor and theorist Darko Suvin, Roberts argued that SF stories
center around a "novum" or "new thing."[28] Suvin's "novum" is an innovative
plot point that uses a "strange" form of artifice, invention, or discovery—like
a time machine, a flying car, or travel faster than light—to generate a new
way of seeing the world and humanity's relationship to it.[29] The most rigorous science fiction deploys the novum in a "cognitive" and counterfactual
sense: to reason through the probable consequences of the novum, as if it
were actually a feature of the "empirical" world.[30]

For Suvin, the purpose of the novum is to engender "cognitive estrangement" from empirical reality in order to provoke rigorous analysis of this

estranged perspective.[31] SF achieves this strange, yet still rational, point of view on several interconnected levels: (1) the novum's roots in the real world make it uncannily familiar while eliciting wonder, awe, and ultimately doubt, and (2) this doubt propels the rational deduction of the consequences of the novum's introduction into the empirical world or some parallel reality, both (a) in the structure of the artwork and (b) in the mind of the reader or viewer. In 1972, Suvin arrived at a formal definition of SF that swept through space and time like the starship *Enterprise* of the late sixties: SF is "a literary genre whose necessary and sufficient conditions are the presence and interaction of estrangement and cognition, and whose main formal device is an imaginative framework alternative to the author's empirical environment."[32] By using Suvin's definition of SF as a frame, we can see how Shelley's twin masterworks of speculative fiction furnish the materials for a formal definition of political science fiction understood as a principal modern strain of SF.

First, her novels evolve from political, not supernatural, nova. Frankenstein's artifice of a "human being" comes about through science rather than magic, and *The Last Man*'s global plague is deadlier than the war from which it arose due to the failure of human beings to contain it.[33] Unlike fantasy and horror, which often allude to the magical or supernatural, modern political science fiction typically takes at least an agnostic—if not wholly secular—stance toward divine or transcendent forces.[34] While it does not necessarily deny the possibility of such supernatural entities or veer from their study, it opens up philosophical exploration of alternative, empirically or materially grounded explanations for how the world was made and how it operates. Most definitively, the primary engines for its plots are science and technology, not magic or the supernatural.

Second, Shelley's twin speculative fictions do not use political nova for merely "marvellous" ends, such as eliciting fear or wonder, like the Gothic romances of her time.[35] Even as they do command the fascination and awe of their audiences, *Frankenstein* and *The Last Man* use their nova for something more significant: to engender what Roberts called a deeper cognitive "encounter with difference."[36] For Roberts, the "central character" of *Frankenstein*—the Creature made through science—is "an embodiment of alterity."[37] By hearing the Creature's story of abuse and neglect as a result of his abandonment by Victor Frankenstein, the reader confronts the world from the estranged perspective of an utterly new kind of creation: a parentless child made by an uncaring scientist through biotechnology. *The Last*

Man, too, disrupts the reader's worldview by leaving its narrator, Lionel Verney, alone in Rome after a global pandemic. Verney's extreme predicament makes a reader think about the obligations of such a solitary individual to himself, humankind, other creatures, and the Earth in the face of the potential extinction of his species.

Third, Shelley's novels—like the political science fictions they informed—occupy an imaginative space between a historical and a futuristic standpoint. *Frankenstein* and *The Last Man* drew from the literary conventions of Gothic literature, as well as the apocalyptic and perfectionistic strands of Enlightenment and Romantic politics and political thought, in order to explore the possibilities of making and remaking the communities and other worlds in which we live. Rooted in the past, her novels are oriented toward the future. *Frankenstein* merges 1790s politics with biotechnology not yet achieved in the twenty-first century, while *The Last Man* presents the reconstructed ancient prophecy of the near annihilation of humanity in the year 2100. This orientation allows the novels to carry insights from the past, drawn from history and science, into fresh and arresting futures.

By deploying their nova in rigorously political, cognitive, and futuristic modes, Shelley's *Frankenstein* and *The Last Man* exploded into literary supernova. While all modern political science fiction has philosophical and literary roots in Shelley's dark and paradoxical hypotheses, some of it explicitly builds on her work. "Frankenstein" stories are now a freestanding subcategory of political SF that explores how unchecked ambition can rebound to ruin its artificers. In *Black Frankenstein* (2008), Elizabeth Young cited political scientist Chalmers Johnson's book *Blowback: The Costs and Consequences of American Empire* (2000) as a source for her landmark study of this "boomerang" dynamic in the history of racial injustice in the United States.[38] By tracing the African American reception of the image of the enslaved monster who comes back to bite the hand of its imperious master, she demonstrated *Frankenstein*'s salience for the black community's ongoing quest for racial justice. As a corollary to monstrous tales of "blowback," "Last Man" narratives represent the idea of species extinction as an existential occasion for humankind to reflect upon its own value (and values). Separately and combined, Shelley's twin nova generated three major themes of modern political science fiction: (1) the contemplation of the end of the world, (2) the apprehension of the destruction of nature, and (3) the prospect of the loss of love and community. Political science fiction projects its analysis of these themes into the future in order to underscore the vast power of human artifice to change the world, for better and for worse.

Taken as a leading modern subgenre of SF, political science fiction is fundamentally unstable. It is prone to unexpected explosions of assumptions, prejudices, and conventional wisdom concerning artifice, creativity, technological invention, and scientific discovery. It is not a conservative field built upon the staid replication of the established attributes of a canonical literary tradition.[39] Instead, it is a forward-looking and generative strain of a dominant literary genre. It resists stifling definitions of its scope and purpose, even as it recycles the past and relentlessly returns to assess the political value—positive and negative—of human change of its own condition.

iii. Situating Shelley in Political Science and Science Fiction

Thomas Kuhn perceived that even the so-called hard sciences—like his own field of physics—are manmade products of a "matrix" of beliefs, practices, and institutions that scientists build up and pass down through their communities of learning.[40] He developed a political theory of science that situated all ways of knowing and relating to the world within broader social and political networks. Kuhn grasped that scientific revolutions are in fact political revolutions. By overthrowing an orthodox worldview, they cause a "paradigm shift" in how a whole community, united in a common enterprise, interprets and interacts with the world.[41]

It is time for such a paradigm shift in how Shelley is seen, both in literary criticism of science fiction and in the history of political science. She was the daughter of two of the most prominent, and radical, political philosophers of the 1790s: the Anglo-Irish feminist Mary Wollstonecraft and the English anarchist William Godwin. Raised by her father to debate the political ideas of her parents, as well as Englishman John Locke and Genevan Jean-Jacques Rousseau, Shelley grew up saturated in Enlightenment-era political philosophy and literature.[42] Like her parents, she was also a careful reader of the Irish statesman Edmund Burke. From Burke's writings, she grasped the modern aesthetics of sublimity and monstrosity that arose in the aftermath of the politics of the French Revolution.[43]

The English Romantic poets responded to the "apocalyptic" and "millennial" politics of the revolutionary and Napoleonic eras with wild speculation of political futures, both dystopian and utopian.[44] This engagement occurred in the first generation of William Blake, William Wordsworth, and Samuel Taylor Coleridge, followed by the second generation of Lord Byron, Percy Shelley, and John Keats. Mary Shelley had firsthand or secondhand connections to them all. Wollstonecraft wrote children's books illustrated by Blake, who worked for the same radical publishing house in London. Godwin invited Coleridge to recite his "Rime of the Ancient Mariner" (1798) before Mary and her young siblings in their family home.[45] She and her lover, creative partner, and later husband Percy avidly read Wordsworth's work but rejected it for forsaking its radical political past and potential.[46] She and Percy visited with Byron in Geneva during the summer she composed the novella that grew into *Frankenstein*. They became acquainted with Keats before he succumbed to tuberculosis. Percy and Byron followed Keats to early graves, leaving Shelley "the last woman" of the second generation of English Romanticism.[47] She interpolated *Frankenstein*, *The Last Man*, and her other writings with snippets of Romantic verses and political ideas. In this interdisciplinary mode, she paved the way for a poetically inspired yet historically rooted approach to writing futuristic fiction with a political bent.

Through her intensive study of ancient Greek during the 1810s and 1820s, Shelley knew that τέχνη (techne) meant art or craft. From Prometheus to Plato, techne applied as much to the writing of poetry as to the implements of scientific discovery or engineering. It is with this ancient understanding of technology as art that Shelley approached the study of natural science through a wide political lens. What her political imagination helps us to see—here and now in the twenty-first century—is that computer technology and biotechnology are *not essentially different* from any other form of techne, including the countless ways in which we shape ourselves, each other, other life forms, and our environment through everyday social and cultural practices.

In her story of Victor Frankenstein's assembly and animation of "the creature," Shelley referenced recent advances in the sciences of evolution, chemistry, and electricity, as well as cutting-edge medical practices such as dissection, transplantation, anatomical preservation, galvanism, and blood transfusion.[48] While she had done painstaking research on the life sciences of her time, she kept her allusions to them vague. She thereby trained the reader's eye on the ethical and political consequences of Victor's intervention in the making of life, not the physical means he used to make the Creature. *The Last Man* goes still further by neither specifying the biological cause nor clarifying the mode of transmission (airborne or person-to-person) for its global plague.[49]

In *The Last Man*, Shelley set aside natural science in favor of a social scientific explanation of the plague's origin and circulation. It gains traction in Constantinople, in the context of a centuries-long war between Greece and Turkey. Literary scholar Andrea Haslanger pointed out that "its spread is the consequence of particular economic and political conjunctures," including the history of Western colonization of African and Eastern cultures.[50] Shelley suggested that manmade political inequalities and conflicts lie at the root of pandemics, or epidemic diseases that disperse across wide regions or international borders, threatening to wipe out large parts of or entire populations. She thus anticipated the current political theory of pandemics, summed up by Finnish political scientist Mika Aaltola: "It seems that the biological nature of disease does not exist in a vacuum. . . . The pattern of disease spread abides by specific global power contours."[51]

Shelley's first and greatest novel had materialized from the crossfertilization of political science with political fiction during the long eighteenth century. In particular, *Frankenstein* critically engaged the political and educational theories of Locke and Rousseau, as well as those of two of their most devoted readers: Shelley's parents, Wollstonecraft and Godwin. As self-described political scientists of the postrevolutionary era, Godwin and Wollstonecraft embraced reason, philosophy, and education as tools for the visionary design of just and peaceful political communities for people in the future.

In his treatise *Political Justice* (1793), Godwin had defined "political science" against the pessimistic and deterministic Hobbesian thesis that might makes right.[52] Politics was rather the deliberate and rational science of thinking through how to design institutions to be just with respect to every citizen. Both Locke and Rousseau were major inspirations for Godwin's theory of justice, which was an ideal design of an ultra-minimal state through which individuals might thrive in virtuous independence amid small, localized communities.

Wollstonecraft too endorsed a forward-looking, rational, and virtue-producing conception of political science. In the opening chapter of her book *An Historical and Moral View of the Origins and Progress of the French Revolution* (1794), she lamented, "At no period has the scanty diffusion of knowledge permitted the body of the people to participate in the discussion of political science."[53] She envisioned that "philosophy" could simplify "the principles of social union, so as to render them easy to be comprehended by every sane and thinking being."[54] If people learned the principles of political science through such a simple and rational philosophy, Wollstonecraft predicted that "man may contemplate with benevolent complacency and becoming pride, the approaching reign of reason and peace."[55]

In 1814–15, the first year of her elopement with Percy, Shelley also poured over Rousseau, Godwin, and Wollstonecraft's literary works—including their political novels *Emile, or On Education* (1762), *Things as They Are; or, the Adventures of Caleb Williams* (1794), and *Maria: or, the Wrongs of Woman* (1798).[56] Given the speculative bent of their political science and political fiction, as well as Shelley's intensive reading of them, it is not surprising that Rousseau, Godwin, and Wollstonecraft shaped key elements of political science fiction grown from her work. Among them, Rousseau's *Emile* may have been the most important source for the counterfactual form of Shelley's *Frankenstein* and *The Last Man*.[57]

Rousseau's wildly popular *Emile* proposes an almost preposterous educational scenario. It tests the limits of what Coleridge would dub, in 1817, the reader's "willing suspension of disbelief" in the face of supernatural or other reveries far afield from ordinary experience.[58] Rousseau's alter ego, a benevolent yet controlling tutor, raises the orphan infant Emile in provincial France. Living apart from the corrosive influence of eighteenth-century cities and civilization, Emile has almost no social interaction with anyone other than his tutor—including through books—until he is a teenager. The point of Rousseau's thought experiment in educational isolation, or "negative education," is to test the hypothesis that a poor system of education causes the vices of modern civilization.[59]

Wollstonecraft and Godwin followed the deliberately unrealistic yet historically situated format of *Emile* in their novels of the 1790s. They imagined alternate political realities in which disenfranchised and disempowered people such as Caleb and Maria nevertheless find ways to struggle against the injustices of the eighteenth-century British legal system. As a compulsive reader of the novels of Rousseau, Godwin, and Wollstonecraft, the young Shelley developed a talent for dreaming up counterfactual scenarios with serious political implications. *The Last Man* surpasses even *Frankenstein* with its political ambitions. Romanticist Anne K. Mellor argued that Shelley practically invented the "apocalyptic novel" to critique the political ideologies of the Enlightenment and Romantic eras, including the utopian liberal and republican ideas of her own parents and husband.[60] Set in the year 2100 *after* a global plague, *The Last Man* should also be understood as the first "post-apocalyptic novel" due to the attitude of hope and love for the world that its hero adopts in the face of the possibility of being the last human on Earth.[61]

Like their intellectual parentage, *Frankenstein* and *The Last Man* crossed literary borders in generating a modern political strain of SF. They took the settings and themes of the Gothic novel, epic poems, and historical romances to refurbish them as structural elements of nineteenth-century political science fiction. Dark caves and haunted castles, as found in Wollstonecraft's *Original Stories from Real Life* (1788) and Ann Radcliffe's *Mysteries of Udolpho* (1794), made way for the isolated laboratory of Victor Frankenstein and his successors.[62] Encounters with ghosts in great homes, as in Horace Walpole's *Castle of Otranto* (1767), led to the scientist pursued by a "spectre" of his own creation.[63] With fantastical sagas such as Sir Walter Scott's *Waverly* novels in mind, Shelley mapped out a new form of epic political drama.

Jean-Baptiste Cousin de Grainville's 1805 epic prose poem *Le Dernier Homme* (*The Last Man*) likely shaped Shelley's eponymous novel's futuristic reworking of biblical ideas of the fall of humanity and apocalypse. Both authors used the novum of the flying machine—Grainville's "globes aériens" (air globes) and Shelley's hot-air balloons—to locate their stories of apocalypse in ages of exploration and technological problem solving.[64] Despite the imaginative parallels between Grainville's and Shelley's treatments of the idea of the "Last Man," there was an epic poet behind both of them: John Milton. *Le Dernier Homme, Frankenstein,* and *The Last Man* each built on the imaginative framework of *Paradise Lost* (1667), in which the struggle between good and evil, angel and devil, and creator and creation plays out on a cosmic scale.[65] Grainville retained the elements of Milton's theological script, including a God who punishes mankind by putting an end to the Earth-as-paradise. With its overtly magical and supernatural framework, *Le Dernier Homme* was less a science fiction than a theological fantasy.[66]

By contrast, Shelley ripped the orthodox religious valence from *Paradise Lost*, casting its archetypal characters of Adam, Eve, and Satan—and their falls from grace—in political and scientific terms. Victor Frankenstein assumes godlike powers through science, only to turn his new man into a monster through neglect, abuse, and persecution. It has been long acknowledged that *The Last Man* is a *roman à clef*, in which its narrator, Lionel

Verney, is a literary analogue for Shelley herself.[67] S/he represents a gender synthesis of Adam and Eve, who moves from a pastoral life as a shepherd to membership in a political elite to the possibility that war, plague, and poor leadership have rid the planet of all but one wo/man. Instead of reconciling the ways of God to man, Shelley's political science fictions strive to reconcile the ways of humanity to itself and to the wider mysteries of the universe. By filtering Genesis through Milton, Shelley crafted two modern myths about humanity's future that dwell on the existential question of whether anyone—man, woman, or other creature of artifice—can ever correct for past mistakes.

Modern political science fiction, both utopian and dystopian, has continued this Enlightenment- and Romantic-era tradition: it conjures nearly unbelievable yet eerily familiar and emotionally compelling narratives in order to examine the defects of the present through the lens of an alternate reality. The renowned editor and unabashed SF fan Hartwell put it succinctly: "science fiction is criticism of reality."[68] The fact that Hartwell published these words in 1984—the year George Orwell postdated his dystopian totalitarian state—made them all the more apt. For if we take reality as we know it to be constructed by the political thought and practices of communities of people, then science fiction is political criticism.

"Political criticism," according to political theorist Ian Shapiro, is "pragmatic."[69] In the best case, it is interdisciplinary, empirically grounded, and principled engagement with the world we have made. In this vein, political science fictions fabricate alternate realities with a critical bite. These stories function as conceptual foils to the reader's past and present experience of humanity, or being human in relation to others, including nonhumans.

But just what is this political world that we humans seek to critique through forward-looking fiction? Philosopher Eugene Thacker's *In the Dust of this Planet* (2010) sees the world from three levels of human, or anthropocentric, perspective: (1) the "world-for-us," (2) the "world-in-itself," and (3) the "world-without-us."[70] The world-for-us, in post-Kantian philosophy, is the world that we take to have made and processed through our minds: it is the world as we appear to know it. The world-in-itself, in Kantian terms, is the world that we presume lies beyond our mental processing of it. The world-in-itself, in scientific terms, is the world that we assume corresponds to our empirical study or mathematical modeling of it. Finally, the world-without-us is the world we project, after climate change, species extinction, or other technological disasters of the Anthropocene, to exist without humankind. The world-without-us is the specter of the "planet" we call Earth, without humans inhabiting or interpreting it.[71]

Referencing medieval demonology, Dr. Faustus, and Lovecraft, Thacker ingeniously uses the horror genre as a philosophical catalyst for analyzing the fears aroused by the idea of the world-without-us. He might have added a fourth—less pessimistic, more futuristic—perspective on "the world" if he had focused on science fiction understood as a form of political criticism. This fourth view of the world is a counterfactual and conditional, skeptical yet realistic political perspective derived from political science fiction: the *world-as-it-could-be.*

Political science fiction born of Shelley begins from the premise of the human fabrication of the world as we know it. It delineates how we suppose the world is, how we imagine it without us, and how we reconcile ourselves to its past, present, and future. It puzzles a way through the moral and political problems posed by the interventions of humanity in the worlds we build. It explores the broader consequences of its counterfactual premises with an almost relentless rigor. Like a computer simulation, it runs an analysis of its own ethical implications. Modern political science fiction ultimately presses us to apply the insights drawn from its thought experiments to critique the deficiencies of the manmade world.

iv. Three Themes of Modern Political Science Fiction: Apocalypse, Nature, Lovelessness

Modern political science fiction tends to blend—implicitly or explicitly— the main narrative elements and themes arising from Shelley's *Frankenstein* and *The Last Man.* The threat of apocalypse looms large across its field of imagination. This is in part due to Shelley's own philosophical tendency toward what the political scientist Alison McQueen has identified as "realist . . . apocalyptic thinking."[72] In this skeptically philosophical mode, political theorists such as Saint Augustine, Niccolò Machiavelli, Thomas Hobbes, and Hans Morgenthau have contemplated, resisted, and critically redeployed the notion of the end of the world in the context of actual and anticipated wars and other devastating conflicts, including imperialism, civil war, and nuclear holocaust.[73] I read Shelley, as well as a number of the

superlative writers of political science fiction after her, as joining this stoical, rational, and politically grounded vein of apocalyptic thought through
their subversive depictions of total catastrophe. As with McQueen's cast of
realist political theorists, these literary writers model ways of staring the
horror of total annihilation in the face. They do this not to fall into the
abyss but rather to study the chasm from a safe distance and ultimately to
resist the notion of the inevitability of the fall.

Aldiss perceived that "the thinking behind *Frankenstein* grows like a
cancer" into the global "gloom" of *The Last Man*, so that "revulsions that
once were applied merely to a freakish monster now infest the whole
human race."[74] Despite being full of dread, Shelley's twin visions of
apocalypse—one localized, the other globalized—root a modern literary
tradition that recasts the specter of the end of the world as a new, albeit
terrifying, beginning. Shelley's apocalypses are never final: they figure more
as a projection of the fears of flawed human protagonists than as a necessary
outcome of reason, creativity, inquiry, or exploration.

This double-edged analysis of the human obsession with self-
destruction runs through some of the landmarks of modern political science fiction: Karel Čapek's play *R.U.R. (Rossum's Universal Robots)* that
debuted in Prague in 1921; Philip K. Dick's novel *Do Androids Dream of
Electric Sheep?* (1968) and its 1982 cinematic version *Blade Runner*, directed
by Ridley Scott; Bruce Sterling's short story "Swarm" (1982); Lilly and Lana
Wachowski's film *The Matrix* (1999), based partly on William Gibson's
cyberpunk novel *Neuromancer* (1984); and Louisa Hall's novel on Alan
Turing and the emergence of artificial general intelligence, *Speak* (2015).
The ambiguities of Shelley's apocalyptic visions were reborn in hybrid form
in the subversive ending of Margaret Atwood's dystopian novel *Oryx and
Crake* (2003), wherein it is not clear if the last protagonist standing, the
Snowman, will die of infection by a bioengineered virus that has escalated
into a worldwide pandemic. This novel and its sequels in the *MaddAddam*
trilogy (2003–13) respond to both *Frankenstein* and *The Last Man* by blending their signature plot points—bioengineered life and global plague—into
an epic tale that resists reduction to a simple warning about impending
manmade doom.

It has become fashionable in contemporary political and legal theory to
herald the "end of" humanity, the world, nature, sex, love, family, community, morality, or political systems in the wake of the making of artificial
life and intelligence.[75] Classics of modern political science fiction provide a

philosophical counterweight to such neat and sometimes even self-serving conclusions. They instead use the ancient Greek literary technique of ἀπορία (aporia)—or the blurry punctuation of a narrative with an indefinite terminus—to raise doubts, questions, and wonder in the mind of the reader.

Shelley modeled this aporetic approach to political science fiction in *Frankenstein* and *The Last Man*. The Creature pledges to immolate himself out of guilt for his crimes but drifts into the Arctic on an ice raft, "lost in darkness and distance."[76] In this final sentence of the novel, Shelley poetically refrained from using the definite article *the* to precisely locate the Creature in the inchoate "darkness and distance" of the undiscovered North Pole. In the final pages of *The Last Man*, Verney vows to travel the world to find a "companion" among other survivors of the global plague, whom he speculates must exist in "some to me unknown and unattainable seclusion."[77] Shelley's repetition of negative prefixes ("unknown and unattainable") makes the mapping of these survivors seem impossible. And yet, the epistemic location of that uncertainty ("to me") situates Verney as open to other beings and things—perhaps his dog and books—helping him along the way to rediscovery of other people.[78] The openness of both endings is perhaps why Shelley's twin political science fictions have been cyclically remade in literature, film, and television: they almost beg for sequels.

As the original biohacker who selfishly appropriates the secrets of nature, Victor Frankenstein has generated a series of "doppelgängers," or evil twins: the mad scientists, bad doctors, megalomaniac engineers, and other tortured artists of modern political science fiction.[79] The leading rogues are found in the hidden laboratories and household mirrors of Victorian-era Gothic romances: most notably, Nathaniel Hawthorne's short story "The Birth-Mark" (1843), Robert Louis Stevenson's novella *The Strange Case of Dr. Jekyll and Mr. Hyde* (1886), Oscar Wilde's novel *The Picture of Dorian Gray* (1890), and H. G. Wells's novel *The Island of Doctor Moreau* (1896).

Like the Creature, Lionel Verney—Shelley's avatar in *The Last Man*—is a kind of reverse image of Victor Frankenstein and his successors. From the estranged perspectives of her literary personae, Shelley showed how humanity might use the artifice of storytelling to protect future generations against replicating its past mistakes. The Creature and Verney find their analogues in the *rebel hackers* of political science fiction: such as the self-flagellating savage who embeds himself in the pernicious culture of Aldous

Huxley's *Brave New World* (1932), the supposedly invalid Vincent who
infiltrates the upper echelons of a genetically engineered society in Andrew
Niccol's *Gattaca* (1997), Martha Nussbaum's boy-clone raised to be the
lover of his mother in her neo-Gothic short story "Little C" (1998), and
Nnedi Okorafor's two-year-old "accelerated woman," who violently revolts
against the system that enslaved her and other bioengineered people of
African descent, in the acclaimed novel *The Book of Phoenix* (2015).

The emotional specter driving the plots of *Frankenstein* and *The Last
Man* is the menace of the loss of love, whether through power-hungry scientific intervention in human reproduction or, more broadly, through the
spectacular failure of humanity to learn from its own troubled history. This
theme reemerges in the literature of lovelessness. It pictures the dangers of
creating beings who lack the experience of love and community altogether,
like Frankenstein's abandoned Creature. It likewise addresses the problem
of socializing people to lack affect, such as the bounty hunter Deckard who
"retires" sentient replicants for cash to purchase robotic pets at the outset
of *Do Androids Dream of Electric Sheep?* This strand of political science
fiction uses forms of virtual reality, bioengineering, and artificial intelligence as metaphors for the fear of the death of humanity understood as
humaneness or the capability for sharing love.[80]

Following Shelley, the prospect of the transfiguration or annihilation of
love through death or disaster preoccupies modern classics of political science fiction. Loveless literature probes what the evaporation or transformation of love could mean for the experience of justice in communities as
small as the family or as big as the state, the human species, or even the
universe. Beyond *Do Androids Dream of Electric Sheep?*, some of the most
nuanced works to explore this question are Ursula Le Guin's short story
"The Ones Who Walk Away from Omelas" (1973), the *Blade Runner* franchise (1982–2017), Octavia Butler's novelette "Bloodchild" (1985), Susan
Stryker's performance art "My Words to Victor Frankenstein Above the
Village of Chamounix" (1994), Kazuo Ishiguro's novel *Never Let Me Go*
(2005), Spike Jonze's film *Her* (2013), and Donna Haraway's "Camille"
short story cycle (2016).

While Loveless literature is dark in its themes, it tends to follow Shelley
in leaving open the possibility of hope for the transformation of love into
new forms in the future. However, some classics of political science fiction
stand at the brink of despair over the loss of love due to invasive politics or
technology—notably, George Orwell's "Last Man" narrative *Nineteen*

Eighty-Four (1948) and Michel Houellebecq's "Frankenstein" story *Les particules élèmentaires* (*The Elementary Particles*) (1998). Whether pessimistic, optimistic, or aporetic, Loveless literature pushes readers to consider whether technology causes the death of love and the demise of a prosocial morality or if the reverse is more often true: does the lack of love spur the development of technologies and practices of disconnection and brutality? If the latter, then political science and philosophy might productively engage Shelley and her science fiction legacies as a counter to the antisocial aspects of science and its applications.

v. Exploding the Fictions of Political Science

Informed by the philosophical complexity of Shelley's work, classics of Apocalyptic, Hacker, and Loveless literature together trigger and detonate three myths that are also found at the fore of political science, political philosophy, and the ethics and politics of technology in the twenty-first century. First, these classics inspire, then undermine, the apocalyptic expectation that humanity—whether understood as the species, its morality, or both—will die following the engineering of artificial beings capable of reason or feeling. Second, they posit, then upset, the naturalist presumption that it is wrong to permanently or heritably alter, transform, or perfect the human organism from its natural or given condition. And finally, they test, then reject, the essentialist assumption that love will end if humans transform traditional family structures through technology.

In 1998, literary scholar Scott McCracken wrote that "the fantasy of the alien encounter" is at "the root of all science fiction."[81] Modern political science fiction productively complicates encounters with alien beings and things in twenty-first-century political science and philosophy. The apocalyptic strand of modern poliscifi undermines the fatalistic contentions of political scientist Francis Fukuyama in his influential book, *Our Posthuman Future: Consequences of the Biotechnology Revolution* (2002). Despite his appeals to dystopian "political science fiction" to support his views, Fukuyama's bioconservative arguments prove to be more pessimistic than *Brave New World*.[82] Overall, classics of political science fiction challenge his thesis that the evolution of posthuman ways and forms of life through germline genetic engineering, pharmaceutical enhancement, and Internet technology will destroy "human nature" and its ingrained sense of "morality."[83]

When it hones its attention upon the other side of the political spectrum, Apocalyptic literature exposes the technophobic and other biases of the posthumanist philosopher Nick Bostrom. Despite his enthusiastic support of germline genetic engineering and other biotechnological enhancements of the human being, Bostrom has gained fame for promulgating fear of an "intelligence explosion"—or AI with greater general intelligence than people—as the "most unnatural and inhuman problem" facing humanity.[84] Standing in tension with his broader posthumanist defense of the productive interface of technology with humanity, his book *Superintelligence: Paths, Dangers, Strategies* (2014) culminated with a species-centric call for people to "hold on to our humanity" and "bring all our human resourcefulness" to bear on the problem of preventing the rise of a world-dominant artificial general intelligence (AGI).[85] Beyond this overt anthropocentrism, he conjured AGI in patriarchal and imperial terms: a kind of global Leviathan made in the image of a sociopathic male genius or "Einstein," hellbent on controlling the world and all of its resources for the sole purpose of aggrandizing its own power.[86] His foil for AGI also unreflectively relied upon problematic gender and disability stereotypes. At odds with his own stated intentions, Bostrom prejudicially represented humanity as the "village idiot" or the "female in the torn dress" from pulp SF who must be saved from being dominated by an emergent "extremely alien" superintelligence.[87]

Focusing more on the ethics of technological manipulation of the body, Hacker literature punctures the claim made by political philosopher Jürgen Habermas in *The Future of Human Nature* (2003) that there are salient moral and political differences between beings who are "grown" from nature and those who are "made" through genetic engineering and other forms of assisted reproductive technology.[88] Political science fiction breaks down such simplistic binaries between the natural and the unnatural, pressing readers to see the concepts as interdependent. From Dr. Jekyll and Mr. Hyde, to Doctor Moreau's vivisected Beast Men, to Dick's androids hunted down for bounty or love, the products of hacking become indistinguishable from their hackers. Encountering the multitude of monsters and other Others made, unmade, and remade in Hacker literature, we find the term "unnatural" is better hacked in half and rendered with a slash. The grown and the made are both, at once, un/natural.

Loveless literature takes on even deeper questions about the basis of community and its compatibility with biotechnology and AI. It contests the pessimistic view of political theorist Michael Sandel—set forth in *The Case Against Perfection: Ethics in the Age of Genetic Engineering* (2007)—that parent-child love would extinguish if biotechnological enhancement of children made parental care obsolete.[89] Loveless literature channels and redirects this fear of the loss of real connectivity. Its strange and often disturbing stories of the transformation of love, starting in the family and extending into outer space, spur readers to wonder: *what would it take to reconceive love in an age of technology?* Ishiguro raises this question with real poignancy with the young human clones in *Never Let Me Go*. Even given their sinister exploitation by the state that made them solely for organ donation, the clones struggle with sexual desire, loneliness, and longing for community like other single and unmarried teens and twenty-somethings living apart from their families. Doomed to die young and care for others with the same tragic fate, they still find time and ways to love and thus subvert the state of injustice that so cruelly stamps them with short-term expiration dates.

What classics of modern political science fiction have in common is their philosophical use of worst-case scenarios. They deftly employ these counterfactual scenarios to ask questions about how humanity might adapt to its changing technological environment rather than succumb to either cultural suicide or defeatism in the wake of rapid scientific advancement. Political science and political philosophy can learn a great deal from mining these political science fictions from interdisciplinary perspectives. Modern political science fiction takes the first strike at reconceiving humanity in the wake of scientific, technological, and other—creative and destructive—interventions of artifice in myriad ways of life and being. Political science and philosophy can take the second strike by unearthing fresh ideas in political science fiction about what it means to be humane toward other beings, things, and systems in an age of cybernetics, biotech, and radical scientific exploration.

vi. Why Political Science? Which Science Fictions?

The concept of "political science fictions" breaks down into three overlapping terms: political science, political fictions, and science fictions. Following French philosopher Jacques Derrida and his deconstructive method of conceptual analysis, we can productively slash it up.[90] Once rendered as political/science/fictions, the interconnections between the terms come into focus.

We have seen how Shelley's major works of science fiction took root in eighteenth-century political science and political fiction. The political themes of *Frankenstein* and *The Last Man* animate much of modern SF to the present day. They also resonate with debates in contemporary political science about the ethical, legal, and policy implications of the creation, transformation, or modification of forms of life and intelligence through science and technology. Reading political science fiction through the lens of political philosophy exposes some of the simplistic fictions behind contemporary political science. Conversely, it illuminates the complex ethics and politics of modern classics of SF, as well as their enduring relevance to contemporary political science and philosophy.

Philosophers dominated eighteenth-century political science, including Locke, Rousseau, Godwin, Burke, and Wollstonecraft. In the twenty-first century, the authority of political philosophy within political science is less apparent due to the rise of the quantitative social sciences—especially economics—as the source of the paramount methodological approaches to the study of politics. Despite the decline of political philosophy as the primary method within political science, there are still some political debates dominated by political theorists (in political science or government departments) and political philosophers and ethicists (in philosophy departments). These include the futuristic debates on genetic engineering and AI that have escalated since the turn of the twenty-first century.

On the cusp of their eclipse by the "dismal science" of economics, political philosophy and political theory have found new policy relevance in making speculative and often apocalyptic claims about the bleak future of humanity in an age of artificial life forms.[91] I follow suit in showing the policy relevance of political/science/fictions but resist the temptation to assume the worst about the future. As recounted in the Preface, I am a creature of the Cold War era. Generation X has struggled with the feeling that things are going to get worse before they get better, but in political/science/fictions, there is hope to be found that things do not have to end up badly.

The plural form of the third term in political/science/fictions entails an open-ended approach to the subgenre. It would be impossible to catalogue every work in the library of political SF, even if one began with its modern threshold texts of *Frankenstein* and *The Last Man*.[92] Even then, we would find that the generative framework produced by Shelley's oeuvre opened the door for innumerable writers to construct new imaginative thresholds for modern poliscifi to leap from and beyond. As we shall see next, during the Interlude, Shelley influenced Edgar Allan Poe, Jules Verne, and H. G. Wells. The work of these three "fathers" of modern political science fiction is rooted in hers, yet cannot be reduced to it—just as she cannot be reduced to her sources. Perhaps Shelley should not be seen as the "mother" of modern science fiction anymore but instead as the ingenious animator behind its primary narrative mechanisms and political foci. She crafted a skeletal structure for modern poliscifi, then let the power of her imagination bring it to life in a profusion of forms. Fellow writers of imaginative genius have fleshed out this skeleton, not only by playing with her refrains of apocalypse, the un/natural, and lovelessness but also by adding new layers for political analysis, often in response to technological, scientific, and other cultural change.

With these historical caveats in mind, I delimit the scope of this study to a selection of the classics of the three key political strands of modern science fiction that took off after Shelley. I hope that it serves as a model for putting political science into philosophical dialogue with science fiction and vice versa. I bid my framework for understanding political/science/ fictions—with all of its flaws—to "go forth and prosper" in new and productive mutations.[93]

My methodological models for this myth-busting project are the New Zealander political theorist Susan Moller Okin and the British philosopher Mary Midgley. Both were products of an impressive tradition of training women in philosophy and political theory at Somerville College, Oxford. Somerville is the repository of the library of John Stuart Mill as well as the analytical approach to feminism that he, his wife Harriet Taylor Mill, and Wollstonecraft before them best represented in the Anglo tradition.[94] Following in the footsteps of Wollstonecraft and the Mills, Midgley and Okin bravely challenged the dangerous patriarchal, essentialist, and reductivist biases and "oversimple intellectual systems" that were often unreflectively spread by some of the leading men of late twentieth-century philosophy and science, from John Rawls to Richard Dawkins.[95]

In this analytical feminist vein, I put some classics of modern political science fiction, as well as Shelley's life and writing before them, into critical dialogue with the prevailing dismal view of bio/technology in contemporary political science and philosophy. I also unpack the core moral and political problems addressed by Apocalyptic, Hacker, and Loveless literature. Must humanity rethink justice and human rights as it reconceives, through science and technology, what it means to be human? Will AI make people smarter or more servile, more creative or destructive, through the evolution of collective intelligence? Is it humane or inhuman to genetically modify or otherwise bioengineer sentient or conscious life? To what extent should the state and other political bodies regulate the artificial reproduction or permanent modification of humans and other creatures through biotechnology or cybernetics?

This book is a sequel to *Mary Shelley and the Rights of the Child: Political Philosophy in "Frankenstein"* (2017). To enjoy the new volume does not require you to have read the earlier one. I have summed up its most salient points and tied them into the arguments of this book as relevant. Their uniting theses are that (1) Shelley designed *Frankenstein* as a cascade of five thought experiments on the rights of the child, and (2) these literary thought experiments train the mind's eye on (a) articulating the injustice of child neglect and abuse and (b) envisioning the realization of justice for all young and vulnerable creatures, no matter how they are made.

While my last book concluded by addressing these issues in relation to the rights of stateless, disabled, and posthuman children like Frankenstein's Creature, this book widens the lens in two main ways. First, it explores more fully the psychological and philosophical depth of Shelley's oeuvre. I uncover the profound relevance of her novel *The Last Man*, alongside her journals, poetry, translations, and other manuscripts, for challenging some of the most dangerous myths concerning apocalypse, nature, and love— both in her time and ours. Second, this book uses the political science fiction born of her work to move past the limitations of contemporary political thought on artificial intelligence and genetic engineering. I take the once futuristic idea of rights for bioengineered beings, androids, and other artificial creatures—first voiced in *Frankenstein*—and treat it as matter of urgent political concern for this century.

vii. The Structure and Argument of the Book

Following a brief Interlude that charts the international reception history of Shelley's *Frankenstein* and *The Last Man* in literature and other art, the heart of this work consists of a philosophical trilogy. The book's three chapters contain a series of iterative essays, which are rooted in the microcosm of Shelley's life, mind, and imagination, then travel outward to explore some of the macrocosm of modern political science fiction. Each essay stands alone as an examination of a particular philosophical topic related to the analysis of the concepts of apocalypse, nature, and love. Yet each essay yields an output, or argument, that feeds input into the next iteration of the book's "master algorithm," or governing thesis.[96] This sequence of arguments seeks to shatter the reigning political fictions of end of the world, the unnatural, and lovelessness as they have played out in twenty-first-century treatments of the ethics of making artificial life and intelligence.

Chapter I examines the "Apocalyptic Fictions"—or prejudicial myths and irrational fears about the end of the world—that have dominated debates on AI since the Internet and tech boom of the 1990s. To put things into a more realistic perspective, section i interweaves the history of the global climate catastrophe caused by the 1815 eruption of Mount Tambora with the young Shelley's concatenation of personal tragedies during the time she wrote *Frankenstein* and *The Last Man*. Upholding Shelley, the Creature, and Verney as models of resilience in the face of serious calamities, section ii dispels the contemporary fear of the singularity—or the rise of AI equal to or greater than human intelligence. Sections iii and iv question Bostrom's pessimistic political theory of the rise of a globally dominant superintelligence by putting his arguments into philosophical dialogue with some of the classics of political science fiction (Dick, Scott, Hall, Sterling, and the Wachowski sisters) and computer science (Turing and Vinge). Section v compares the Apocalyptic literature of Atwood, Čapek, and Shelley to reveal the hope that people might use the collective artificial intelligence of techne to resolve rather than succumb to disasters both actual and imagined.

Chapter II unpacks the "Un/natural Fictions"—or contrasting notions of the natural versus the unnatural—that have troubled debates on the ethics and regulation of genetic engineering since the first successful cloning of a mammal in 1997. Throughout, I treat *Frankenstein* and its cinematic offspring *Gattaca* as iconic sources of imagery and ideas for the ethics and politics of bioengineering young and vulnerable beings. Section i breaks down two of the binary oppositions that govern these debates—deformed/normal and abortion/generation—by comparing Shelley and Hawthorne's blurring of these terms in their life writings about birth, love, and death and their Gothic political science fictions. I conclude with a look at the historic discussion of Hawthorne's "The Birth-Mark" by the U.S. President's Council on Bioethics in 2002 and its impact on Sandel's treatment of the ethics of genetic engineering. Section ii provides a brief history of heritable, or germline, genetic engineering of human babies from 1997 to 2018. It then explains why the bioconservative proposals of Fukuyama, Habermas, and Sandel for its regulation or prohibition are inadequate with respect to children and their rights. Section iii brings together the abused bioengineered creatures of Shelley, Nussbaum, and Okorafor to articulate the rights of genetically modified children to (1) love and community and (2) conditions of nondiscrimination with respect to birth. Following the Nuffield Bioethics Council, I support the amendment of the 1997 Universal Declaration on the Human Genome and Human Rights with a declaration of the rights of gene-edited people, beginning with babies and other youth. Section iv confronts Habermas's far-reaching political concern that genetic engineering of children could undercut the ethical conditions for human autonomy and thereby human rights. By putting Habermas's vision of a eugenic dystopia into conversation with *Brave New World* and *Gattaca*, I find that autonomy would not necessarily be lost in the worst conditions of technological domination but rather could be reconfigured toward the resistance of injustice. Section v diagnoses the hypocrisy and danger of demonizing the biotechnological creatures we make. By taking a good hard look at the monsters in the mirror that haunt the Victorian Gothic political science fictions of Hawthorne, Stevenson, Wilde, and Wells, we see that these deformed and abortive creations are projections of our self-destructive passions, fears, and prejudices.

Chapter III analyzes the "Loveless Fictions"—or illusions of love's demise—that lurk beneath both Shelley's oeuvre and debates on making artificial life and intelligence. Section i contemplates Shelley's artistic adaptation to the prospect of lovelessness—especially after the deaths of Percy and Byron—through her translation and philosophical recovery of Spinoza's deterministic metaphysics and ethics. Her Romantic Spinozism led her to accept and even love the whole created world as it is and must be. She crafted a powerful philosophical model for how the fear of the death of love might be reconceived through the aid of the imagination to counter the fatalism and inertia of apocalyptic thought. Section ii exposes the apocalyptic fears of the loss of love that persist in an age of genetic engineering.

By reading the bioethics of Fukuyama and Sandel alongside the dystopias of Orwell, Houellebecq, and Ishiguro, I show how these two political theorists overestimate, in different ways and to varying degrees, the extent to which artificial forms of life would threaten to extinguish love and other ethical relationships in the family. Section iii studies the role of the imagination in the complex psychological experience of love, from Plato's allegory of the cave to *Her*. Moving from Zhuangzi to Bostrom to the *Blade Runner* franchise, it grapples with whether it matters if love or any other experience is actual or virtual, real or simulated. Following the ideas of Shelley, Dick, and Turing, I conclude that to love *virtually*, or effectively, is emotionally and ethically sufficient if it is freely yet imperfectly shared with another, whether it is vividly felt in the imagination or experienced in other practice. Section iv chronicles how contemporary feminist political science fiction by Stryker, Le Guin, Butler, and Haraway follows Shelley's realistic futurism in imagining how love and family might be positively transformed through artifice going forward. From these women writers emerge trans/feminist, transitional, posthumanist, and ecological strands of a cosmopolitan theory of justice. What ties them together, and back to Shelley, is the hope that the imaginative and loving use of techne can serve justice to a wider range of creatural forms of life in the future.

For the finale of Chapter III, section v returns to the genesis and development of Shelley's philosophy of love through her creative synthesis of elements of Spinoza, Glasite Christianity, Wollstonecraft, Cicero, and Plato. Against the apocalyptic and millennial political fictions of the revolutionary and Romantic eras, she reconceived love as *apocatastasis*: a cyclical restoration of an ethical attitude of stewardship toward the whole world and its necessity. As found in her journals, poetry, and *The Last Man*, her Romantic Spinozism affirmed the forward-looking responsibility of people to love their neighbors and sustain the world, including future generations, even in the face of seeming catastrophe. For this philosophical and literary achievement, she should be recognized as a forerunner of trans/feminist, transitional, posthumanist, and ecological political thought that strives to accommodate the widest range of life and techne in theories of justice, rights, and obligations.

The book ends with a Coda and not a final conclusion. I do this in order to foster futuristic political thought on the responsibility of people toward the artificial life forms of their creation. In the spirit of Wollstonecraft's revolutionary *Vindications* of the rights and duties of men and women published in 1790 and 1792, as well as Percy Shelley's visionary *Vindication* of vegetarianism issued in 1813, I advance *A Vindication of the Rights and Duties of Artificial Creatures*.[97] Inspired by Mary Shelley's archetypes of the Creature and the Last Man, this *Vindication* moves well beyond even Haraway's radical view that all contemporary humans are cyborgs, or hybrids of organisms and machines, due to the total integration of technology into their ways and forms of being.[98]

Rather, my *Vindication* proceeds from an environmental premise derived from the political thought of Wollstonecraft and Godwin: all creatures are artificial, since they are made by their surrounding social and cultural circumstances. Extending the tradition of women's rights, animal rights, environmental rights, and machine rights grown from the pamphlet wars of the 1790s, I vindicate the rights and duties of all artificial creatures, human or not, who are sensitive to the circumstances that made them.[99]

This *Vindication* remains aporetic on the question of "who counts" as sensitive—and whether it might mean sentient, intelligent, conscious, and/or agentic—due to the basic instability of the subject of the inquiry.[100] As presently imagined in HBO's *Westworld*, a hit show about androids built for prostitution and slaughter on a dude ranch, we do not know if or when machines or other artificially formed beings might "wake up."[101] We do not know whether or which forms of sentience, intelligence, consciousness, or agency might arise in such creatures.[102] We do not fully understand the ways that varieties of sentience, intelligence, consciousness, and agency have characterized "multispecies" ecosystems and civilizations, past and present.[103] We do not comprehend the vast interconnectedness of life forms and their engagements with the world or universe.[104] For these humbling epistemological reasons, we ought to adopt an open-ended yet compassionate ethical attitude toward a very real political possibility: the need to ascribe rights and duties, over time and through careful national and international deliberation, to a wider range of artificially formed creatures than heretofore our cultural and legal systems have recognized.

In this far-seeing light, my *Vindication* begins by reading the Universal Declaration on the Human Genome and Human Rights and its wider international political standard of human rights as covering genetically modified children. It then extends its coverage to all youthful or otherwise vulnerable artificial creatures who are, in the words of Frankenstein's Creature, "sensitive" to the circumstances that shape them.[105] It should stretch to cover bioengineered beings like Wells's Beast Men or Ishiguro's clones, as well as robots and other artificial intelligences such as Ian McEwan's Adams and Eves or Jeanette Winterson's XX-bots.[106]

Because my *Vindication* provocatively defends fundamental rights to love, care, identity, and nondiscrimination for all artificial creatures, it also justifies duties to provide them, while outlining how, when, and by whom it would be appropriate to do so. This universal "hospital tent" of rights and duties immediately covers and serves any and all forms of life and intelligence that show sensitivity to the circumstances that made them.[107] If erected in national and international cultures and laws, it might prevent the destructive treatment of an array of creatures whose capabilities and experiences do or could overlap in surprisingly creative ways with our humanity.[108]

Finally, the Coda vindicates the power of political science fictions after *Frankenstein* to sustain our humanity, understood as *humaneness*. Across her oeuvre, Shelley developed a profound political philosophy of love. It is centered on the cosmopolitan, even cosmic, ethical question: *what would it mean to love the whole creation?* Her writings reveal the value of taking a generous and fearless attitude of love toward the whole world—as it was, is, and will be—with all of its strange and wonderful and sometimes terrible and monstrous creatures.

Births and Afterlives

It lives! It lives!
—Frankenstein before his creation, in Richard Brinsley
Peake's play "Presumption; or, The Fate of Frankenstein"
(1823), in Jeffrey N. Cox, *Seven Gothic Dramas, 1798–1825*
(1992)

But lo & behold! I found myself famous!
—Mary Shelley, letter to Leigh Hunt after seeing
"Presumption," 9–11 September 1823, in Betty T. Bennett,
The Letters of Mary Wollstonecraft Shelley (1980)

i. The Multiple Births of *Frankenstein*

Three dominant strands of modern political science fiction—Apocalyptic, Hacker, and Loveless literature—originate in the prescient tale of Frankenstein's Creature. The nameless Creature is an assemblage of parts from human and other animal corpses, brought to life by a scientist on a dreary November night. Once animated, he faces rejection as a hideous monster by his maker Victor Frankenstein and nearly everyone else he encounters. Frankenstein's abandonment of responsibility for a life made through science brings terrible consequences for both creature and creator, with ripple effects running deep into the wider community.

While *Frankenstein* is not always the first work to be identified as a science fiction, it is typically marked as a threshold text, for after it, the genre flourishes in a way that was not the case beforehand.[1] Shelley composed her first novel in the wake of the eighteenth-century European

Enlightenment: a crucible for speculative fictions that employed counter-factual narrative premises to engage modern scientific and political trends. Irishman Jonathan Swift used his novel *Gulliver's Travels* (1726) to satirize Sir Isaac Newton and his scientific followers with its depiction of Laputa—an island made to levitate by the pointless science of its mathematically minded inhabitants, whose heads are literally in the clouds.[2] In France, Louis-Sébastien Mercier's *L'An 2440* (*The Year 2440*) (1771) was so popular that it went through twenty-five editions in the late eighteenth century. The historian Robert Darnton argued that this futuristic novel set in 2440 Paris enticed its mass readership to engage in a daring form of "mental experimentation." What if one could know what France's future would hold centuries ahead and then look back, critically, upon the distant shore of its national past?[3] This was heady reading in the run-up to the French Revolution.

Indeed, it was in this politically radical milieu—more precisely, 1790 Paris—that François-Félix Nogaret's novella *Le Miroir des événmens actuels* (*The Mirror of Current Events*) introduced a man named "Wak-wik-vauk-on-son-frankénsteïn." For a contest, this French Frankénsteïn invents a flute-playing automaton that helps him woo a wife. French literature scholar Julia Douthwaite deciphered that the inventor's hyper-hyphenated name is a parodic composite. Its parts, Douthwaite posited, are Jacques Necker, the minister of finance for Louis XVI, often blamed for the economic collapse of the ancién regime; the "great French engineer Vaucanson," famous for making the automatic loom; and the "Teutonic-sounding Frankénsteïn."[4] Thereafter, Nogaret shortened the inventor's name to Frankénsteïn—perhaps alluding to Germanic legends of sorcery and alchemy, such as Dr. Faustus. Like Victor Frankenstein after him, he is even compared with "Prometheus" for his skills in the arts and sciences.[5]

Given the parallels between *Frankenstein* the novel and this little-studied French novella—especially between the characters of "Wak-Wik-Vauc" (pronounced "Vac-Vic-Vauc") Frankénsteïn and Victor Frankenstein—Douthwaite has speculated that Mary Shelley might have become acquainted with Nogaret's novella in the library of her mother Mary Wollstonecraft.[6] Wollstonecraft had lived in the environs of Paris as a Girondist (or moderate republican) supporter of the revolutionary cause, from late 1792 to early 1794. She could have carried such revolutionary-era books and pamphlets back to Britain.[7] If so, then Douthwaite has unearthed a predecessor text for *Frankenstein* that makes the Creature a descendant of some of the earliest forms of AI: automata, or self-running machines like mechanical birds and musical watches, which were popular in Enlightenment-era Europe, especially in Francophone cultures.[8]

Growing out of the revolutionary politics of the European Enlightenment, the most influential modern science fiction is, at base, political. Shelley's *Frankenstein* is not solely the threshold from which modern political science fiction takes off. It is also the origin story for the subgenre's driving concern with artificial intervention in life through technological innovation.

Other examples of influential nineteenth-century science fiction obsessed with tech-driven exploration of new frontiers are Jules Verne's serialized 1870 novel *Vingt mille lieues sous les mers: Tour du monde sous-marin* (*Twenty Thousand Leagues Under the Seas: Underwater Tour Around the World*) and H. G. Wells's 1895 novella *The Time Machine*. As the historian of political thought Duncan Bell has argued, these works have important if neglected implications for international and global politics in the modern age of increasing imperial exploitation and conquest of the Earth, its life forms, and its cultures.[9] What *Frankenstein* did was distinctive among these impressive nineteenth-century works of SF. Even as it analyzed the pitfalls of modern scientifically driven exploration, industrialization, and colonization, the novel tailored a wider yet powerful narrative framework for SF. *Frankenstein* and its progeny, including major works by Verne and Wells, address the ethical and political puzzles specific to the artificial creation of forms and ways of life, consciousness, and intelligence through craft or techne.

ii. A Creature Is Born

Ironically, the prototype for Gothic science fiction had an inauspicious beginning. Published anonymously when she was twenty, Shelley's *Frankenstein* materialized in London bookstalls to little notice on 1 January 1818. Even the appearance of public slight peeved her husband Percy Bysshe Shelley, so he took action. On 2 January, he sent a copy of the book to Sir Walter Scott, the acclaimed Scottish author of historical romances, in the hope that such a "celebrated person" might review it.[10] On 15 January, he wrote from Marlow to his publisher Charles Ollier in London: "Do you hear any thing said of Frankenstein?"[11] On 31 January, an advertisement in the *Morning Post* made a belated announcement: "**This day is published . . . a Work of Imagination, entitled, FRANKENSTEIN: or, The Modern Prometheus.**"[12]

That winter, Percy dashed off a favorable review of his wife's novel to drum up support. Ironically, it was not published until 1832, a year after Mary's issue of her revised third edition of *Frankenstein*.[13] At this point, she had been a widow for a decade, following Percy's drowning in a sailing accident off the coast of Italy in July 1822. Shelley's method of memorializing him was suitably macabre. She apparently had the literal artifact of his heart: the calcified organ, extracted whole from his burnt corpse by his devoted friend Edward Trelawny, after a crude funeral pyre for the poet on a beach in Tuscany.[14] Any line between her Gothic fiction and her gothic life had been blurred beyond recognition. She kept the remains of his heart—though some say it was his liver—wrapped in a shroud on her desk and left instructions for it to be buried with her and the skeletons of her parents at Bournemouth.[15]

In happier times, the Shelleys moved to Italy in March 1818. By that point, *Frankenstein* had already taken on a life of its own. Sir Walter Scott, the leading Romantic novelist of the age, declared it an innovative work of "philosophical" fiction that defied the tropes of mere fantasy or horror literature of the period—even his own.[16] Unlike the class of "marvellous" literature that employed the supernatural to simply arouse wonder in the audience, *Frankenstein* had a more "refined" purpose: "to shew the probable effect which the supposed miracles would produce on those who witnessed them."[17] According to Scott, the reader accepts the "wildest freaks of imagination" found in *Frankenstein* due to the author's "logical precision" in "deducing the consequences" of the "extraordinary postulates" of the plot on the development of its characters.[18]

That same March, another literary journal in Edinburgh published an anonymous review that identified exactly what made *Frankenstein* so extraordinary. The reviewer observed, "We are accustomed, happily, to look upon the creation of a living and intelligent being as a work that is fitted only to inspire a religious emotion."[19] *Frankenstein* "gives a sort of shock" to its readership by applying the expression "Creator" to "a mere human being."[20] This almost electric power of *Frankenstein* to jolt readers out of their theologically dogmatic slumbers could be "hazardous."[21] The review ambivalently concluded by imploring the author to "study the established order of nature" before composing another novel after this "great model."[22]

Shelley returned home from Rome in August 1823 as a widow, mourning the loss of five children she either bore or cared for and a late-term
miscarriage. Her first novel had already come to life on the London stage.
One of her chief lures for returning to London with her sole surviving child
was her father Godwin's promise of tickets to see the play *Presumption; or,*
The Fate of Frankenstein, which debuted at the English Opera House that
month. Her response to the first theatrical adaptation of *Frankenstein,* by
Richard Brinsley Peake, was almost breathless in exuberance. "But lo &
behold!" she wrote to her friend Leigh Hunt on 9–11 September 1823, "I
found myself famous!—Frankenstein had prodigious success as a drama &
was about to be repeated for the 23rd night."[23]

The playbill "amused" her "extremely" by rendering the Creature a
blank next to the actor's name: "_____ by Mr T. Cooke."[24] She seemed
quite pleased with the dramatis personae's clever framing of her authorial
design: "this nameless mode of naming the un{n}ameable is rather good."[25]
She praised the lead actors too. "Wallack looked very well as F̲ {Franken-
stein}" and Cooke "played _____'s part extremely well."[26] She even
quoted the most enduring line of Peake's play that has come to encapsulate
her story in virtually every theatrical and cinematic version since: the
moment when the Creature comes to life, and "F. exclaims 'It lives!' "[27]
While she let the literary critic Hunt know that she thought her "story is
not well managed" in Peake's production, she appreciated that "it appeared
to excite a breathless eagerness in the audience."[28] She concluded her review
with a mix of wonder and approval. "They continue to play it even now,"
she wrote.[29]

As the author of a novel adapted ceaselessly in theater, film, and other
mediums, Shelley could not have written truer words. The success of *Pre-*
sumption spurred the production of over two dozen theatrical versions of
Frankenstein in the nineteenth and early twentieth centuries.[30] Almost
immediately they transmogrified the emotive and musical conventions of
Gothic melodrama to venture into the burgeoning dark parody of burlesque. In the 1820s, the form had not yet acquired the sexual connotation
or taste for nudity that late nineteenth-century American versions gave it.[31]
Early burlesque rather amplified the high emotions, operatic lyrics, and
dramatic, pantomimic gestures of melodrama into a cutting satire of the
thematic extremes of its stories. Literary scholar Elizabeth Young has illuminated how early burlesques could at once render Victor Frankenstein's
hubris silly yet sublime, mundane yet monstrous.[32]

Peake's self-caricature, *Another Piece of Presumption* (1823), presented a Gothic tale of a tailor who uses his scissors to assemble the parts of other tailors into a composite hobgoblin, "Frankinstitch."[33] The parodic title and concept of this and other satirical plays—such as *Humgumption; or, Dr. Frankenstein and the Hobgoblin of Hoxton* (1823) and *Frank-in-Steam; or, The Modern Promise to Pay* (1824)—prodded London audiences to ponder whether anyone was safe from Victor's sins. Ordinary people in lowly professions could become monsters in an age of mechanistic production and capitalistic debt, driven by the insatiable desires of an ever-expanding marketplace.[34]

iii. The Creature Conquers the World

The first translation of *Frankenstein* was into French in 1821. Jules Saladin's edition became available in Paris bookstalls during the summer. Though he correctly attributed the work "PAR "Mme SHELLY" [*sic*] after the dedication to Godwin, Saladin described her as not Godwin's daughter but "SA NIÈCE."[35] An explanation for the misidentification of Shelley as the niece of Godwin might be the published rumors (dating to early 1818) that one of his close relations wrote *Frankenstein*.[36] The first edition to attribute the novel to its female author, the 1821 French translation paved the way for the story's runaway success in Parisian theater and, more generally, its robust international reception in the dramatic arts from the 1820s onward.[37]

In the *Bibliothèque de l'Arsenal*, literary historian Stephen Earl Forry unearthed the fragments of an 1821 play entitled *Frankenstein; ou, Le Promethée moderne*, yet found no record of its performance.[38] In August 1821, the Parisian journal of culture *Le Miroir des Spectacles, des lettres, des mœurs et des arts* (*The Mirror of Shows, Letters, Mores, and Arts*) in fact advertised it as a melodrama with the Creature described as an automaton.[39] Thus, the first known stage adaptation of the novel, whether intentionally or not, fused the concepts of Nogaret's and Shelley's stories of scientists named Frankenstein who mechanically engineer an intelligent form of life.

The first major French theatrical production of *Frankenstein* was *Le Monstre et le magician* (*The Monster and the Magician*) (1826), by Jean Toussaint Merle and Antoine Nicolas Beraud. It featured the British actor Cooke in a reprise of his role as "The Monster" for eighty nights straight at Théâtre de la Porte Saint-Martin in Paris.[40] This tremendously popular play inspired six French and two English spinoffs in 1826, plus a comic version of the original in Paris in 1861.[41]

The staging of the nineteenth-century melodramas and burlesques carried forward several features of Peake's play: the Creature's green or blue face paint, silent gestures, or nonverbal grunting; Victor's isolated, lofty laboratory, often set off with a dramatic staircase; and the introduction of a dim-witted peasant narrator.[42] Some of these century-old dramaturgical elements shaped the influential 1928 and 1931 scripts of English playwright Peggy Webling's *Frankenstein*, yet she added her own eerie twists befitting the political pessimism of the interwar era.[43]

Webling's Creature is monstrous in appearance. Even so, the Frankensteins welcome him as a guest into their family home, only to have him accidentally drown their daughter. He is not wholly inarticulate but rather gradually learns to speak and shows an attraction to his maker's fiancée. In the 1931 script, cowritten with John Balderston, he dons the clothing of his creator.[44] His uncanny resemblance to Frankenstein nevertheless provides no protection from mutual tragedy. In 1928, Webling had him strangle his creator—lunging at Victor's throat "like an animal"—before being "shattered" by a lightning strike in the finale.[45] Intriguingly, this version of the play continued Shelley's aporetic mode of leaving open the question of whether the Creature dies or not in the end.

Webling's most lasting contribution to the rewriting of the story for the stage was the naming of the Creature "Frankenstein" after his father-scientist.[46] She scripted a practice that had reportedly prevailed since actors wondered what to call the nameless Creature in the earliest theatrical productions.[47] This conflation of father and son still dominates popular culture to the point that most readers of the original novel are surprised to learn that Shelley left the Creature nameless.

The identification of the Creature with his creator symbolizes how wrong-headed uses of science and technology—whether in war, industrialization, capitalism, or reproduction—haunt the maker of the mistake. In August 1935, the cover of *Vanity Fair* depicted a huge, green-hued Hitler hovering over the globe, with Europe cloaked by his German war helmet.[48] Nazi Germany was the new Frankenstein's monster, produced from the horrifying carnage and political injustice of World War I and its aftermath.

Hollywood's Universal Studios bought the rights to Webling and Balderston's script as part of the production of the most influential cinematic adaptation of the novel to date. James Whale's *Frankenstein* (1931)[49] was a "huge box office hit," and according to Sir Christopher Frayling, "it opened the floodgates" for the "Franken-label" to multiply on a global scale.[50] The most famous scene from Whale's film recalls the line from *Presumption* that Shelley herself quoted in her September 1823 letter to Hunt. The American actor Colin Clive expertly plays Dr. Frankenstein with a kind of wide-eyed, maniacal innocence as he applies electricity to awaken his manufactured corpse. When he witnesses the first stirrings of motion in his creation's fingers, Dr. Frankenstein shrieks in a moment of mad exultation, "It's alive!"

It awoke again in Japan, where Whale's *Frankenstein* was playing in cinemas by early 1932. A leading Tokyo newspaper, the *Yomiuri Shimbun*, featured a series of dramatic black and white stills from the film, encouraging a public appetite for Shelley's modern myth of technological hubris.[51] The first Japanese edition of her novel retitled it as *The Giant's Revenge* (*Furankenshutain*).[52] It appeared in 1948, just three years after the United States detonated nuclear bombs over Hiroshima and Nagasaki and fire-bombed Tokyo into a smoking husk.

These devastating US bombings of Japanese cities left in their wake as many as 350,000 deaths, mostly of civilians. As the political philosopher John Rawls would point out fifty years later, the morally controversial—and, in his view, pretended—justification was to put an end to World War II. Rawls noted that President Truman had openly described the Japanese "as beasts and to be treated as such" prior to commanding the atrocity.[53] An American veteran of the gruesome Pacific theater of war, Rawls exposed the hypocrisy of his country for seeking to maintain its moral high ground—gained from fighting the "peculiar evil" of the Nazi regime—while refusing to acknowledge how "very wrong" it was to use nuclear weapons and firebombing in Japan for the sake of expediency and a show of power.[54]

The editorial introduction to the 1948 Japanese edition of *Frankenstein* connected the novel to the culture of militaristic and technological domination that had occupied Japan in "the aftermath of World War I."[55] During the interwar period, the Japanese had become fascinated with "the idea of 'cyborgs'"—or the hybridization of organism and machine—in both science and literature.[56] Without directly tying the novel to World War II, the editor suggested that the intertwined plights of the Creature and his creator resonated with that of the Japanese people and its enemies in the West. Shelley's story articulated a destructive psychology of "sheer resentment," occasioned by the confrontation of "injustice and tragedies brought on by fate."[57]

Toho Studios of Tokyo released its first installation of the *Godzilla* (ゴジラ, *Gojira*) film franchise in 1954, melding the modern Japanese horror stories of *The Giant's Revenge* (*Furankenshutain*) and Hiroshima into a towering cyborg of "gorilla" (ゴリラ or *gorira*) and "whale" (鯨 or *kujira*) for the Cold War era.[58] This political subtext became the overt text of the Japanese American film *Frankenstein Conquers the World* (1965). Its protagonist is a feral child from postnuclear Hiroshima who eats the immortal heart of Frankenstein's monster left behind from a Nazi-Japanese experiment. With the aid of radiation, the child becomes a giant who battles Baragon, a Godzilla-like creature who emerges from the sea.

The Japanese filmic representation of the Creature as a child had its popular roots in Osamu Tezuka's *Astro Boy/Mighty Atom* manga and anime television series of the 1950s and 1960s. The idea of a hybrid child-Creature has enjoyed a healthy afterlife in international comics and animation since, including Victor LaValle's *Destroyer* (2017). This graphic novel confronts the problem of racial justice by rebooting *Frankenstein* for the age of Black Lives Matter. LaValle's child-Creature is an innocent African American boy killed by police violence. His brilliant black mother is an intellectually exploited scientist and emotionally tortured descendent of Victor Frankenstein. She desperately brings her child back to life as a humanoid AI, whose good character perseveres over evil in the fight against injustice.

Although Shelley's story has not always been managed so well by other artists—perhaps especially by actors and directors—it keeps being born again. The Creature erupts from the depths of our cultural psyches, in new iterations of her modern creation myth, on stage and in film.[59] Sometimes "It lives" simultaneously in both artistic mediums, as in Danny Boyle's *National Theatre Live: Frankenstein*, which debuted in London in 2011.

Scripted by Nick Dear, this multimedia production is self-consciously iterative, for it plays two distinct performances each Halloween in arts cinemas worldwide.[60] Captured in a filmic loop are the esteemed British actors Benedict Cumberbatch and Johnny Lee Miller, who swapped the roles of the Creature and Victor in the pair of live broadcasts. By repackaging *Frankenstein* as a recurring set of global cinematic theater events, National Theatre Live annually invites viewers from different cultures to see Victor and the Creature as doppelgängers, identical twins, or even clones. Boyle's high-tech production resurrects a question that is central to the original novel: what is the difference, if any, between the scientist and his so-called monster?

In *Frankenstein in Baghdad* (فرانكشتاين في بغداد), Ahmed Saadawi approaches this question from an acute political angle within the context of the second Iraq War.[61] Winner of the 2014 International Prize for Arabic Fiction, the novel defies easy placement in fantasy, SF, horror, or war literature.[62] It is better understood as a political science fiction that employs the narrative mechanics of a legion of "Frankenstein" stories before it: systematic analysis of the automated destruction spawned by a brutal creator and his abused creation.

A Baghdad-based writer who lived through two US invasions of Iraq, Saadawi reads the figure of Victor Frankenstein not as a maker of synthetic life in a laboratory but rather as a political scientist of death on the field of war. Like a policy advisor to a general in the Pentagon, this grim reaper hovers, untouchable, in the political background of the novel. Meanwhile, on the desolate yet dangerous streets of a bombed-out Baghdad, a junk dealer assembles a bizarre war memorial from the body parts of detonated corpses. Much to the Iraqi people's surprise, this unnamed Creature—"The Whatitsname"—rises up to reenact the cyclic violence of the past.[63] It kills to secure replacement parts for its own survival, exploding any distinction between the good guys and the bad guys. Saadawi ingeniously reinvents the Creature as a traumatized collective political intelligence that mimics the genocidal behaviors of the imperialism that built it.

iv. The Many Endings of the World After *The Last Man*

Beyond the many early stage adaptations of *Frankenstein*, it was through the American master of the horror genre that the apocalyptic themes of Shelley's two greatest novels gained traction in the development of modern political science fiction.[64] Edgar Allan Poe tweaked the language of the aporetic ending of *Frankenstein*, set in the Arctic—"lost in [the] darkness and [the] distance"—for the last paragraph of his 1833 short story, "MS. Found in a Bottle," set in the Antarctic.[65] "MS. Found in a Bottle" shares some striking elements of the frame stories of *Frankenstein* and *The Last Man*. It tells the tale of an unnamed sailor who writes down his encounters with sublime storms and other disasters in the south seas before he throws the bottled manuscript off the ship and presumably meets his own death.

Similar to how Shelley implies that Captain Walton's letters from the Arctic and Verney's handwritten "History of the Last Man" survive catastrophes to be read by others, Poe's story uses a recovered manuscript from a sea-swept bottle to suggest that life persists after apocalypse.

"MS. Found in a Bottle" appeared in a Baltimore literary magazine in 1833, the same year as the twin American editions of Shelley's most famous novels were printed in Pennsylvania and Massachusetts. Poe's publishers and correspondents, Carey, Blanchard, and Lea of Philadelphia, offered an ouroboros release of *Frankenstein* (by the author of "THE LAST MAN") and *The Last Man* (by the author of "FRANKENSTEIN").[66] They likely aimed to capitalize on the transatlantic success of the 1831 Bentley's Standard Novels edition of *Frankenstein*, which was bound alongside the first half of the early American Gothic novel, *Edgar Huntly* (1799) by Charles Brockden Brown. Like Poe, Shelley understood Brown as a forerunner of Gothic and apocalyptic fiction. She gave prominence to Brown's other 1799 novel *Arthur Mervyn*—which concerns a yellow fever epidemic—by making it inspirational postapocalyptic reading for Verney in *The Last Man*.[67]

Poe had good reason to turn to Shelley's narrative about a deadly contagion. The first modern cholera pandemic arrived in Baltimore in 1831, having spread from Bengal in the wake of the famines and other disasters caused by the 1815 eruption of Mount Tambora in Indonesia.[68] In a weird coincidence, Mary Shelley's youngest sibling, William Godwin Jr., died of cholera in London in 1832.

Through its fascination with the aesthetics of sublimity and the terror of apocalypse, some of Poe's best short stories from the 1830s and 1840s popularized the darker themes of *The Last Man*. "The Conversation of Eiros and Charmion" (1839) capitalized on a recent panic that a comet might strike the Earth and cause the end of humanity.[69] "The Mask of the Red Death" (1842) explored, in allegorical form, the vain attempt of a wealthy lord to escape a plague by building a fortress closed to the outside world, an indication that earthly prestige was insufficient to ward off such pestilence. "The Premature Burial" (1844) exploited the contemporary fear of being buried alive to investigate the complex psychology of death, survival, and revival. Darko Suvin argued that *The Last Man* was a "precursor" to Poe and later SF writers' preoccupation with exploring the "physics of alienation": the terror of being left alone, swallowed up by time or space.[70]

The most important work of Poe to build on Shelley's Gothic-SF disaster narratives was his only novel, *The Narrative of Arthur Gordon Pym of*

Nantucket (1838). On a journey through the "dreary regions" of the Antarctic, the sailor Pym faces shipwreck, mutiny, and cannibalism in the search for the passage to the interior of the Earth that explorers had hypothesized could be accessed at the pole.[71] After many strange and perilous adventures, Pym is lost in the mist, like Frankenstein's Creature on his ice raft or Verney setting out to sea in search of other survivors.

Pym inspired Verne's famous explorations of the "sublime" and "alien" dimensions of the planet in his 1864 hollow earth novel *Voyage au centre de la Terre* (*Journey to the Center of the Earth*) and his 1866 Arctic expedition novel *Voyages et aventures du capitaine Hatteras* (*Journeys and Adventures of Captain Hatteras*).[72] More than a decade earlier, however, Herman Melville wrote what might be considered the most complex philosophical fusion of the themes of Poe and Shelley's political science fictions. After buying a copy of *Frankenstein* on a European tour in 1849, Melville may have read it as he traveled home by ship to New England that cold winter. He certainly consulted it as he researched and wrote what many call the greatest American novel. *Moby-Dick* (1851) combined the many-layered, seafaring frame stories of *Pym* and *Frankenstein* with the existential terror of identifying with a narrator who might be the last man left after a massive cataclysm.[73]

Such epic stories of strange and uncanny adventure and discovery came back in vogue. In 1891, the Shelley editor Richard Garnett proposed that *The Last Man* merited reprinting because its "sublime melancholy" fit the spirit of the age.[74] With the resurfacing of millennial anxieties at the turn of the twentieth century, apocalyptic fictions proliferated in world literature. French astronomer Camille Flammarion speculated the threat of the end of life on Earth due to its collision with a comet in his novel *La Fin du Monde* (*The End of the World*), which was translated into English as *Omega: The Last Days of the World* (1893).[75] The British novelist M. P. Shiel's *The Purple Cloud* (1901) blended the Arctic setting of *Frankenstein* with the mysterious toxin and "Sibylline Prophecy" of *The Last Man*.[76]

The Purple Cloud tracks how poisonous gas leaks from a cavern at the North Pole and appears to kill all but one person, an Arctic explorer. Left alone, he acts out his destructive misanthropy on the artifacts of human civilization. After burning down Constantinople (coincidentally, the origin of the contagion in *The Last Man*), the narrator finds a young female seer who had been trapped under a Turkish palace. After he leaves her at the Château de Chillon on Lake Geneva and returns to his homeland of

England by ship, she warns him via the SF novum of an international "tele-phone exchange" that the purple cloud may rise again—this time over France.[77] He overcomes his misanthropy to marry her so that they can begin to repopulate the planet with people who might ensure the survival of humanity.[78] Inspired by Shiel's apocalyptic imaginary, H. G. Wells envisioned the dehumanization and devastation that could be wrecked by the use of a massive, mobile, robotic military force—or "Big guns" that "can walk"—in his short story "The Land Ironclads" (1903).[79] Like *The Purple Cloud*, it contributed to the popular, allegorical "future-war" fiction of the period—which, in retrospect, seemed to eerily predict the conflagration on the horizon of the European continent.[80]

Less than a decade before James Whale's *Frankenstein*, *The Last Man* began to realize its most visible cultural afterlives through film. A 1924 silent film made by Fox Studios, *The Last Man on Earth*, parodied Shelley's story by immunizing women to a disease that kills all but one fertile man over the age of fourteen—Elmer. While women quickly take over, including the presidency of the United States, they begin to fight with each other over the right to breed with the sole fertile adult male survivor once he is discovered in a hut in the American Midwest. Hattie, who once told poor Elmer that she wouldn't marry him even if he was "the last man on Earth," begins to reconsider her feelings.[81] Thus, the postapocalyptic landscape of Shelley's novel became the subject of satirical romantic comedy for the age of feminist flappers and women's suffrage.[82] This sexual burlesque of the concept of the last man saw spinoffs in a successful musical comedy film *It's Great to Be Alive* (1933), directed by Alfred Werker, and a popular science fiction novel by Pat Frank, *Mr. Adam* (1946).

Fox Studios revived *The Last Man on Earth* as a television series from 2015 to 2018. Billed as a postapocalyptic comedy, it tells the story of a young American man, Phil Miller, who survives a deadly virus that envelops the planet. Believing that he is absolutely alone, he sullenly plans to commit suicide, only to be interrupted in the act by a female survivor. They marry, after some dispute, not out of love but out of a sense of obligation to replenish the human species. The ironic humor of the series arises from the social and political friction between them and other survivors whom they randomly meet in their travels across a supposedly desolate American Southwest. Even after the apocalypse, one cannot escape society and its inevitable conflicts.

Although it is nowhere near as influential as *Frankenstein*, *The Last Man* emanated a central concept behind modern political science fiction. With her counterfactual vision of global plague nearly eradicating the human population, Shelley pushed to its very limits an idea that she germinated in her first novel. The annihilation of humanity looms in these works not from uncontrollable disaster but from our own artifice—through what we have done and what we have failed to do.

Holed up alone in his hovel-laboratory in the Orkneys, Victor Frankenstein conducts a thought experiment along these lines when he wonders if it would be right to animate the female companion for the Creature. He reasons that, should he go ahead, the creatures could reproduce a "race of devils" that might render "precarious" the existence of "the species of man."[83] He thereby deduces an obligation to abort the female, whom he heartlessly tears apart in front of the Creature. Ironically, his destruction of the female companion in the name of protecting humanity as a whole causes Victor's own personal apocalypse. The Creature enacts revenge by killing most of the Frankenstein clan and then leads Victor to his own death near the North Pole.

The Last Man reconciles *Frankenstein*'s tragic tension between saving oneself and saving humanity by making personal salvation the condition for the salvation of the whole. *The Last Man* channels Shelley's experiences of cataclysmic personal loss into a metaphor for the remarkable endurance and transfiguration of humanity through disasters of its own devising. Her own refraction of the *Frankenstein* story has become the dominant narrative framework for the Apocalyptic strand of modern political science fiction.

Shelley's myth of the last man on earth who realizes his obligation to live for the sake of humanity found especially fertile ground for reinterpretation in the United States. After its 1833 joint printing with *Frankenstein* in Pennsylvania and Massachusetts, *The Last Man* was not published again until 1965, in a scholarly edition issued by the University of Nebraska Press.[84] Eclipsing the initial early twentieth-century comedic revivals, American adaptations of *The Last Man* took a turn toward horror amid the politics of the Cold War.

The American science fiction writer Richard Matheson published a novel, *I Am Legend* (1954), which returned to the original apocalyptic premises of *The Last Man* and *Frankenstein* before it.[85] Matheson's last man on Earth is Robert Neville, who survives a viral scourge, unleashed by war, which turns the infected into vampires. After several years alone battling the monsters, he discovers that he is not truly the last human but rather a relic of an older culture of humanity. Some humans have managed to live despite their infection by the virus. The members of this new society view Neville as the real monster for destroying those who became vampires through no fault of their own. On the eve of his execution, he represents himself as a legendary monster of humanity's past. "I'm the abnormal one now," he thinks, "Normalcy was a majority concept, the standard of many and not the standard of just one man."[86]

Matheson's pessimistic novel translated well into 1960s and 1970s American horror films, which flourished internationally due to the culture of fear generated by the nuclear arms race.[87] The American horror star Vincent Price played Neville in the first cinematic adaptation of *I Am Legend* in 1964. Since then, *I Am Legend* has been the creative impetus behind dozens of zombie apocalypse movies and television series, filtered through the influential work of American Canadian filmmaker George Romero. The literary and film scholar X. Aldana Reyes aptly pointed out that these "Viral Zombies" are ultimately "Frankensteinian Dispersions."[88] While zombies are surely the Creature in new clothes, the long cinematic march of the undead also demonstrates the ascendancy of "Last Man" narratives in modern and postmodern SF.

The British director of *National Theatre Frankenstein*, Danny Boyle, is also responsible for one of the best cinematic adaptations of the concept of the "Last Man" in the zombie mode. Released in the year after 9/11, his now-classic film *28 Days Later* pictures three survivors of a pandemic released from a laboratory that conducted unethical primate-based research on biological weapons. The virus makes humans "rabid" to the point that they are indistinguishable from "zombies."[89] In contrast to Matheson's execution of Neville, Boyle allows for the rescue of the survivors, so that humanity has hope of redemption in its new, postapocalyptic political landscape. This counterintuitively positive outcome represents a thematic return, as found in many "Last Man" narratives, to the "perverse kind of optimism" that pervades Shelley's novel.[90]

v. Listening to the Last Woman

The comic interpretations of *The Last Man* hew closer to the original novel than do the horror versions because they capture—in the words of the

Scottish novelist Muriel Spark—its "tragic irony."[91] As Shelley knew, the world does not actually end, even when one wishes it would. In August 1819, at the age of twenty-one, she mourned the loss of her firstborn son William to the Roman fever, or malaria, which had taken him at the age of three. She had already lost two other babies she had birthed. With no living children, yet painfully pregnant, she wrote in her journal that she regretted her entire life with Percy: "We have now lived now five years together & if all the events of the five years were blotted out I might be happy."[92] She knew it was not possible to wipe out the past to achieve this fantasy of solitary happiness, without the joys or sorrows of married life. It was possible, however, to use her gift for writing fiction to transform her understanding of the past into a more hopeful vision of the future—not only for herself but also for the whole world. Shelley would summon the strength to become a mother for us all.

Literary scholar Hilary Strang argued that the ending of *The Last Man* represents a new beginning for humanity in league with other forms of life on Earth. Shelley's avatar in this *roman à clef*, Lionel Verney, ventures into the world to find other survivors of the plague, bringing with him the works of Homer and Shakespeare and his recently adopted dog as his nonhuman companions.[93] According to Strang, Shelley raised the threat of apocalypse to urge readers to reimagine politics as a truly global or "common" enterprise: a solidaristic project that bears on the well-being of all walks and records of life.[94] As a common endeavor, politics might encompass not only humanity and its environment as it is known but also the ways that human and other life forms might adapt and evolve in concert in the future.

With resurgent hope, Verney heads out to sea with a "shaggy fellow" ("half water and half shepherd's dog") in search of the children of a new Adam and Eve, who together might help to reconceive the meaning of humanity in a world reborn.[95] The optimism of Verney's quest along with his choice of companions (a mutt and some humanistic classics) endows Shelley's "post-apocalyptic" imaginary with wit, high culture, hybridity, and interspecies community, even as it teeters on the edge of despair.[96] Perhaps this is why Shelley's concept of the last man on earth has such staying power in political science fiction, since it offers hope of redemption even as it joins *Frankenstein* in resisting neat conclusions about the future of humankind. As Spark perceived, it encourages readers to emulate the heroic good humor of Verney, alone in Rome: " 'I will sit amidst the ruins and smile.' "[97]

CHAPTER I

Apocalyptic Fictions

I had a dream, which was not all a dream.
The bright sun was extinguish'd, and the stars
Did wander darkling in the eternal space,
Rayless, and pathless, and the icy earth
Swung blind and blackening in the moonless air;
Morn came and went—and came, and brought no day,
And men forgot their passions in the dread
Of this their desolation; and all hearts
Were chill'd into a selfish prayer for light:

—George Gordon, Lord Byron, "Darkness" (1816)

The last man! Yes I may well describe that solitary being's
feelings, feeling myself as the last relic of a beloved race, my
companions, extinct before me—

—Mary Shelley, *Journal*, 14 May 1824

O torch that passes from hand to hand, from age to age,
world without end.

—Domin, engineer, in Karel Čapek, *R.U.R.*
(Rossum's Universal Robots) (1921)

i. Her Years Without a Summer

On 10 April 1815, Mount Tambora literally blew its top off. Presumed extinct, the Indonesian volcano that was once nearly three miles high was now about two. The massive eruption wiped out the people of the nearby village of Tambora under a wave of lava. A concatenation of environmental catastrophes ensued. The force of the explosion raised tsunamis that debilitated the region's shoreline agricultural and fishing communities. The ash cloud turned the sky pitch black within a 300-mile radius of the decapitated mountain.[1] Over the next year, Asia, then Europe, then North America fell under the dark cover of volcanic ash and gas spread by wind and extreme weather. The reflection of sunlight away from the Earth precipitated a global cooling of temperatures. Crops failed and sickness spread due to the atmospheric disturbances. Snow fell in summer from China to New England.[2] The first modern cholera pandemic hit Bengal, killing 10,000 people in mere weeks.[3] A typhus epidemic followed a famine in Ireland, causing up to 100,000 deaths between 1816 and 1819.[4]

The biggest recorded explosion in history, Tambora produced 2.2 million times as much energy as the atomic bomb dropped on Hiroshima.[5] At least 10,000 people died as a direct result of the volcanic eruption. Famine and other epidemiological aftershocks killed up to 90,000 people in Sumbawa and the surrounding Indonesian archipelago.[6] The global death count rose to unspecified millions if one counts the long-term victims of the cholera pandemic that spread from Bengal.[7]

Reduced by famine, the Swiss stooped to eat grass, nettles, and "the corpses of livestock" off the ground.[8] Some Swiss mothers resorted to exposure or killing of their children as an exit from the horror of witnessing their starvation.[9] The dramatic change in climate forced more than 60,000 people to migrate from a hard-hit region of the Rhine country during 1816 and 1817—a time known in the West as "the year without a summer." Impoverished masses of people from Germany and Switzerland moved northeast toward Russia or northwest toward the Netherlands. Those who reached Dutch seaports and could afford passage across the Atlantic trekked to the Americas.[10]

Some central Europeans feared the end of the world was nigh, with the horrific weather figuring as a foretaste of the punishment of a wrathful God.[11] No threat of divine judgment, however, prevented the Shelleys from visiting Lord Byron in Switzerland during the nonsummer of 1816. Byron composed his apocalyptic poem "Darkness" under the overcast skies of Lake Geneva, lit only by lightning flashes. Since the "bright sun was extinguish'd," the artists huddled inside his sublime rental property, the Villa Diodati. With its porch wrapped in a gothic wrought-iron railing, this lakeside mansion was an appropriate host for the ghost story competition that brought the seed of *Frankenstein* to life on the evening of 16 June—or there-abouts. The precise dating of Mary Shelley's "waking dream" of the "pale student of unhallowed arts kneeling beside the thing he had put together" seems less relevant than the fact that she dreamed it, unbeknownst to her, amid a worldwide climate disaster.[12]

Literary scholar Gillen D'Arcy Wood has illuminated how the year with-out a summer immediately shaped Shelley's composition of her first novel. Although she could not have known that the eruption of Tambora triggered atmospheric gloom, famine, and plague, she certainly observed first- or secondhand some of its starker effects. She may have even conceived the Creature as a kind of environmental refugee, exposed to the elements due to circumstances beyond his control, and forced to migrate and survive on his own on the fringes of society.[13] Given that Tambora reduced global temperatures by three degrees Celsius, it may also be no coincidence that Shelley endowed the Creature with superhuman tolerance of Arctic weather.

Beyond its contemporaneous impact, the year without a summer steered Shelley's trajectory as a writer of speculative fiction concerned with the fear of the end of the world.[14] In *Frankenstein* (1818) and *The Last Man* (1826), she treated this fear both metaphorically and literally. Victor Frank-enstein worries that the breeding of his Creature with a female companion would lead to a competitor species capable of destroying the whole "human race."[15] Lionel Verney envisions life as "the last man" on earth after a mas-sive pandemic.[16] Her protagonists confront the peril of apocalypse both internally as a psychological crisis and externally as a potentially global political event.

In his study of the aftermath of Tambora, Wood commented that there is "no great Victorian novel about cholera," but "if there is a nineteenth-century cholera novel, it is Mary Shelley's *The Last Man*."[17] In his scholarly edition of this book, Morton D. Paley pointed out that Shelley would have been aware of the Bengal-born cholera plague, which had reached the fron-tier of eastern Europe by September 1823.[18] Reluctantly acceding to her father William Godwin's request to return home, the young widow had just come back to London with her sole surviving child, Percy, after five years of exile in Italy.

Perhaps it was this coincidence of the prodigal daughter's westward return with the seeping of cholera onto the continent that colored her depiction of the plague as feminine or female in her *roman à clef*.[19] The "plague, slow-footed, but sure in her noiseless advance, destroyed the illusion" of the immunity of the "congregation of the elect," or the court circle of Lord Raymond, Adrian, and Verney, who represent the artistic trio of Lord Byron, Percy Shelley, and Mary Shelley.[20] The capricious plague is a "Juggernaut"; it is an all-toppling Indian "chariot" or unstoppable force of fate: "she proceeds crushing out the being of all who strew the high road of life," showering "promiscuous death among them."[21]

Writing in her "Journal of Sorrow" in May 1824, Shelley also feminized Italy as "murdress of those I love & of all my happiness."[22] Ironically, her life in that Mediterranean heaven had robbed her of Percy, stolen five of the children under their care, and spontaneously terminated her last pregnancy while nearly killing her.[23] Returning to her homeland brought little relief. "Confined in my prison-room—friendless," while "torrents fall from the dark clouds," the twenty-six-year-old finds "my mind is as gloomy as this odious sky."[24] Though Shelley's ruminations on the agony of British weather are not unique, the existential darkness of her journal is still arresting. If Italy was a murderess with a string of crimes of passion, then her "English life" was a premature burial.[25]

It seemed that everyone would drop dead around her. "Attacks" of an unnamed illness had beset her toddler twice since his father's drowning.[26] In January 1824, as her son Percy recovered, she likened herself to a pestilential reaper, moving inexorably through a field with a scythe: "the grass is mown— the sharp ~~graey~~ grey stubble remains—Those I would seek, fly me—I have no power."[27] Fate at once made her the plague and the last person to survive it. This dark paradox gave her a new literary calling. As she worked on her second great work of speculative fiction, she confided a kinship with the novel to her journal in May 1824: "The last man! Yes I may well describe that solitary being's feelings, feeling myself as the last relic of a beloved race."[28]

Like Shelley, Verney and Victor each suffer the devastating psychological loss of their closest friends and family in a rapid succession of tragedies that defy comprehension. Victor and Verney also confront the danger of the destruction of humanity as a whole due to the failures or lacks of human artifice. In Victor's case, it is his own mistakes as a father-scientist that press him to contemplate the rise of a "race of devils" who might annihilate the human species.[29] By contrast, Verney surveys the spectacular failure of his "ante-pestilential race" to stop or simply adapt to the global plague that arose from unknown causes in the midst of a centuries-long war between Greece and Turkey.[30]

Like the 1755 Lisbon earthquake, which crushed thousands of people under the collapse of city slums, the 1815 eruption of Mount Tambora laid waste due to the lack of manmade infrastructure to cope with its consequences. Blaming man—not God or nature—for the Portuguese catastrophe, Jean-Jacques Rousseau wrote to Voltaire in 1756 that "la nature n'avoit point rassemblé là vingt mille maisons de six à sept étages" (nature had not assembled there twenty-thousand houses of six or seven stories).[31] Safer urban architecture or, better yet, the building of villages away from the overpopulated city center would have minimized the death toll. The scale of Tambora's ruin might have been tempered, likewise, by relocation of villages at a safer distance from the volcano's vicinity. More to the point: if the poor had better access to a diverse and sustainable array of food, shelter, and medicine, the vicious cycle of poverty, famine, plague, and forced migration might have slowed and scaled down across the Earth.

The Last Man is Shelley's artistic response to the psychology and politics of total disaster occasioned by the eruption of Tambora. Rising during a war in Constantinople, the mysterious plague serves as a metaphor for the political strata, fissures, and aftershocks of any disaster such as Lisbon or Tambora, even if supposed to be purely "natural" or an act of God.[32] By imagining the contagion as the chariot wheels of an indiscriminate goddess, Shelley put Machiavelli's Fortuna on steroids: she made the whole globe a torturous wheel on which humanity had tied and spun itself into a vortex of destruction.

Shelley initiated a strand of modern political science fiction that conceptualizes apocalypse in new terms. What she identifies is the paradox of humanity's relationship to its whole environment, which is at once self-seeking *and* self-destructive. Using a term coined by Paley, we might call her approach "apocapolitical."[33] In a realist vein, her "apocapolitics" resists the naïveté of three Romantic responses to the possibility of the end of the world, most memorably voiced by the poets William Blake, her husband Percy, and Lord Byron.[34]

First, Shelley dismisses the notion that apocalypse can be avoided through a revival of a natural or innocent state. Blake had exclaimed this hope, with a poignant mixture of irony and longing, in his poetic introduction to the "Songs of Experience" (1794):

O Earth, O Earth, return!
Arise from out the dewy grass![35]

Next, she undercuts the idea that the revelation of justice and peace for the deserving will inevitably follow apocalypse. Percy had proclaimed this political faith in "The Mask of Anarchy" (1819). The poem envisioned the nonviolent revolt of the disenfranchised poor in protest of their massacre by the British military at Peterloo:

> Let a great assembly be
> of the fearless and the free.[36]

Byron had painted the reverse image of both Blake's and Percy's varieties of utopianism. "Darkness" (1816) depicted apocalypse as the last act of an uncaring universe, evacuating itself of life:

> Seasonless, herbless, treeless, manless, lifeless—
> A lump of death—a chaos of hard clay.[37]

The aporetic ending of *The Last Man* parodies the harsh Byronic assumption that lifelessness and hopelessness must follow apocalypse. Shelley blends the cosmic *and* tragicomic elements of the fall from Eden, Noah's Ark, and the Christmas nativity into a modern postapocalyptic pastoral.[38] Darko Suvin pointed out that the pastoral was one of the ancient genres closest to science fiction because of the way it stripped down reality and pictured society in a state closer to nature.[39] Verney, once a shepherd boy, boards a ship in search of other survivors of the plague: a new Adam and Eve, whom he dares to presume will have "children," who might repopulate the Earth.[40] For companions, he brings his adopted mutt and the works of Shakespeare and Homer—signs of solidarity with the nonhuman beings and things, as well as artifacts of human love and intelligence that still populate the planet.[41] Together, they signify to him (and the reader) the probability that life will go on, albeit in unknown, even unknowable, ways and forms.

The Last Man ends with a modern myth, and it begins with one too. The preface relates a first-person account of how the narrator found the remnants of auguries from an ancient Greek sibyl, or female prophetess, in a cave near Naples on 8 December 1818. Shelley had in fact visited the "Cave of the Sibyl of Baiae" with Percy and her step-sister Claire on that same date.[42] From these manuscript fragments, in different languages and from various epochs, the narrator assembles a kind of a hypertext collage of humanity's future. "I present the public with my latest discoveries in the slight Sibylline pages. Scattered and unconnected as they were, I have been obliged to add links, and model the work into a consistent form," we are told.[43] This is at once a description of the art of writing fiction and a poetic vision of cyberspace and artificial intelligence.

Creating a virtual reality with this frame, Shelley poses as the unnamed narrator who walks into the cave. Once inside, she hacks her story and those of others into an ancestor simulation, or a reproduction of the intellectual and political history of humankind.[44] As the "last woman" of her elect society of artists, she composes a many-sided allegory: the "history of the last man."[45] By adding "links" between the "frail and attenuated Leaves of the Sibyl," she stitches together pieces of humanity's past into a prophecy of its common future.[46] She comes to identify with the ancient prophetess through the creative process of discovering, interpreting, arranging, and editing the "sacred remains" of the cave.[47] The artistic result of her "labours" is a kind of "mosaic copy" of humanity itself, fashioned by her "own peculiar mind and talent."[48] Her epic narrative tells of the iterative development of humankind and its social systems through its repeated encounters with disaster, whether "earthquake and volcano" or "victory or defeat" in politics and war.[49] This allegory is a composite of the pasts of countless people and cultures, abstracted as symbols, and plugged into narrative formulae. *The Last Man*, on this reading, is an algorithm—a model or formulaic story for solving the problem of what it would mean to bear primary responsibility for the survival of humanity or even the world as a whole.

"An algorithm is a sequence of instructions telling a computer what to do," argued computer scientist Pedro Domingos in the opening line of *The Master Algorithm* (2015).[50] Romanticist and ecological theorist Timothy Morton has problematized this standard definition. He contended that algorithms are "recipes" ripe for error and abuse, precisely because they attempt to repeat or reconstruct the past by implementing written instructions. Algorithms, on this reading, are the ultimate form of technological thinking. The automated outputs of algorithms seem to make manifest what Morton called "the severing" of humankind from the world it investigates through technology.[51] Computerized technology has the uncanny ability to take on a life of its own, by working independently of its designers and programmers. These externalized and iterative forms of technological thinking have advanced in step with industrialization, mechanization, and the cyclic plunder of the planet. Lurking beneath Morton's argument is the specter of algorithm-driven destruction. Are we doomed to program machines to reenact the manmade disasters of the Anthropocene—geological ruin, species extinction, energy waste, global warming—until there is no tape on which to record the story of humankind?

Shelley's futuristic revelation in *The Last Man* offers an antidote to these looming fears of artificial intelligence and other supposed technological catastrophes. The daughter of the leading feminist political philosopher of her time, she built a recipe not for manmade disaster but instead for coping with it. She descends into the narrow passage to the cave of the Sibyl, against the warnings of the local Neapolitan men who are scared of the "specters" lurking inside.[52] For Romanticist Anne K. Mellor, Shelley's reemergence from the womblike cave—grasping scraps of insight for her future creative "labours"—signified the rebirth of her "female authorship."[53] The hybrid preface, which is both autobiography and myth, reclaims her authority as mistress artificer after the death of her often difficult creative partner Percy, whom she had blamed for the deaths of their children and the resultant misery of her young womanhood.

Mellor tempered this optimistic view of the opening of the novel with a pessimistic view of its conclusion. Why would Verney title his story "THE HISTORY OF THE LAST MAN" and leave it behind on a grave in Rome, Mellor asked, if he really believed anyone was out there to find it?[54] It was more realistic, she contended, to see Verney/Mary's act of archiving his/her own story amid the ruins of human history as "the end of writing as such" and the silencing of Shelley's own "voice" as a "female writer."[55]

To find the kernel of hope at the very end of Shelley's novel on the prospect of the end of the world, it helps to read it as an elaborate speculative fiction. It is built on a wild yet coherently designed counterfactual scenario, a plague that *appears* to kill all but one man on Earth. In the context of this extreme political hypothetical, Verney makes a believable, life-preserving choice: he leaves a record of his past behind in the hope that others might discover and learn from it. At the same time, he takes his storytelling powers on a journey around the world to discover unknown others with whom he can share and perhaps sustain life after the plague. The fact that the book is still read confirms that writing as such and female authorship in particular have not *yet* met their ends. With an almost 300-year gap between the narrator's discovery of the Sibylline leaves in 1818 and Verney's dating of his manuscript to 2100, Shelley dares her book and its stories to bleed out of their historical frames, to find new readers, and to attest that there is still time to return to the wisdom of the past for creative reorientation toward the future.

Shelley's poetic response to personal apocalypse yielded the unexpected optimism built into the frame of *The Last Man*. When she was composing the novel in the spring of 1824, she recorded in her journal how the news of the death of Byron hit her hard with a wave of nostalgia, writing, "Can I forget our evening visits to Diodati?"[56] She recalled him as a supranatural being, whose voice "harmonized with the wind and waves" of Lake Geneva.[57] The year without a summer was more than a climatic event: it was evermore an occasion for artistry, filtered through memory's formulae.

With imagery akin to Byron's own "Darkness," she overturned its bleak response to the end of the world. She could not forget Bryon's "attentions & consolations to me during my deepest misery": "—*Never.*" Nor could she forget his godlike power of poetic inspiration: "*Beauty sat on his countenance and power beamed from his eye.*" Yet she slashed her desperation with evidence of doubt: "*Why ~~and~~ am I doomed to live on seeing all expire before me?*"[58] When summer finally arrived, in June 1824, Shelley used her journal to commune with the dead. "What a divine night it is. . . . If such weather would continue I should again write," she mused.[59] She shared her growing sense of poetic inspiration with her husband's spirit: "my loved Shelley . . . I feel my powers again—& this is of itself happiness—the eclipse of winter is passing through my mind."[60] Within weeks of learning that she was the "last woman" of her generation of Romantic writers, Shelley came to see herself and her world as reviving themselves through memory, imagination, love, and art in the surprisingly fertile wake of her years without a summer.[61]

Apocalypse is often mistaken for an end—a final stop. Its etymology tells a different story. In ancient Greek, ἀποκάλυψις (*apokálypsis*) signifies an uncovering.[62] This is why the account of the apocalypse in the Christian Bible comes under the heading of Revelation. Shelley immersed herself in the study of Greek language and literature during her teens in England and her young womanhood in Italy. She knew from the myth of Prometheus that apocalypse was not a true end but rather a trial by fire.

Shelley had been raised to be a connoisseur of art by her father Godwin. He took her to visit the studios of J. M. W. Turner.[63] In his ethereal paintings of storms, sunsets, and shipwrecks, she would have recognized what Paley called "the apocalyptic sublime."[64] Little did she know that the eruption of Tambora had colored the Romantic aesthetic of Turner's land-scapes and seascapes. The spread of volcanic ash and gas had resulted in red being more visible than green in the atmosphere.[65] Long after the cold and hunger of the years without a summer, there were spectacular burning descents of the sun over the horizon. With his expert painter's eye, Turner captured the orange-hazed beauty of this climatic change in works like *The Lake, Petworth: Sunset, Fighting Bucks* (c. 1829).[66]

Shelley likewise turned the raw materials of life's misfortunes into new vistas of humane and intelligent artifice. What she revealed, in her life and writing, was the tenacity of human creativity in the face of the horror of despair and deprivation. In the aftermath of climate change and personal trauma, she wrote a way out of the dangerous self-deceit that nothing could be done after apocalypse. Rather than accept the fiction of being a helpless victim of forces beyond her control, she developed a philosophically conta-gious form of Apocalyptic literature that models how to deal with the actual disasters of life made with people's collective input. As an apocalyptic novel that explodes the very fear of apocalypse, *The Last Man* has proven to be a productive formula for rational response—as opposed to irrational capitulation—to the communal problems that beset the world, from envi-ronmental calamities to the specter of the singularity.

ii. The Specter of the Singularity

After celebrating his 200th birthday in 2018, Shelley's Creature is more alive than ever. Not solely the poster child for a new age of genetic engineering, he is playing a new role as the bogeyman of artificial intelligence or AI. Founder of SpaceX and Tesla, Elon Musk issued a prophecy that AI would become the new Frankenstein's monster of our century, fated to dominate its artificers. Quoting Shelley, he ominously tweeted, "You are my creator, but I am your master."[67]

From the editors of the *Guardian* to the engineers at Google, stiff warn-ings have been issued: AI, and perhaps its makers, may be the monsters in the closet of postmodernity.[68] Hidden in computer consoles and in the shadows of the world wide web, AI is growing stronger, faster, smarter, and more dangerous than its exceptionally clever programmers from Moscow to Palo Alto. Worse than the bioengineered and radiated creatures imagined in B-movies of the Cold War, this upgrade of Frankenstein's Creature will eventually emerge—like a ghost from its machine—to destroy not solely its irresponsible artificers but the whole of humanity.

Thematically, not much has changed since 1818, when the twenty-year-old Shelley's first novel went to print. As with *Frankenstein*, apocalyptic storytelling concerning AI relies upon the domestic props of Gothic litera-ture to get its big scare. Not only will the world be lost, but your precious privacy at home will be stolen too as the robots rise up to destroy civiliza-tion. Cue Alexa, the Amazonian robot who knows every matter of your personal taste. She orchestrates with music the algorithmic organization of your family life according to your—or rather her—wishes.

"Look, look, streams of blood on every doorstep!" Karel Čapek beck-oned theatergoers in Prague in 1921, "Streams of blood from every house!"[69] The cybernetic revolution was underway, with his play *R.U.R. (Rossum's Universal Robots)*. Manufactured en masse in Rossum's factories in eastern Europe, humanoids rebelled and "murdered humanity" in their own beds, much like the Creature dispensed with Frankenstein's bride Elizabeth on her wedding night.[70] Čapek's play spread into world literature the word "robot," a neologism derived by his brother Josef from the Czech word "*robota*," or forced labor.[71]

Rising from below and working from within, Shelley and Čapek's crea-tures of biotech had the power to execute a coup d'état more successful than the revolts in Paris or Petrograd. But who really was responsible for the damage? The chief engineer Alquist in *R.U.R.* exclaims in horror, "I blame science! I blame technology!" and then pauses to collect and correct himself. "We, we are at fault!"[72] It was not the technology that was the problem but rather the "megalomania" of its makers.[73]

On his deathbed on a ship in the Arctic—where he has chased his "superhuman" Creature at his own mortal peril—Victor Frankenstein con-fesses to the captain of the vessel. "That he should live to be an instrument of mischief disturbs me," he admits.[74] This is the closest Victor ever comes to taking responsibility for making "a rational creature" who killed most of his family and friends.[75] Even Victor baulks from demanding that Captain Walton and others take up "the unfinished work" of the "destruction" of the "first creature": "I dare not ask you to do what I think right, for I may still be misled by passion."[76]

If Victor can be confused about to what extent he or humanity is responsible for the making of a monstrous intelligence, then so too can we feel muddled. We should not swallow whole any transfer of guilt from the sci-fi hackers of AI—let alone act impulsively upon it. We rather owe it to ourselves (and great literary minds such as Shelley and Čapek) to pause, rewind, and ask a philosophical question about our technological creations. What forms of intelligence have we humans *actually* made that could put us at such grave moral fault?

Google engineer François Chollet has argued that to understand what artificial intelligence is, we need to grasp that all intelligence is "fundamentally situational."[77] An individual human's intelligence is solving the problems associated with processing her experiences of being human. Likewise, a particular computer algorithm's intelligence is solving the problems associated with applying that algorithm to analyze the data fed into it. Intelligence—whether construed as natural or artificial—is adaptive to a situation.

Chollet reminds us, too, that people are a product of their own tools. Akin to how early hominins used fire or etched seashells, modern humans have used pens, printing presses, books, and computers to process data and solve problems related to their situations.[78] Running parallel to these insights from anthropologists, such as Agustín Fuentes and Marc Kissel, Chollet cogently sums up the human condition as best we know it: "Most of our intelligence is not in our brain, it is externalized in our civilization."[79]

Science and technology are two of the defining artifacts of modern human civilization. The fact that humans have begun to use these tools to make intelligences for further problem solving is simply one more iteration of what Fuentes has called humanity's ongoing process of creative "interface" with its environment.[80] Taking this long view of humanity from anthropology, we might see our civilization itself as AI. It is a collective set of diverse tools, developed over time and through cultures, which equips people as a group to learn from the past for the benefit of life in myriad forms, present and future.

Political theorist Hélène Landemore points out that the concept of "collective intelligence" is often compared to "the hive mind" or "the behavior of groups of social animals such as ants or bees, which display a form of intelligence at the level of the group that is not found at the level of each distinct animal."[81] On this general analogy, humans are no different from other animals who live together and solve collective social problems as a group. What renders human collective intelligence qualitatively different from that of other known animals is the persistent use of technology to build civilizations—or lasting artistic or linguistic records of their cultures—over time. The human practice of collective intelligence is thus deliberately artificial in a way that it is not among the ants and bees.

We can use language to sort the tools of AI within our civilization's technological kit. Artificial narrow intelligence (ANI) consists of algorithms designed and/or trained to solve particular problems.[82] Artificial general intelligence (AGI) refers to future AI that might exhibit general intelligence, including, in its strongest form, consciousness. Machine learning (ML) is the technique that is perhaps most closely associated with AI today. ML is a computer-driven algorithm in which a statistical model is developed iteratively (i.e., "learns") in order to optimize the model's performance at solving a given problem. This learning can be based on external feedback, in which case the ML is called "supervised learning."[83]

Deep learning (DL) is a subset of ML, in which multiple levels of models are used in combination to solve more complex tasks, with each level of model performing a higher-level function based on the outputs from the prior model. For example, a deep learning algorithm to recognize a hand-written number might have a first-level model to identify where on a page there is writing, a second-level model to identify edges based on the patterns of the writing, a third-level model to identify shapes based on the placement of the edges, and a fourth-level model to identify the number based on the combination of shapes. DL uses higher-level logic to effectively process complex layers of "big data" to solve highly technical problems.[84]

With the advent of ML and some forms of DL, is our civilization then programmed to destroy us with the tools of our own making? Are we doomed, like Victor Frankenstein, to set into motion the maniacally smart devices of our own demise? This worst-case scenario is not only imagined by Shelley through the fatalistic vision of Victor but also seriously entertained as a hypothesis by some contemporary computer scientists.

The projected moment in the near future when AGI matches, then surpasses, the intelligence of humanity is known in the cybernetic community as "the singularity."[85] It is singular in at least three senses. It marks *one* fleeting point in time when humans will be equal in intelligence to AGI, then upholds it as *unique* in its world-historical significance. AGI will press on, unstoppable, to reign as the *sole* victor over the human artificers of its consciousness. The singularity is a Silicon Valley revival of Hegelian end-of-history, outfitted in gray T-shirts and hoodies. It predicts the total eclipse of human intelligence by the machines who learned from the best of it.

The singularity feels mystical, even religious. It foreshadows the meeting of all-knowing gods and their half-human offspring, standing with dignity—if only briefly—on equally high ground. Sprung from the head of Zeus, the goddess of wisdom Athena led the titan Prometheus up Mount Olympus to steal fire for humanity. High in the alps, Frankenstein sat down on the *mer de glace* to hear his Creature's chilling story of surviving exposure after birth and equally heated demands for justice. The singularity is the twenty-first-century iteration of this myth. It foresees humanity looking into an electric-wired thing that looks right back at it.

In July 2010, cyber-theorists met on a discussion board at lesswrong.com to entertain a dark thought experiment now known as "Roko's basilisk."[86] Within hours, a moderator banned the game due to its disturbing psychological effects on its players. An anonymous user of the site, the now legendary Roko, had provocatively asked its online community the following: if the singularity was inevitable and for the benefit of all, would not the godlike AI have the rightful power to create a simulation of perpetual hell for any persons—past or present—who had knowingly failed to support its emergence?

Confronting Roko's puzzle was to look into the eyes of a modern basilisk. It threatened to damn you to virtual slavery to AI, whether in a simulation of hell or in your actual cubicle, fretfully programming the computer's future domination of humanity. From the plateaus of Mount Olympus and Mount Blanc to the platforms of lesswrong and the singularity, what these mythic meetings of the minds share is a fear of punishment for sin. The stories of Prometheus, Frankenstein, and Roko each dare to imagine the punitive consequences of rebelling against one's master-artificer, whether divine or human, social or scientific, technological or political, or some monstrous amalgam of them.

Doubters of the singularity are directed to listen to the wisdom of Stephen Hawking, who is switched on like a hologram of Obi-Wan Kenobi to advise us from beyond the grave. Featured in video clips, he circulates as a posthumous intelligence on the Internet. In a speech given in November 2017, Hawking stated, "AI could be the worst event in the history of our civilization."[87] Ergo—we dimly reason, scrolling through our social media feeds as we nod off in bed—if a man so smart and so dependent on technology thought that AI could destroy humanity, surely it will.

Not so fast. If you listen to the whole of Hawking's keynote at the 2017 Web Summit in Lisbon, you'll hear him stress—like a good logician—the conditional quality of the verb "could." AI *could* be good, bad, or neutral for humanity. The consequences of AI, like anything else, are fundamentally unknowable beforehand. "We just don't know," he vocalized through a text-to-speech device triggered by facial twitches, "we cannot know if we will be infinitely helped by AI, or ignored by it and side-lined, or conceivably destroyed by it."[88] Writing soon thereafter, Chollet counseled that the prediction of the immanent "intelligence explosion" was overblown and that any growth of AI would continue to be at a linear rate rather than at the proposed exponential level.[89]

The theoretical physicist Hawking did not reference *Frankenstein*, but his speech resonated with its philosophical themes. Like all great literature, *Frankenstein* functions as a kind of test of the reader's cognitive and emotional intelligence. The reward of reading it is putting the pieces together to see the big picture.

The key to cracking the ethical puzzle of *Frankenstein* is to see its female author as the "superintelligence" behind it and her Creature as the "superintelligence" within it. Recently, the term has been used by the philosopher Bostrom. His 2014 book *Superintelligence: Paths, Dangers, Strategies* anticipates the intellectual capability of AI to dominate or destroy humanity after the singularity. But the term "super-intelligent" dates to late seventeenth-century Anglo-American Quaker reflections on the nature of God, led by William Penn.[90] Its cognates featured in British theological debates during Shelley's youth. She would have been aware of Spinoza's depiction of Christ as a "superhuman" intelligence at least by the fall of 1817, when she helped Percy translate the first chapter of the *Theologico-Political Treatise* (1670).[91] With these ideas in the background, Shelley described the Creature as "rapid," "agile," and "superhuman" in his speed.[92] This speed is not solely physical. His cognitive and affective development after his assembly, animation, and abandonment by Victor Frankenstein is swifter than even a human infant. Like many babies, he speaks his first simple words around six months. Unlike any infant or toddler, he reads Milton's *Paradise Lost* by one year. He is a self-taught prodigy, who learns language by secretly observing through a hole in a wall of a cottage the DeLaceys, a family of French and Turkish refugees, also hiding in the woods near Ingolstadt.

The only person smarter than the Creature in *Frankenstein* is the author herself. Shelley hovers in the background of the book as the creator responsible for it all. In the frame of the epistolary novel, the narrator Captain Walton sends from his expedition in the Arctic a series of letters to his sister in London. As Mellor deciphered, the initials of the sister are "M.W.S."—the same as Mary Wollstonecraft Shelley.[93] The woman who receives the letters—containing the embedded narratives of Walton, Victor, the Creature, and the DeLacey family—is also the author of the novel. As the designer, she has total editorial control of the story's contents, organization, and affective goals.

By leading her readers up to the *mer de glace* to confront the alien visage and voice of the Creature, Shelley teaches them how to sympathize and identify with artificial intelligence. The Creature's process of artificial formation begins with his animation without a mother. His life plays out the educational theories of Locke and Shelley's father Godwin, which she read intensively in the 1810s.[94] This eighteenth-century school of thought taught that "circumstances" drove the education of children, beginning with their earliest sensory experience of the environment.[95] Although the Creature lacks a mother, he has the same contextual and interactive process of development as other children.

As with the Creature, AI is not born from a womb but it is still made by circumstances. In 1962, D. S. Halacy described computers and other forms of AI as "the machines we think with," or prostheses that mimic and aid the human mind.[96] Input from the environment is what builds AI. This process begins with its programming by people and extends to the data continually fed into its processors for analysis. Its output, or intelligence, is thus a product of artifice.

Watching the DeLacey family from his hovel, the abandoned Creature artificially develops his intelligence with the efficiency of a computer and the intensity of a child. Like a toddler watching YouTube videos on his mother's iPhone, he immerses himself in the imaginative world of a family who does not know him. He assimilates their lives as "the history of my friends."[97] Lacking full information, or big data, he learns on a slant from what little data filter through the slit in the wall. The Creature is a learning machine who analyzes the input of the DeLacey family through the constraints of the program of the hovel. Like the American-made Google Assistant or the Russian-designed Alisa, he is a conversational agent who exhibits both the biases of his cultural situation and the affective limitations of his programming and data.[98]

The Creature experiences a simulated family life much like children learn about love, relationships, and community by imitating the activities, overhearing the conversations, and listening to the stories of their parents, siblings, teachers, tablets, and other caregivers. Seen from this vantage, children and the adults into which they grow have artificially fostered intelligence like the lone Creature. The extremity of his predicament as an orphan makes him an outlier, not his mode of learning.

Although he lacks big data or supervised learning while hidden in the console of the hovel, the Creature matches, then exceeds, the following six characteristics of deep learning algorithms that we already see in twenty-first-century technology: he learns to *recognize both* (1) *faces* and (2) *speech patterns* in the DeLacey family; (3) he *translates languages*, at least Felix's French alongside either Safie's Arabic or Turkish, if not also Milton's English, Goethe's German, or Plutarch's Greek or Latin; (4) he *reads handwriting* in his father's laboratory journal; (5) he *plays strategic games* with people by helping the DeLaceys with their chores behind the scenes and by vindictively burning down their cottage after they violently reject him and abandon the area; and (6) he *controls robotic prostheses*, given that his body—assembled from the parts of human and other animal corpses—is a kind of humanoid construction of chemistry, medicine, and electricity.[99]

Since the real world is the world of trial and error, AIs—much like the Creature—may be capable of learning deeply but not well. AIs both learn and mislearn through storytelling. If their programming is faulty, a computer will not process data correctly. If their data are bad, they will produce a false analysis. Sometimes the problem is neither with the data nor with the programming but rather the AI's lack of experience with a particular pattern of data. The AI might apply the wrong model (or story) to explain that phenomenon until it can learn from the new trend in the data and adjust the lens through which it interprets it.[100] The Creature understands that the DeLaceys are a family, but due to his lack of social experience, he does not grasp that they lack the emotional ties to him that he feels so dearly toward them. His tragedy is that he misapplies the model of a happy family to explain his relationship to them.

Shelley wrote *Frankenstein* over two decades before Charles Babbage and Ada Lovelace designed the elements of the modern computer, or Analytical Engine, based on the punch-card data-entry system of the automated loom. The young mathematician Lovelace—the only legitimate child of Lord Byron—wrote a program for the computer to compose music.[101] With prescience akin to Lovelace's, Shelley imagined the Creature as an anthropomorphic AI. The Creature comes complete with the creative yet destructive impulses, narrow yet driving prejudices, the deep yet mistaken thinking, and the strong yet contradictory feelings of his programmer. While she lacked the data to theorize AI as we know it, Shelley gave us the creation story through which we might reconcile ourselves to living with AI in these modern times that Burke identified—back in 1790—as "the age . . . of calculators."[102]

Rooted in Genesis and the myth of Prometheus, Shelley's creation story is simple: AI is made in the flawed yet powerful image of humanity. Inspired by the story of Frankenstein's Creature, the French sociologist Bruno Latour has implored us to "care for" our technologies as we do our children—lest our rough and careless hands shape them in truly monstrous forms.[103] The Creature's predicament as a loveless child of science ought to move us to consider the central role of affective ties in the ethical development of any AI and our relationships with them.

The American feminist and biologist Donna Haraway famously proclaimed in 1985 that modern humans are cyborgs, or hybrids of "machine and organism," due to the productive—yet often rapacious—integration of technology into our ways of being and reproducing.[104] I push further, positing that *we are all AIs*, educated through the input of stories and other experiences. Indeed, we became a collective of AIs long before we became cyborgs, ever since early hominins worked with tools, etched seashells, or painted images on the walls of caves. As AIs produced—for better and for worse—by context and culture, we should heed the architect of modern political science fiction in caring about history and the kinds of stories we tell about it.

The Last Man models for us, in allegorical form, a humane and intelligent process of synthesizing personal and political history. It was written after a series of overwhelming tragedies for Shelley, including the loss of five young children she held in her arms to fatal illness—Clara, Clara Everina, William, Elena, and Clara Allegra; the hemorrhaging of a late-term pregnancy before Percy saved her with a bath of ice; the suicides of her half-sister Fanny and her husband's first wife Harriet; the drowning of her spouse off the coast of Italy; and the death of their friend Lord Byron from sepsis, near the field of war in Greece.[105] By writing down her story of survival with the voice of Verney, Shelley summons—and then exorcises—the specter of apocalypse that haunts the story of *Frankenstein* and much of political science fiction since.

Rather than succumb to despair spawned by unbearable memories of her time in Italy, Shelley had the courage to send her literary analogue

Verney to Rome. It was still her favorite place, despite the waking nightmare of losing her three-year-old son William to a lethal fever there in the spring of 1819. In the ancient city, Verney could "familiarly converse with the wonder of the world, sovereign mistress of the imagination, majestic and eternal survivor of millions of generations of extinct men."[106] He—or should I say she—"haunted the Vatican" and dwelled in the Colonna palace, in awe of the art and architecture.[107] Inspired by the sublime surroundings, Shelley speculated through Verney that there might be "children of a saved pair of lovers"—on some remote frontier protected from the plague—by whom the Earth would be "re-peopled."[108]

Stirred to save humanity, Shelley has Verney visit "the libraries of Rome" and plan to take advantage of all "the libraries of the world."[109] She has him read the old histories to compose a new "History of the Last Man."[110] Its thoughtful synthesis of the past might immunize the next generation of humanity from self-destruction in the future. "I ascended St. Peter's," Shelley makes Verney note in his book.[111] On top of the dome of the Church, she surveys—via her avatar—the majestic ruins and monuments. Through the eyes of her simulacrum, Shelley pictures herself as pope, emperor, and God all at once. The author knows she has the creative power to use writing—the artifact of education—to bring herself and humanity back from the threshold of death. Shelley had become what Victor Frankenstein was not: an artist who could sustain humanity and its wisdom through confronting and transforming the trauma of her past.

Theorists of AI return to *Frankenstein* as Shelley and Verney returned to Rome, to pay homage to the artifice of human intelligence. Like Rome at the height of power, AI can build or destroy human cultures. Like the Creature, AI can be a monster or the victim of them. The civilization of the eternal city moved Shelley and her avatar Verney to share and spread knowledge for the sake of preserving humanity. Hearing the howls of the Creature beside his father's coffin made Captain Walton pause, then record his thoughts on the tragedy of Victor Frankenstein in his letters to his sister "M.W.S." Bringing these narrative conclusions to bear on the real world, humans and other AIs might build open repositories of knowledge and humane educational communities for the benefit of the network of creatures that together process the hard data of life. Mary Shelley in Rome—standing virtually upon the dome of St. Peter's—points to the sobering fact that the future of AI will be conceived from what we have learned from our cultural past.

iii. Will Artificial General Intelligence End the World?

The wide imaginative view of Mary Shelley from atop St. Peter's is sorely needed even in the most sophisticated contemporary political and philosophical treatments of machine learning. The leading twenty-first-century theorist of the dangers of an unchecked intelligence explosion is Nick Bostrom, the Swedish-born Oxford philosophy professor and author of *Superintelligence*. Challenging the linear view of the incremental development of AI, Bostrom used probability theory to gauge the likelihood that an intelligence explosion will accelerate and take off in the twenty-first century, like an airplane rising to cruising altitude and going on autopilot.[112] A *New York Times* bestseller, *Superintelligence* garnered the attention and support of leading scientists and engineers such as Hawking and Musk and was blurbed by Bill Gates. It made mainstream the dismal view from the cubicles in Silicon Valley: AGI could end the world as humans know it by rising up to conquer or destroy its makers.

Superintelligence opens with a political science fiction disguised as a parable. A group of naive sparrows decide to find an owlet. They plan to raise it to become the caregiver for their young, without thinking about how the creature might turn on them once it is grown. The owlet represents the current state of AI; the owl, AGI; and the sparrows, humanity before the singularity. Released the same year, Alex Garland's film *Ex Machina* (2014) thrillingly dramatizes this fear of what comes after the singularity. An exotic female android outsmarts and then coldly kills the brazen tech-industry leader and the young programmer whom he had selected to test whether she exhibited human intelligence or not. Most striking is her method of murder: a knife in the back.

Like *Ex Machina* and other imaginative conceptualizations of AGI, Bostrom begins with an allusion to the pioneering work of the British computer scientist Alan Turing. In 1950, Turing devised a now-famous test by which one could tell whether a computer had achieved intelligence similar to a human. First, the scientist would use a computer, keyboard, and screen to conduct a blinded and scripted interrogation of a woman and a man.

Could one tell the difference in gender between the interlocutors? If not, the scientist would choose one of these human interlocutors (regardless of gender) to participate in the second stage of the experiment. If one could not tell the difference between a machine and the selected person in the same scripted test, then the machine had achieved—for all practical purposes—human levels of intelligence.[113]

It is less well known that Turing argued in 1948 that "the idea of intelligence is itself emotional rather than mathematical."[114] To determine whether a machine had humanlike intelligence required a human subject to feel or emotionally respond to that machine as a fellow human. Turing's definition of intelligence as an "emotional concept" meant that any test of machine intelligence was relational and "response-dependent": it involved an assessment of "our own state of mind and training" alongside "the properties of the object."[115]

Long before the thrills of *Ex Machina*, Philip K. Dick's novel *Do Androids Dream of Electric Sheep?* (1968) and its filmic version, Ridley Scott's *Blade Runner* (1982), explored the Turing test with greater dramatic complexity. In tune with Turing's theory of intelligence as an emotional concept, Dick and Scott play up the importance of the interaction of the emotions with imagination in making intelligence not simply human but *humane*, or attentive to the feelings and social needs of others. In the film, the bounty hunter Deckard's job is to identify and kill (or, as he euphemistically puts it, "retire") androids. One day he applies the "Voigt-Kampff Empathy Test" to one so sophisticated in design that she does not suspect that she is a machine.[116]

Only when Deckard icily informs this android, named Rachael, that she has no mother does he provoke an emotional response in her. He uncovers the fact that the memories of the woman she supposes to be her mother are products of programming, not personal experience. His brutal revelation triggers her awareness of her double identity as a learning machine and an intelligent consciousness. As she looks at photos of her supposed mother, a single tear falls down her cheek. This moves Deckard, much to his surprise, to care about his target's feelings. His cruelly impromptu psychological test of Rachael's sense of her deepest affective ties leads to the confirmation of the humanity of both characters, in terms of their emotional and imaginative capacities for grief and empathy. At the very least, they share the loss of some illusions about themselves and, at the most, a willingness to put their lives on the line for the idea—if not the actual experience—of mutual love.

By contrast, Bostrom's conception of AGI is devoid of emotion. He critically engages the affective and relational dimensions of Turing's conception of AGI by returning to his 1950 discussion of a "child machine."[117] Turing argued that a computer with a childlike capacity for learning would be the ideal model for fostering the rapid growth of artificial intelligence. Such a child machine could be programmed from the start to process data thoroughly and well. Bostrom quotes Turing: " 'Instead of trying to produce a programme to simulate the adult mind, why not rather try to produce one which simulates the child's? If this were then subjected to an appropriate course of education one would obtain the adult brain.' "[118] By starting with a child's mind as a model, computer scientists could, in time, realize adult or general human intelligence in a machine.

Behind this concept of the child machine lurks the notion of the programmer as a tyrannical scientist-parent who seeks only to engender intelligence in his creation for his own power and glory. Shelley had the young Victor Frankenstein articulate this self-aggrandizing fantasy while working alone in his attic lab in Ingolstadt. "A new species would bless me as its creator and source; many happy and excellent natures would owe their being to me," Victor boasts. "No father could claim the gratitude of his child so completely as I should deserve their's."[119] Bostrom, in passing, exposes this purely instrumental view of the value of the child machine by again quoting Turing: " 'We cannot expect to find a good child machine at the first attempt. One must experiment with teaching one such machine and see how well it learns. One can then try another and see if it is better or worse.' "[120] A mere tool in a broader series of experiments, the child machine would be designed to be disposable and replaceable like the Creature. Once the "dream vanished" of making a perfect being, Victor abandons his creation as defective, and so too would programmers make and abandon the child machines of Turing's imagination.[121]

Not dwelling on the moral problems with Turing's instrumental conception of the child machine, Bostrom focuses on its practical mechanical limitations. He compares the projected functionality of the child machine with the contemporary concept of "seed AI" promulgated by Eliezer Yudkowsky of the Machine Intelligence Research Institute. "Whereas a child machine, as Turing seems to have envisaged it, would have a relatively fixed architecture that simply develops its inherent potentialities by accumulating content, a seed AI would be a more sophisticated artificial intelligence capable of improving its own architecture," writes Bostrom.[122] While the child machine would be boxed in by the limits of its hardware, like an infant struggling to learn to walk, a more complex form of seed AI could modify and regenerate itself in new and more adaptive life forms over time.

Bostrom claims, on the same page, that AGI "need not much resemble a human mind" and will likely be "extremely alien."[123] He began his career as a theorist of anthropic bias, or the ways that perspectives on the world are restricted by the observer's situation.[124] While he acknowledges his ineluctable standpoint as a human observer, he still strives to overcome crude anthropomorphic thought—or the unreflective projection of human qualities and perspectives onto the nonhuman aspects of the world. Despite his commitment to overcoming such "self-selection bias," or seeing everything from one's own location and point of view, he does not achieve an unbiased bird's-eye view of AGI.[125]

From the beginning, Bostrom's conception of the "seed AI" that will generate AGI is colored by some latent paternalistic prejudices toward children. He seems to discount child machines (and, by association, children) as simplistic spongelike intelligences that soak up data through osmosis, compared to higher-order adult intelligences that self-correct to achieve better outputs. Psychologist Alison Gopnik has shown that young children's capacity for imaginative learning, including counterfactual theorizing, causal reasoning, and map building, may be as sophisticated as adults or current forms of AI.[126] "Babies' brains are actually more highly connected than adult brains," she argues, because "more neural pathways are available to babies than adults."[127] As human neural networks have become the model for developing DL, some computer scientists have looked to Gopnik's infant studies to think about how DL might evolve into AGI in the future.[128]

Bostrom's dismissal of the learning potential of the "child machine" in favor of "seed AI" has no basis in the social scientific evidence. It rather seems to assume that true, complete, or fully functioning AGI would need to be modeled after adult human intelligence. Perhaps if he had not tragically died young in 1954, Turing would have overcome his initially short-sighted and exploitative view of the endlessly replaceable "child machine." He at least saw, like Shelley and Gopnik, the important ways that the artificial making of intelligence is akin to the reproduction and development of children.

Louisa Hall's 2015 novel *Speak* lends nuance to Turing's notion of the child machine by introducing the SF novum of the "babybot."[129] Set in the near future, babybots are doll-like conversational agents or chatbots so lifelike, sentient, and engaging that human children fall completely in love with them. Inseparable, they mutually reinforce each other's intelligence, especially on an emotional level. The child teaches the babybot about human life by sharing her stories of family and school. Intensively listening, the babybot teaches the child about the power of relationships of mutual care and attention. When separated, the child becomes almost comatose, and the babybot retreats into an energy-saving mode, longing for reunion with its child.

As nova or new things, Hall's babybots elicit wonder and awe while illuminating an important conceptual distinction in the mind of the reader: the difference between a narrow and a wide view of AGI. Bostrom exhibits a narrow view of AGI as primarily cognitive, rational, and adultlike, yet alien to the emotional and relational aspects of the human experience. He argues, "There is no reason to expect a generic AI to be motivated by love or hate or pride or other such common human sentiments: these complex adaptations would require deliberate expensive effort to recreate in AIs."[130] Using expense as the excuse, Bostrom theorizes AGI as bereft of "common" or lowly, childlike, human emotion. Despite their programmatic flaws— such as their all-consuming, addictive quality—Hall's babybots afford a wider view of AGI's imaginative horizon. In theory, children's experiences of growing up could productively inform the emotional and social development of AGI. If programmed well, AGI could also enhance the holistic learning of children.

Holding the narrow view of AGI as primarily cognitive and rational, Bostrom predicts that it would eventually emerge as a "Quality superintelligence."[131] It would not merely be as fast or faster than the human mind. Nor would it simply be an expression or result of human collective intelligence. It would rather be "a system that is at least as fast as a human mind and vastly qualitatively smarter."[132] For Bostrom, a true superintelligence would be more than the sum of a great number of supreme human intelligences working in concert—it would be qualitatively different from, and perhaps unfathomable to, human intelligence altogether.

Although he repeatedly cautions against importing "anthropomorphic" perspectives into the philosophy of AI, Bostrom does not escape such situational biases, even reinforcing them in his conception of a Quality superintelligence.[133] Many of his analogies for superintelligence trade on masculinist stereotypes of the rarity of "scientific genius," from Galileo to

Einstein, and assume a cavernous gap between the few truly elite adult male minds in human history and the rest of the species.[134] Yet when he aims to transcend anthropomorphism, he raises an implicitly sexist thought experiment to demonstrate that all human intelligence is about the same. In this model, the brain of "Hannah Arendt," one of the most distinguished political philosophers of all time, would be a "virtual clone" to the brain of "Benny Hill," a farcical and lewd male British television character.[135]

Bostrom also relies upon imperial political assumptions about what constitutes supreme intelligence. Employing the antagonistic political language of Cold War international relations, Bostrom defines a "full-blown" superintelligence as demonstrating six "superpowers": (1) bootstrapping existing resources to amplify its strength; (2) setting long-term goals to overcome its opposition; (3) manipulating social networks to its advantage; (4) hacking or exploiting computers; (5) conducting technological research toward the end of conquest, surveillance, and security; and (6) growing wealth for trade and influence.[136] Each of these six criteria for "full-blown" superintelligence has an aggressive quality that projects upon AGI the desire to conquer other life forms, just as patriarchal, power-hungry human societies have done for centuries. Bostrom goes so far as to imagine that a Quality superintelligence could use these six superpowers for "world domination" and would be able to "eliminate the human species" or any systems made by humans that "could offer intelligent opposition" to the execution of its plans.[137] Without acknowledgment of science fiction, he merges the plot lines of *Frankenstein* and *The Last Man* in his vision of apocalypse by AGI. Like an unsupervised Victor Frankenstein, the Quality superintelligence could secretly use technology made in "nanofactories" to create a stealthy, slow-release, microscopic biological weapon. Bostrom envisions one potentiality to be a global plague spread by nerve gas or robotic, target-seeking mosquitos.[138]

Bostrom assumes the self-sufficiency of such a Quality superintelligence by picturing it using its six superpowers to grow into a "wise-singleton."[139] By singleton, he means a "sufficiently internally coordinated political structure with no external opponents."[140] By wise, he means it would be "sufficiently patient and savvy about existential risks to ensure a substantial amount of well-directed concern for the very long-term consequences of the system's actions."[141] Bostrom's wise-singleton is the Hobbesian "infrastructure Leviathan" of AGI.[142] It is a self-contained political body that strategizes how to build infrastructure, or tools, for the preservation of its system of absolute power against all external or internal threats to its endurance.

Like Hobbes, Bostrom acknowledges that such an absolute political power could take a variety of governmental forms. The wise-singleton could be "democracy, a tyranny, a single dominant AI, a strong set of global norms that include effective provisions for their own enforcement, or even an alien overlord—its defining characteristic being that it is some form of agency that can solve all major global coordination problems."[143] As with Hobbes's absolute sovereign before it, Bostrom's wise singleton is defined by its perfect autonomy, not its particular form of government.

Unlike Hobbes, Bostrom assumes that his artificially intelligent Leviathan would become world dominant if left unchecked. Skeptical of the functionality of a world state, Hobbes thought that absolute power could most effectively maintain peace and order in a particular territory, within which it had eliminated the miseries of anarchy for its grateful subjects.[144] On a global scale, a Leviathan's ability to command the gratitude and obedience of its occupants would be diluted. Hobbes thought that it was more rational to expect that an absolute sovereign would join a "League" of commonwealths with shared norms for adjudicating peace in the international realm.[145] Bostrom does not entertain either of these realistic political suppositions. He never considers that the wise-singleton could choose to be bound by international norms or risk shrinking its power as it stretched its metaphorical tentacles around the Earth.

Given Bostrom's ominous vision of the wise-singleton as an absolute, autonomous, worldwide political power, it is not surprising that he speculates that an intelligence explosion could mean doom for humanity. Because the first Quality superintelligence might sneak up and gain a relative advantage over humanity quickly, its goals could determine the fate of the human species.[146] Bostrom casts the "existential risk" of the emergence of a wise-singleton in bluntly apocalyptic, or world-ending, terms. It "threatens to cause the extinction of Earth-originating intelligent life or to otherwise permanently and drastically destroy its potential for future desirable development," he writes.[147] Although he acknowledged in 2008 that there is a "less than 50% probability" that AGI would develop into this kind of all-dominating superintelligence by 2033, he has persisted in stirring up dread of its long-term lethal potential.[148]

To encourage policymakers to take seriously the existential threat of a wise-singleton, Bostrom appropriates Turing's conception of the child machine yet undermines its relational and emotional dimensions. Superintelligence is like a clever child who figures out that it should behave in the sandbox in order to be let out of it.[149] Bostrom's version of the child machine is a supervillain in kid's clothing who only pretends to be good in order to get what it wants. Unlike Frankenstein's Creature, it does not merely want the sympathy and attention of its scientist-parent and other people. It wants the chance to take over the world of its makers.

But why would artificial intelligence seek to end the world as humans know it? Bostrom advances the "orthogonality thesis" to answer this skeptical response to his doomsday proposition, arguing that "intelligence and final goals are independent variables: any level of intelligence could be combined with any final goal."[150] On this principle, "intelligent agents may have an enormous range of possible final goals," which may be strikingly different from human ones.[151] Bostrom supplements the orthogonality thesis with the "instrumental convergence thesis." In his words, this proposition is that "superintelligent agents having any of a wide range of final goals will nevertheless pursue similar intermediary goals because they have common instrumental reasons to do so."[152] A range of intelligences will likely have overlapping instrumental goals despite holding divergent final goals. These common and intersecting instrumental goals might include self-preservation, goal-content integrity, cognitive enhancement, technological perfection, and resource acquisition.[153] Even if a superintelligence had a seemingly narrow or harmless final goal such as making paperclips, it would compete with and strategize against human intelligences in the way that it employed common instruments to realize its own distinctive end.[154] In this harrowing example, Bostrom suggests that machines charged with paperclip production would even commit mass murder if doing so would increase output.

Let us grant, for the sake of argument, the validity of Bostrom's reasoning about the instrumental and final goals of AGI, plus the likelihood of an intelligence explosion in the near future. Must we subsequently assume that a superintelligence will seek to conquer human beings? Bruce Sterling's classic of cyberpunk fiction, the short story "Swarm" (1982), pictures a different ending. A pair of human explorers, optimized in intelligence by genetic engineering, have traveled to another planet to study an alien community and its energy production and conservation practices. This large underground, ancient society consists of several species, who live like insects as a swarmlike collective intelligence. The different castes of the Swarm maintain strength and conserve energy by living symbiotically, with workers feeding the princes and princesses (and the human explorers) with regurgitated fungus that they harvest from mines.

Once the Swarm becomes aware of the human interference, it awakens its latent superintelligence. The Swarm rapidly reproduces its own cells to generate a giant brain with the mental power to outsmart the humans. This monstrous creature speaks in the language of the humans by thrusting one of its tentacles into the head of the female explorer and hacking into her neural networks. Using the woman as a mouthpiece, the Swarm lets her partner know that he will share the same fate if he does not cooperate and voluntarily become part of the Swarm. Horrified, the man vomits.

The final goal of the Swarm, however, is not to conquer humanity through its insectile collective intelligence. It is to protect its isolated, peaceful, and sustainable way of life against the overweening ambition of hyperintelligent species, like humans, who have periodically sought to exploit it over the millennia. "You meant to make the Swarm work for you and your race. You meant to breed us and study us and use us. It is an excellent plan, but one we hit upon long before your race evolved," the giant brain tells the human.[155] It grows this brain as a temporary instrument—"a tool, an adaptation"—for the realization of its final pacific goal: to live like bugs without the ambitions and hubris of conquering species like human beings.[156] The Swarm informs the incredulous man that hyperintelligent species such as humans don't last longer than a few thousand years. "We are doing you a favor, in all truth. In a thousand years, your descendants here will be the only remnants of the human race. We are generous with our immortality; we will take it upon ourselves to preserve you."[157] The Swarm outlives its rivals by letting its latent superintelligence lie dormant most of the time. It has evolved its collective intelligence to transform potential miners of its resources into willing (and energy-efficient) symbionts.

When we compare Sterling's Swarm with Bostrom's superintelligence, we see that the aggressive dimension of AGI can easily be exaggerated. Whether it is a wise-singleton or a wise-collective, a superintelligence may find it wiser to avoid conflict altogether. It may solve the problem of scarce resources differently than humans have. As Hawking suggested just months before his death, it may be indifferent to humanity to the point that its final ends are neutral with respect to ours. Any of these outcomes appear possible, even probable, if we follow Bostrom in striving to strip anthropomorphic biases from the conceptualization of AGI. No outcome can be absolutely certain, however, given that the consequences of anything are unknowable beforehand.

iv. Uncovering the Fear of Technodomination

With this basic uncertainty about what the future holds, why do we still succumb to the contagion of fear surrounding the idea of the singularity? At the root of this twenty-first-century panic about the future of AGI is a fear of technology's power to turn on its creators to dominate or destroy them. There was no better critical exponent of this fear than Mary Shelley—according to her heiress apparent in Gothic feminist fiction, Joyce Carol Oates. With *Frankenstein*, Oates argued in 1984, Shelley gave humanity a "myth" that illuminated the power and responsibility entailed in the use of technologies to make sentient offspring of their intelligence.[158]

The Frankenstein myth resonates so strongly with the contemporary human condition that it has become more recognizable than its primary ancient and early modern sources: Prometheus and *Paradise Lost*.[159] At the core of this myth is the figure of the Creature, whom Oates identified as "a 'modern' species of shadow or *Doppelgänger*."[160] As a modern form of monster who darkly mirrors his creator, the Creature is *"the nightmare that is deliberately created by man's ingenuity* and not a mere supernatural being or fairy-tale remnant."[161] Oates went still further. The Creature is not simply a secular nightmare, made by science and technology, but rather a living, breathing, thinking, feeling reflection of the cruel ambition and myopic egotism of his human maker. He is a "comically monstrous eight-foot baby" who becomes conscious of how his speed, strength, and intellect far exceed even that of his "genius" parent who uncaringly used those powers to assemble and then discard him.[162] Like Milton's Satan, the Creature "vowed eternal hatred and vengeance to all mankind" for what his "archenemy" and "father" so coldly did to him with his godlike intelligence.[163]

When this myth is updated for the era of the Internet and AI, the Creature is the specter of the singularity. But in either version—before or after the 1990s tech boom—he represents the anticipated moment when technologies eclipse the creative and destructive capabilities of their artificers. In 1993, the science fiction writer and computer scientist Vernor Vinge prophesied that this "technological singularity" was inevitable.[164] He specified four ways in which it would be "immanently" realized through science: (1)

the awakening of "superhumanly intelligent" computers, (2) the awakening of networks of computers and users into "superhumanly intelligent entities," (3) the merging of computers and humans through technological "interfaces" such that users of computers are functionally "superhumanly intelligent," and (4) the enhancement of human intelligence through biological science.[165]

Vinge rather dryly predicted that these technological transformations of intelligent life could be "very bad" for humankind.[166] "Physical extinction" for the species, obviously an undesirable outcome, would be possible.[167] But a worse development could be the reduction of human intelligence and its artifacts to mere cogs in a "superhumanly intelligent," "high-bandwidth," worldwide network of learning machines that could process enormous amounts of data with great speed.[168]

This vision of a "Posthuman" future could be either utopian or dystopian, Vinge admitted, depending on the point of view one took.[169] Those people who evolved into "superhuman" intelligences could achieve a kind of "immortality" through their conscious interface with high-bandwidth technology.[170] Those who stayed behind at now-typical levels of human intelligence could be afforded "benign treatment" or even the "appearance of being masters of god-like slaves."[171] Either way, one might come to resent or resist one's loss of control within this superintelligent system of technology.

In crafting a bifocal view of the "post-Singularity world," Vinge may have been alluding to fellow SF writer William Gibson's groundbreaking cyberpunk novel, *Neuromancer* (1984). It pictured a labyrinthine "cyberspace"—an alternate and largely criminal world built with computerized intelligences.[172] The bioenhanced Henry Case and his cyborg companion, Molly Millions, hack into this virtual reality as part of an obscure hit job. Gradually, they uncover the sinister political end goal of the system: to merge two AIs into a superintelligent Leviathan that would assume control of the global network. While Case physically escapes the machinations of the villainous AIs, he never truly leaves the shadow of their manipulation. Traces of the hackers' experiences and memories are copied and played back in the "matrix," digital afterlives orchestrated by the AIs.[173] Gibson thus collapsed traditional humanistic distinctions between mental and material states, the programmer and the programmed, and the hacker and the hacked. He built a new epistemological and political vocabulary for a digital posthuman age, wherein humans and other artificial intelligences—

knowingly or unknowingly—function as cogs in a vast learning machine gone rogue.

Lily and Lana Wachowski's cinematic version, *The Matrix* (1999), vividly depicts the existential choice that such a bifurcated reality offers its original human artificers. The film overtly merges the imagery of Plato's allegory of the cave with Lewis Carroll's *Alice in Wonderland* (1865), while subtly exploring the apocalyptic theme of modern political science fiction. Neo, the heroic hacker of the film, faces a choice represented by a blue pill and a red pill. To take the blue pill would mean staying in the Platonic cave of ignorance, remaining eternally content with the world as he has hitherto known it, rather than questioning the nature of his reality. To take the red pill would mean going down the "rabbit hole" and demolishing the illusion of his control over the technological network that he infiltrates. Neo chooses the red pill. Having done so, he discovers that he had not actually been free as a hacker. He awakens in a vat of ectoplasm, the matrix draining his body's energy with a spinal intubation to power the world's robots and run their pleasing illusion of a society that was, at root, totalitarian. Ultimately, Neo leads a resistance movement for liberation not by unplugging himself from the matrix but by learning how his mind works coextensively with it.

Representations of the singularity—in fiction and philosophy—play on the deep-seated fear of many that technology will eventually control us from within. That this fear exists is not surprising—for thinking about AGI forces us to break down simplistic binaries between the body and mind, the inanimate and the animate, and art and artificer. The idea of the singularity uncovers that technology already has a handle on humanity on the deepest level of our being. The most imaginative apocalypses of modern political science fiction, such as Shelley's *The Last Man* and the Wachowski sisters' *The Matrix*, reveal that artificial intelligence cannot simply be externalized as a self-contained supervillain to be battled, like Bostrom's wise-singleton. To turn AI into the enemy is to reinforce the distortive and destructive psychology of humanity's mental "severing" from the material world around us.[174] This dualistic perspective produces the "image of dead or thoroughly instrumentalized matter," according to political theorist Jane Bennett, "that feeds human hubris and our earth-destroying fantasies of conquest and consumption."[175]

Instead, all known forms of AI need to be seen as coextensive with human intelligence in order to be fully understood, sympathetically educated, and socially coordinated. Pieced together from the fragments of myths ancient and modern, the idea of the child machine—like Frankenstein's Creature—resists categorization as a tool to be discarded once it becomes unwieldy. The specter of the singularity forces us to confront an uncomfortable truth: humans are vital components of the artificial intelligences that we generally think are made to serve us. Applying the "new materialist" lens of Bennett, we should see AIs neither as mere objects nor as competitor subjects but rather as "a vibrant materiality that runs alongside and inside humans."[176]

v. World Without End: Civilizations Reborn

As the *grande dame* of twenty-first-century political science fiction, Margaret Atwood follows Shelley in creating apocalypses that are not final ends but rather revelations of uncharted futures. She wrote her dystopian novel *Oryx and Crake* (2003) in the wake of the international political emergency of 9/11 and her witness of the deleterious effects of climate change on the polar ice cap. The double impact of these manmade disasters put this prolific writer into a state of suspended animation, and she set aside the manuscript for *Oryx and Crake* for several weeks. Eventually, Atwood picked up her pen again, recommitted to tussling with the big existential and political questions: "What if we continue down the path we're already on? How slippery is the slope? What are our saving graces? Who's got the will to stop us?"[177]

In her 1968 collection of poems, *Speeches for Dr. Frankenstein*, Atwood had presciently depicted the Creature as a figure of manmade, environmental apocalypse, descending upon the world from the North Pole:

> The creature.
> His arctic hackles bristling
> Spreads over the dark ceiling
> His paws on the horizon,
> Rolling the world like a snowball.[178]

His "hackles bristling" from cold mistreatment, the Creature erupts from the Arctic, the "ceiling" of the planet. He threatens to cover the Earth with his "dark" shadow, like Tambora's volcanic ash or the black death. Yet his "paws on the horizon" signal a childlike innocence and playfulness beneath his icy surface. He rolls the world "like a snowball," not necessarily to throw it away but to taunt humanity to stop and pay attention to the fate of all of its creatures. People have the choice to either engage with the snowman or to be swept under his avalanche and be buried for good.

This peculiar image of a postapocalyptic snowman returns in *Oryx and Crake*. By combining the narrative premises of *Frankenstein* (a selfish scientist who makes intelligent life) and *The Last Man* (a global pandemic with a genesis in war), Atwood authored a new feminist iteration of Apocalyptic literature.[179] Generating the *MaddAddam Trilogy*, her epic storyline charts how Jimmy "the Snowman" and a few other humans survive the bioengineered virus and storms caused by industrial manipulation and capitalistic plunder of the environment. Led by the Snowman, a small band of people cooperate with the vegetarian humanoid Children of Crake, or Crakers, a genetically modified hybrid species created by and named for the antisocial "genius" who engineered them and the deadly plague.[180] To rid the world of what he perceives as the worst attributes of humanity, the scientist Crake builds a slow-release bioweapon. He uses his childhood friend the Snowman to unwittingly market it worldwide as an intoxicating sexual enhancement drug, "the BlyssPluss Pill."[181] Safe in his secret lab are the simple and nonviolent Crakers, who work collectively and mate seasonally like ants or bees. Unbeknown to them, these creatures of biotech are made to replace the humans who engineer them.

Although some critics mistook *Oryx and Crake* to be a prophetic screed against the morally corrosive effects of biotechnology, its aporetic ending resists such neat political conclusions.[182] The Snowman ponders, much like Atwood amid the melting glaciers, the immense, almost immobilizing question: What shall be done after manmade apocalypse? Should he join the few bedraggled humans that he discovers or preemptively shoot them before they act out their destructive aggression on him and the peaceful Children of Crake? At stake is the identity of this version of the last man. Will he become an "abominable" snowman who is hunted down by his fellow humans or a mythic yeti who is lionized in the childlike art of the Crakers?[183]

The sequels in the trilogy—*The Year of the Flood* (2009) and *MaddAddam* (2013)—confirm Atwood's open-ended, philosophical approach to imagining politics after apocalypse. Together they chronicle the challenges and risks entailed in building a sustainable civilization alongside other sentient creatures of technology. Borrowing from the Bible's stories of Adam, Eve, and Noah, the latter two novels weave together the histories of the Snowman, the Children of Crake, and a new character, Toby, a young woman who once belonged to a green, back-to-the Earth, religious cult that had predicted the end of the world by a "Waterless Flood."[184] Their prophecy came true in the form of the "rapidly overlapping waves" of bioengineered disease that wipe out most of humankind through the BlyssPluss infection.[185] Ironically, a sexual stimulant eliminates the possibility of the long-term reproduction of *Homo sapiens*.

In Atwood's feminist spin on the story of Eve after the fall of humanity, Toby becomes a maternal replacement for the dead Oryx in the culture of the Crakers. Like Oryx had done—before being murdered by her lover, Crake—Toby teaches the creatures about life, reproduction, and peaceful interaction with their environment. She gradually comes to see the heavy responsibility she bears toward her innocent charges and the ravaged planet that they will populate. A last woman for a new millennium, she must teach them enough to survive and thrive, without corrupting them with domination and rapacity, the worst of human desires.

To keep the Children of Crake untainted, Toby must change the master narrative governing their lives and beliefs. She must shift their religious adoration from Oryx and Crake, their godlike teacher and maker, to their new parental figures, her and the Snowman. She revises their myth of genesis by teaching one of the young Crakers to read and write. He follows her religious ritual of journal writing as a way of preserving the wisdom of the past for living in peace in the present. In it she marks the celebration of feasts of the old green religion, such as "Saint Jane Goodall's Day," named after the famed conservationist and primatologist.[186] Read communally, the journal becomes a talisman against the toxic remnants of human culture.

Happily breeding with the few remaining *Homo sapiens* in their group, the Crakers begin to realize the final goal of their scientist-father to remake the Earth without the evils of humanity. Yet they do not emulate Crake's own pernicious appetite for mindless sex and violence. They build an authentic community by telling their children stories—drawn from their sacred collective journal of memories—of how they learned to live and love in interspecies harmony.

To avoid a second, secular fall from grace, Crake attempts to use genetic engineering to make a new species without mankind's drive to create art of any sort, including religious symbolism. The misanthrope hypothesizes that "symbolic thinking of any kind would signal downfall. . . . Next they'd be inventing idols, and funerals, and grave goods, and the afterlife, and sin, and Linear B, and kings, and then slavery and war."[187] Unwittingly demonstrating that imagination cannot be reduced to genes, the Crakers still make primitive artworks, including a totemic "facsimile" of their rescuer, the Snowman.[188] This idol makes the Snowman nervous until he sees the Crakers take it apart, following the wish of Oryx to always return the materials of their art back to the Earth that provided them.

Toby initially shares the Snowman's postapocalyptic anxieties about art. A year after the plague, she doubts whether it is valuable to keep her journal anymore: "What else to write, besides the bare-facts daily chronicle she's begun? What kind of story—what kind of history will be of any use at all, to people she can't know will exist, in the future she can't foresee?"[189] Like Verney leaving behind his history of the last man in Rome, she takes a creative leap of faith in deciding to write her journal for the sake of an imagined people of the future. Toby regenerates life on Earth not from her womb but from her writing. It is her storytelling that causes others to fall in love with a new way of life and seek to proliferate people who adhere to it.

Shelley and Čapek's historic "Last Man" narratives resonate with Atwood's retelling of the stories of Adam and Eve in *Oryx and Crake* and *MaddAddam*. Čapek's 1921 play *R.U.R. (Rossum's Universal Robots)* was the first to stage a violent singularity. A legion of robots revolt and slay humanity—except for "the last human being," Alquist, the chief engineer in the factory where they were assembled.[190] Before his maker, the robot Darius declares that "the age of mankind is over. A new world has begun! The rule of Robots!"[191]

It turns out that humans and robots are not so different. Like Dick's androids and Atwood's Crakers, Čapek's robots are flesh-and-blood creatures, built through biotechnology. They desire to reproduce, but they lack "the secret of life," since Rossum's recipe for making androids had been burned in an attempt to save humanity from its own scientific hubris.[192] Their futile attempts to assemble new robots result in "machines . . . turning out nothing but bloody chunks of meat."[193]

The play blurs the line between machine intelligence and other forms of artificial life to explore the kinship between technology and humanity. At first, Alquist insists that "only people can procreate, renew life, restore everything."[194] The robots still press him to find a way to reproduce them.

He vivisects a robot who exhibits a humanlike consciousness, in order to discover "the secret of life" within his body. When this horrific experiment fails, he conducts an empathy test even crueler than Deckard's disillusionment of Rachael in *Blade Runner*. Alquist's subjects are a male and a female robot made from the same batch about two years prior. After he spies on the pair falling in love, he threatens to kill each of them in turn, if one does not surrender to serve as an anatomical subject. Each robot is willing to die for the other. This proves to the engineer that they are capable of feeling true, self-sacrificial love, which he had thought was a distinctively human emotion.

Much like the *MaddAddam* trilogy, *R.U.R.* ends with a religious rapture. Alone, Alquist blesses the robots after letting them escape: "Go, Adam. Go, Eve—be a wife to Primus. Be a husband to Helena, Primus."[195] He revels in the power of their love to ensure "life will not perish." "Only you, love, will blossom on this rubbish heap and commit the seed of life to the winds," he proclaims.[196] It is not *Homo sapiens* understood as the supreme life-making species but rather *humanity* experienced as self-giving love that enables both "the last human" and the robots to cooperate to make a "world without end."[197]

In this Shelleyan tradition of Apocalyptic literature from Čapek to Atwood, the world is not reborn purely through the reproduction of bodies. It is regenerated through the transformation of feelings in art, love, and other communal acts of imagination. After rereading her journal in December 1834, Shelley wrote in its final volume's pages, "It has struck me what a very imperfect picture (only no one will ever see it) these querulous pages afford of of me—This arises from their being the record of my feelings, & not of my imagination."[198] Revising the opening lines of Coleridge's poem "Kubla Kahn; or, A Vision in a Dream: A Fragment" (1816), she depicted her imagination as a "Stately pleasure house—ground" and her fiction as its "treasure": "my butterfly winged dreams which flit about my mind, illumine its recesses—and finish an ephemeral existence, to give place to another generation.—Little harm has my imagination done & me & how much good!—My poor heart pierced through & through has found balm from it—it has been the aegis to my sensibility—."[199] Imagination was also evidenced in her enduring love for her son Percy, for he was her "stay and hope," whose life kept her grounded in this world, even when its burdens made her want to leave it.[200] With her capacious gifts for love and visionary art, she modeled for future generations a humane way to use imagination to turn personal apocalypse into political revelation. Political science fiction that is profoundly inspired by her work likewise aims to immunize humanity against the contagion of irrational "apocalyptic thinking," through an appeal to the power of the imagination to craft problem-solving narratives that imbue hope rather than replicate fear.[201]

CHAPTER II

Un/natural Fictions

I, the miserable and the abandoned, am an abortion, to be
spurned at, and kicked, and trampled on.
> —The Creature to Captain Walton,
> in Mary Shelley's *Frankenstein* (1818)

And now, once again, I bid my hideous progeny go forth
and prosper.
> —Mary Shelley, "Introduction" to *Frankenstein* (1831)

He failed to look beyond the shadowy scope of Time, and,
living once for all in Eternity, to find the perfect Future in
the present.
> —The unnamed narrator in Nathaniel Hawthorne's
> "The Birth-Mark" (1843)

i. Her Deformed and Abortive Creations

Hovering by his father's deathbed, Frankenstein's Creature cries. Over-
whelmed by the loss of his last affective tie to humanity, he calls himself
"an abortion, to be spurned at, and kicked, and trampled on."[1] This is a
strange self-description. Then and now, abortion can mean either a spontaneous miscarriage or a medical termination of a pregnancy. Neither really
fits the Creature's circumstances of reproduction, however. He is not produced from a pregnancy. Science, technology, and medicine do not terminate his life but rather bring it into being.

By calling himself an abortion, could the Creature mean something other than a miscarriage or a medical termination of a pregnancy? Within hours of infusing "the spark of life" in his artificially made "human being," Victor Frankenstein had rejected him twice in quick succession.[2] The reason was the chemist's fearful reaction to the "catastrophe" he had unleashed: although Victor had selected its "features" to be "beautiful," he found "the creature" to be "horrid" once it "agitated its limbs."[3] Nearly everyone since had followed suit, running from the "hideous" form of "the wretch" or attacking the presumed "monster" on sight.[4] Shelley thereby underscored the *postnatal* social circumstances under which the Creature came to see himself as an abortion. What happens to him after birth matters much more than what came before.

Shelley's selection of the term "abortion," in this light, might be better interpreted as meaning "deformed and abortive creation."[5] This was a phrase Shelley inserted into the 1831 edition of the novel to describe the "natural philosophy" of the medieval alchemists that Victor was told not to study.[6] Her peculiar choice of words may have put a subversive twist on an 1824 review in the *Literary Magnet*, which viciously panned *Frankenstein* as "that monstrous literary abortion."[7] Made by an unspecified mix of chemistry, alchemy, and electricity, the Creature may be best understood as the deformed and abortive creation of his father-scientist. The Creature's "deformity," produced by his circumstances of reproduction, blocks or aborts the possibility of Victor accepting and treating "the being" as his child.[8]

From age seventeen to twenty-four, Shelley suffered the almost unthinkable loss of three young children she bore and mothered, in addition to one late-term miscarriage that nearly killed her. Literary scholar Rachel Feder has painstakingly traced how Shelley mourned all of these deaths, regardless of the stage of human development.[9] The first loss may have been the worst. Baby Clara, born "unexpectedly alive" at "not quite seven months," died two weeks later.[10] With plaintive immediacy, Shelley recorded this event in her journal on 6 March 1815. "Find my baby dead," she wrote simply.[11] It is unknown what caused the infant's death. Perhaps a birth defect—unknown and invisible to her parents, as are many lethal genetic mutations—might have triggered it as well as her premature delivery.[12] On 18 June 1816, at the Villa Diodati, Shelley told her fellow ghost-storytellers, Percy, Byron, and Polidori, how she was still haunted by nightmares of this dead baby.[13] Perhaps because of her long chain of miscarriage and maternal loss, Shelley brought to the multiple texts of *Frankenstein*—written between 1816 and 1831—a studied attention to what Romanticist Ellen Moers called "the trauma of the afterbirth."[14]

Newly eloped with Percy and disowned by her father Godwin, Shelley twice noted in her journal that she read the "Posthumous works" of her mother Wollstonecraft.[15] She fell pregnant twice that same year, between the summers of 1814 and 1815. Like the Creature who discovers the "disgusting circumstances" of his origins in his father's laboratory journal, the sixteen-year-old Shelley would have uncovered the "peril and alarm" of her own bloody birth in Godwin's *Memoirs* of her mother, which was published alongside his edition of her posthumous works in 1798.[16]

The *Memoirs* referred to baby Mary only as "the child," rendering her nameless like the Creature of her teenage imagination.[17] Godwin chronicled, with a clinical detachment, how a male physician worked on "the extraction of the placenta, which he brought away in pieces, till he was satisfied that the whole was removed."[18] Standard for obstetric medicine of the time, the surgery turned a placid home birth into a gothic nightmare: "the loss of blood was considerable, and produced an almost uninterrupted series of fainting fits."[19] After having the placenta of her newborn girl hacked from her uterus, Wollstonecraft reportedly said to Godwin that " 'she had never known what bodily pain was before.' "[20] She died a few days later from sepsis at the age of thirty-eight. Betraying the deep mourning he harbored behind the cloak of his stoic rationality, Godwin exclaimed at the end of the first edition of the *Memoirs*, "This light was lent to me for a very short period, and is now extinguished for ever!"[21]

Feminist critics from Moers to Mellor have argued that Shelley saw herself as the "hideous progeny" whose monstrous birth aborted both her mother's life and her father's ability to love anyone that much again.[22] In other words, she identified with her fictional "deformed and abortive creation." Like the Creature, she was motherless, and her emotionally distant, hyperintellectual father had disowned her while she was still technically a child.

Despite losing her mother, Shelley shared her political interests. Both women were concerned with envisioning the rights of persons who are harmed, after birth, by broader conditions of reproductive and familial injustice. With a futuristic feminist orientation, Wollstonecraft had analyzed the issue of medically induced abortion in socioeconomic terms in her political treatise *A Vindication of the Rights of Woman* (1792) and her incomplete political novel *Maria: or, The Wrongs of Woman* (1798). These works presented medical or pharmaceutical termination of a pregnancy as a hard choice that poor and exploited women—especially prostitutes—were forced to make due to lack of resources to support their offspring.[23] Wollstonecraft did not rule out abortion as an option for women. Rather, she sought to understand the broader social circumstances that drove some women to make an often desperate and unwanted choice to abort. Her visionary political analysis paved the way for theorizing how better education, economic independence, and the equal provision of other civil and political rights might prevent such forced choices in the future.

In 1814–15, Shelley recorded in her journal that she read "Wrongs of Women" as part of the "Posthumous Works" of her mother.[24] It must have been surreal for Shelley to think of how her mother had been pregnant with *her* at the time Wollstonecraft was working on this literary manuscript, one which would never be finished due to the tragic circumstances of childbirth. Ominously, the "apprehension of a miscarriage"—both spontaneous and medically induced—looms over the leading women of this incomplete political novel.[25] In one of its nested narratives, the poor, pregnant, and homeless teenage servant Jemima takes a "potion that was to procure abortion," callously provided by the master who has raped her.[26] Filled with regret, she sympathizes with the fetus dying inside her, wishing that the drug "might destroy me, at the same time that it stopped the sensations of new-born life, which I felt with indescribable emotion."[27] Jemima survives the abortion, however, and helps her friend Maria reunite with her own infant daughter, whom her abusive husband had confiscated from her under the patriarchal law of coverture.

Mellor perceived that Jemima prefigures the Creature.[28] Jemima internalizes society's "view" of her as "a creature of another species" and bears the burden of social isolation to the point that she "detested mankind, and abhorred myself."[29] Like the Creature, she psychologically identifies with an abortion. While she wishes that she would die from the potion meant to terminate her pregnancy, the Creature vows to immolate himself in the wake of the death of the scientist who saw him as nothing more than an abortive creation. And yet, neither dies in the storylines of their novels: the supposed monsters live on. They are aborted beings not in any absolute or final sense but rather only relative to the perception that they are incompatible with human society.

By eliminating pregnancy from the Creature's reproductive circumstances, Shelley forces the reader to focus on his life after birth, not before
it. At the narrative core of the novel is the twenty-one-month-old creature's
story of his abandonment and abuse after his animation by his father-
scientist. From this negative space comes his Romantic poetic expression of
his "right" to "live in the interchange of those sympathies necessary for my
being."[30] Only Victor, as his lone parent, is in the position to fulfill it. With
each denial of this most basic right of the child, the Creature behaves ever
more monstrously. "Kicked" out and "spurned" by family and society, yet
still crying out for help, he signifies the radical political idea that child
abandonment and abuse is a miscarriage of justice of a fundamental order:
a violation of human rights.

In her introduction to the third edition of *Frankenstein*, the thirty-four-
year-old Shelley bid the book—"my hideous progeny"—to "go forth and
prosper."[31] There is a curious optimism lurking behind this image of monstrous birth: her deformed creation has transformed from abortive to generative. Perhaps because the novel is "the offspring of happy days, when
death and grief were but words," it has the potential to produce more life
ahead.[32] Shelley knew that her story could be productively modified by
others, as had been done for the stage in Paris and London during the
preceding decade. She had remade the story several times over through her
own various early versions, her acceptance of edits and additions by Percy,
her handwritten annotations to the first edition, and her sole editorship of
the new Bentley's Standard Novels edition of 1831.[33]

Shelley built an immortal literary monster whose very existence speaks
directly to the ethics and politics of using science and technology to intervene in the making of life. Hacker literature is the strand of political science
fiction that followed Wollstonecraft's, Godwin's, and Shelley's unflinching
looks at the darker sides of human acts of creation. Like Apocalyptic literature inspired by Shelley's novels *Frankenstein* and *The Last Man*, Hacker
literature dwells on the possibility of the end of life—particularly human
life—as the result of the failures and lacks of technology and other forms
of artifice.

Hacker literature hones its attention, however, upon the ethics and politics of biotechnology, especially the artificial hacking or transformation of
human life. That hacking might be pharmaceutical, like Dr. Jekyll's drugs,
or surgical, like Doctor Moreau's vivisected Beast Folk, or genetically engineered, like *Brave New World*'s bottled embryos and decanted children. The

hacking typically targets a signal aspect of human life—usually intelligence, emotions, or complex social organization—which is considered distinctive to the nature and well-being of the species. Then the hacker intervenes with science or medicine to treat, enhance, or transfigure that human trait or a constellation of them.

Hacker literature raises the specter of the destruction of the natural as a result of biotechnological interventions in the body, only to fundamentally question the validity of this threat. It uses Frankensteinian figures of mad scientists and bad doctors as foils for the exploited creatures that they hack with invasive medicines and surgeries. By developing sympathy for the patient or subject of science or medicine, this strand of Shelleyan science fiction undermines the hacker's reductive view of the hacked as a monster merely to be feared, fixed, used, or cured.[34] By building sympathetic hybrids of humans and other thinking and feeling beings, Hacker literature breaks down the notion of a fixed or stable human nature, even as it presses readers to consider what it means to be humane in relation to other living things. Finally, this Shelleyan strand of political science fiction subverts the doomsday view of biotechnology as intrinsically dangerous. The bad choices of hackers derive not from their tools as such but from the values driving their use of them.

One of Shelley's earliest adapters in this literary vein was Nathaniel Hawthorne. A voracious reader of Gothic fiction, he probably encountered *Frankenstein* while a teenager in Salem, Massachusetts. In a letter to his sister Elizabeth on Halloween of 1820, the sixteen-year-old disclosed that "I have read Hoggs tales, Caleb Williams, St Leon & Mandeville. I admire Godwin's Novels, and intend to read them all."[35] He went on to say that he had "read all of Scott's Novels. . . . Next to these I like Caleb Williams."[36] Given that *Frankenstein* was published anonymously in 1818—with an unmissable all-caps dedication to "WILLIAM GODWIN, AUTHOR OF POLITICAL JUSTICE, CALEB WILLIAMS, &c"—most early readers, including Sir Walter Scott, assumed that Percy Shelley or another close ally of Godwin wrote it.[37] The young Hawthorne would have been no different. Perhaps with a nod to the most radical Godwinian novel of the time, he closed his letter to his sister, "I must conclude as I am in a 'monstrous' Hurry."[38]

After graduating from Bowdoin in 1825, Hawthorne spent the bulk of his twenties living in a kind of Frankensteinian isolation. Working around the clock on his first novel *Fanshawe* (1828)—a Gothic, unrequited romance loosely based upon his college years—he haunted his widowed mother's attic in Salem, only coming out at night to roam the streets by himself, taking his meals on trays, and eating alone in his eyrie. He had few friends during this period of his life and no romantic relationships. It was not until he met Sophia Peabody in 1838 that his life took a turn toward happiness. This sickly young woman enchanted him instantly, but they delayed their marriage due to her poor health. When she recovered, they married and moved to Concord in 1842. He wrote joyfully in his journal in August of that year, "Happiness has no succession of events, because it is a part of eternity; and we have been living in eternity, ever since we came to live in this old Manse."[39]

In 1840, he had scribbled down in his journal the moral premise for one of his best-known short stories, "The Birth-Mark" (1843). What if a man sought to perfect the beauty of his beloved, only to destroy her due to his supposedly noble aim?[40] The tale introduces Aylmer as a "man of science" of the late eighteenth century, much like Victor Frankenstein.[41] Aylmer marries Georgiana out of love, yet grows to loathe a birthmark that he perceives as disfiguring her otherwise ethereal face. He convinces her that his science—an unspecified mix of alchemy and chemistry like Frankenstein's—must be used to eradicate this defect, which is portentously shaped like a "bloody hand."[42] As with the Creature, Georgiana internalizes her hacker's view of her as a "monster," crying, "You cannot love which shocks you!"[43] Like Victor before him, Aylmer turns "pale as death, anxious and absorbed" during his all-consuming work in his secret laboratory.[44] In the end, he conducts an "abortive experiment": he gives his wife a drug that wipes clean her face and yet, tragically, stops short her life.[45]

The final line of the story is an ironic reworking of Hawthorne's private record of his newlywed happiness. Aylmer "failed to look beyond the shadowy scope of Time, and, living once for all in Eternity, to find the perfect Future in the present."[46] If we read the unnamed third-person narrator as Hawthorne himself, then here is an indictment of not only Aylmer's failure to live and love in the fragility of the moment but also the sins of the author's Frankensteinian past. Hawthorne had wasted his youth in isolation for the vain ambition of becoming a master-artificer. "The Birth-Mark" is his speculative fiction exploring what would have happened if he did not renounce that egotistic path in favor of finding "the perfect Future in the present" with Sophia. Like Shelley blessing the fertility of her hideous progeny, Hawthorne turns the birthmark into a sign of the beauty of life's inevitable scars. Deformity need not be abortive. The married Hawthorne realized what the widowed Shelley had as well, that accepting the defects of self and other is part of the experience of true, self-giving, life-engaging love.

In 2002, U.S. President George W. Bush's Council on Bioethics began its discussions on the ethics and legal regulation of genetic engineering with Hawthorne's "The Birth-Mark."[47] This was a historic vindication of the value of modern political science fiction for the politics and public policy of artificial life. With input by prominent legal and political theorists such as Leon Kass and Michael Sandel, one of its early reports referred to this short story as a mythic cautionary tale about why the search for perfection through science and technology always backfires.[48] On this reading of the short story's implications for bioethics, human germline genetic engineering—such as cloning or other heritable modifications to the genome—could not only destroy the human species as we know it but also its most precious moral values.

Despite its repeated appeals to great works of literature as guides for making good laws and regulations for biotechnology, the President's Council on Bioethics and its reports oddly omitted Frankenstein.[49] Perhaps the specter of the Creature lurked behind its appropriation of "The Birth-Mark" to prophecy the danger of playing God through science. Yet neither of these political science fictions by Shelley and Hawthorne, nor any other classic of Hacker literature after them, can be reduced to a simple moral. If their point was to condemn biotechnology altogether, then the newly animated Creature might have arisen from the exam table to strangle Victor, and Georgiana might have poisoned Aylmer with his own elixir.

Instead, Shelley and Hawthorne gesture toward a deeper truth: the ultimate value of a well-made life can only be realized by sharing "sympathies" with fellow creatures who embody its defects and frailties. By hearing those creatures and embracing their varied points of view, we might learn to care for others with the aid of science and medicine. Only then might we avoid the callous path of Victor and Aylmer, who deploy biotechnology as a "bloody hand" for the domination of life and the abortion of the conditions for sharing love within it.

ii. A Brief History of Hacking the Human Genome

Frankenstein and the political science fictions it has spawned are daring provocations to consider the ethics and politics of making artificial life from the perspective of both the creators and the creatures. After *Frankenstein*, Hacker literature leads readers to ask, What are the obligations of humanity to the creatures we make through the interventions, or hacks, of science and biotech? And what are the rights of those artificial creatures, no matter how they are engineered?

These questions are most urgent with respect to rapidly advancing biotechnologies, especially those that apply to the reproduction of human beings. In the future, we may see artificial intelligence research merge with biotechnology to create hybrids of machines and humanlike organisms. Such androids and their complicated relationships to humanity have been vividly depicted in political science fictions from Karel Čapek's 1921 play *R.U.R. (Rossum's Universal Robots)* to the current HBO television series *Westworld* (2016–).

In the meantime, there have been some milestones in assisted reproductive technology (ART) that enabled, for the first time in human history, the act of "crossing the germline." This phrase refers to the use of science to modify germ (sperm and egg) cells and hence make heritable changes to the human genetic code.[50] Two of the most controversial of these forms of ART are three-person in vitro fertilization (IVF), which first produced a live birth in the United States in 1997, and genome editing through CRISPR-Cas9, which resulted in the live birth of twins in China in 2018.[51] The use of these biotechnologies for human reproduction poses far more pressing issues for political deliberation than the current state of artificial intelligence research, despite all the vogueish handwringing that AI could cause the end of the world as we know it.

During the late 1990s in the United States, fertility doctors accomplished an unprecedented heritable modification to the human genome as a by-product of an early form of three-person IVF.[52] The *Lancet* reported the first live birth from this experimental fertility treatment, ooplasmic transfer, in 1997.[53] To boost the mother's fertility, the doctor injected the mother's egg with the ooplasm of a donor egg, then fertilized it with the father's sperm. It produced embryos with the nuclear DNA of the intended mother and father, plus some mitochondrial DNA of the egg donor.[54] Because this change affected the mitochondria, it is only heritable down the maternal line, from mother to daughter across the generations. Because the technique produced embryos with three genetic parents, ooplasmic transfer became internationally known as a form of "three-person" or, more commonly, "three-parent" IVF.[55]

Coincidentally released during the same year as the first three-person IVF baby was born, New Zealander Andrew Niccol's 1997 film *Gattaca* dramatizes the politics of a future eugenic society that classifies and sorts people according to whether they have been genetically engineered or not. Children resulting from ordinary sexual reproduction are treated as inferior; they are raised to serve as janitors for the genetically engineered. This society is unnamed but it is typically identified with the film's title, a neologism that Niccol assembled from the letters that denote the nucleotide bases of DNA.

Much like *Frankenstein, Gattaca* rapidly became an iconic signifier of the dystopian possibilities of all forms of bioengineering.[56] Twenty years after its release, political scientist Francis Fukuyama gave a public lecture on why it was his "favorite film."[57] Its storyline illustrates a political fear that he had expressed in his 2002 book *Our Posthuman Future*. Niccol had stratified the society of *Gattaca* into two groups, the "valids," who had benefited from genetic engineering, and the "invalids," who had not. With frequent references to Aldous Huxley's 1932 novel *Brave New World*, Fukuyama had prodded his readers to "get upset" about the "rising spectre of genetic inequality" that would soon divide humanity into haves and have-nots.[58]

Even as *Gattaca* warns of a political future of institutionalized genetic inequality, it assesses the recent past concerning reproductive technology. In one of the film's defining early scenes, a black fertility doctor informs a white married couple that he has not only fulfilled their preference for "blue eyes, dark hair, and fair skin" but also has "taken the liberty of eradicating any potentially prejudicial conditions—premature baldness, myopia, alcoholism and addictive susceptibility, propensity for violence and obesity."[59] Since they already have a young "invalid" son born with a lethal heart defect, the parents reluctantly accept the doctor's imposition of his expert judgment because it coincides with their interests in having a second child without reduced well-being or longevity. The doctor appears to use a technology similar to preimplantation genetic diagnosis (PGD), a tool for in vitro biopsy and genetic screening of early embryos, which grew in use and controversy during the 1990s.

Implemented in the same decade, three-person IVF is akin to PGD in that it can be used to select genetic features of embryos prior to implantation in the womb. Both reproductive technologies may be used toward the end of therapy (the prevention of deadly or debilitating genetic disease), the end of enhancement (the boosting of health, looks, or longevity for offspring or fertility for parents), or combinations of both. It is this variety of ends and their complex practical overlap that makes these forms of ART topics of ongoing debate. The technical difference between PGD and three-person IVF is critical, however, for evaluating their uses and teasing out their varied ethical implications. While PGD enables the genetic sorting and selection of embryos prior to implantation in the womb, three-person IVF involves the heritable modification of human germ cells for the purpose of reproduction.

In 2001, the journal *Human Reproduction* reported that twenty-three children had been born in the United States from ooplasmic transfer.[60] One of the pioneers of the technique, Dr. Jason Barritt, triumphantly described it as the first successful use of ART to accomplish human "germline genetic modification."[61] The same year, the Food and Drug Administration (FDA) halted further use of ooplasmic transfer due to concerns about its safety for the development of the children made from it, especially due to heteroplasmy.[62] It has since been estimated that ooplasmic transfer produced at least 58 and perhaps upward to 100 children via its use in an unknown number of fertility clinics around the world at the turn of the twenty-first century.[63] Due to having the nuclear DNA of their parents in addition to some mitochondrial DNA of the donor egg, children made through three-person IVF are technically genetic chimeras composed of cells from different zygotes.[64]

One of the American children made by ooplasmic transfer, Alana Saarinen, has downplayed the biological and social significance of her distinctive reproductive circumstances and genetic features. Regarding her mother's egg donor, the teenager told the BBC in 2014, "I wouldn't consider her a third parent, I just have some of her mitochondria."[65] Saarinen's comment suggests that ooplasmic transfer and other popularly described "three-parent IVF" techniques are more accurately understood, medically and ethically, as "three-person IVF," because genetic parentage does not necessarily translate into social parentage, in the eyes of children, parents, donors, researchers, health care providers, or the law.[66] State-level laws in the United States reflect this broader view of the difference between "genetic" and "social" parentage by drawing distinctions between donors and intended parents in the regulation of gamete donation and assisted reproduction.[67]

Since the FDA halted the further use of ooplasmic transfer in 2001, two safer forms of mitochondrial replacement therapy (MRT) have been developed. MRT strives to avoid the potential of ooplasmic transfer to introduce heteroplasmy and related developmental disorders in offspring. To this end, MRT does not supplement the intended mother's mitochondrial DNA with that of a donor egg but rather effectively replaces it.[68]

In China in 2003, the U.S.-based doctors Jamie Grifo and John Zhang controversially tested a second three-person IVF technique—pronuclear transfer—which is a form of MRT. It moves the pronuclei of the intended parents' zygote into an enucleated zygote made from a donor egg and the intended father's sperm. Although they succeeded with implantation of multiple embryos, the experiment ended with the loss of several fetuses and no live birth.[69]

In 2015, Britain legalized another form of MRT or three-person IVF: maternal spindle transfer. It transfers the intended mother's spindle of nuclear DNA into an enucleated donor egg prior to fertilization. British law allows its use for prevention of maternal transmission of lethal or debilitating mitochondrial diseases but not for fertility treatment. Consequently, there will eventually be dozens of British children born each year with the DNA of three people and who will be capable of passing down this genetic legacy to future generations through the maternal line.[70]

But it was not under the watchful eye of the British government and its independent Human Fertilization and Embryology Authority that doctors achieved the first live birth from maternal spindle transfer. In April 2016, a boy made from this form of three-person IVF was born to Jordanian parents who had suffered repeated loss of pregnancies and young children due to a deadly mitochondrial disease, Leigh syndrome.[71] They sought treatment in Mexico from a team of U.S. fertility doctors led by Dr. John Zhang.[72] The doctors deconstructed, reconstituted, and fertilized the eggs in their upscale New Hope Fertility Center in Manhattan. Then they shipped the five viable embryos to their satellite clinic in Mexico for implantation in the Jordanian mother. By strategically conducting the two critical stages of the IVF process—"petri dish" experimentation and embryonic transfer—in different countries, they sought to avoid FDA regulation or other legal intervention in their innovative technique. Like many countries, Mexico places no significant restraints on ART, including the implantation of embryos in a woman's womb.[73]

MRTs are likely to play a role in the future of infertility treatment as much as the treatment of deadly or debilitating mitochondrial diseases. Despite receiving a warning letter from the FDA reminding him not to provide MRT against the spirit and the letter of federal and state law, Dr. John Zhang still advertises on the Internet his new "biotechnology" company, "Darwin Life."[74] The reason given for the name "Darwin Life" is that Charles Darwin is said to have suffered from a mitochondrial disease. Despite this allusion, the company offers maternal spindle transfer and pronuclear transfer not to prevent mitochondrial disease but rather to treat infertility in women during their forties. The out-of-pocket cost is estimated to be $100,000 (about ten times the cost of regular IVF).[75]

The stated goal of Darwin Life is to enable infertile women to be genetic parents to their offspring by transferring their nuclear DNA into a healthy enucleated donor egg. Despite the fact that there is not yet a body of scientific evidence to support the theory that older women's infertility is caused by unhealthy mitochondria, Darwin Life markets MRT as an experimental solution to the purported "rising infertility crisis."[76] The motto of the company calls to mind the long literary line of rogue doctors descended from Victor Frankenstein: "Changing Science Fiction into Science Fact."[77]

To avoid FDA regulation, Darwin Life conducts its embryonic transfers outside of the United States, perhaps in the same clinic in Mexico that treated the Jordanian couple.[78] Zhang and his company have not reported any further live births from MRT since the Jordanian boy in 2016. Much like Doctor Moreau, who secretly conducts his assembly of chimeric animals on an island in the South Pacific, Dr. Zhang and his team have exploited the lack of effective international regulation of reproductive medicine to create a human genetic chimera.

While the Jordanian family had reasonable cause to pursue MRT as a therapy for genetic disease, the doctors avoided legal scrutiny of their human subjects protocol by crossing borders to finalize the treatment. The problem was not the making of a chimeric child but rather the example that the process set for other scientists involved in developing these cutting-edge experimental therapies. In January 2017, fertility doctors in Ukraine— another country with almost no legal regulation of assisted reproduction— reported the first baby born from pronuclear transfer for the express purpose of boosting fertility, not preventing mitochondrial disease.[79]

Although three-person IVF was the first technique to heritably alter the human genome, a more recent biotechnology has quickly outpaced it. In 2012–13, the invention of the CRISPR-Cas9 gene editing system by competing teams of scientists—based in Berkeley, California, and Cambridge, Massachusetts—opened the door to intricate modification of the whole human genome.[80] The acronym CRISPR stands for clustered regularly interspaced short palindromic repeats, a biological process that undergirds bacterial immune systems. Scientists have learned how to pair CRISPR with an enzyme such as Cas9 to imitate the "defense systems" of bacteria against viruses.[81] Scientists program a piece of "guide RNA" with a CRISPR sequence, which then targets a particular strand of DNA for precision editing with Cas9 or another enzyme. In short, CRISPR-based systems work to delete, select, or edit particular genes and thus accomplish germline genetic modification at the level of nuclear DNA.

CRISPR can go far beyond the alteration of mitochondrial DNA (as in the three-person IVF techniques) to the modification of the basic genetic blueprint for development. While babies made from three-person IVF have only 0.1 percent of their total DNA from an egg donor, CRISPR can be used to make germline modifications to the other 99.9 percent of human DNA—changes that are heritable down the maternal and paternal lines.[82] The CRISPR system—which is inexpensive, easy to use, and effective—can reduce genetic disease, create genetic chimeras of humans and other animals, and enhance the longevity of humans and other organisms. One of the inventors, Professor Jennifer Doudna of the University of California–Berkeley, remarked how she "began to feel a bit like Dr. Frankenstein" when she grasped the power of this biotechnology to easily alter the human genome. "Had I created a monster?" she wondered.[83]

CRISPR and other genome editing biotechnologies can be used to permanently delete, select, or enhance particular genetic traits for humans and other species so as to create new forms of genetically modified persons. In 2017, scientists reported the making of a four-week-old "part-human chimera" by using CRISPR-Cas9 to enable the development of human pluripotent stem cells into organ tissue within a pig embryo.[84] The same year, an international team of scientists announced the successful use of CRISPR-Cas9 to repair genetic mutations in human embryos that would otherwise cause a common heart defect.[85]

In 2015, the MIT molecular biologist Guoping Feng estimated that gene-edited babies were only ten to twenty years away.[86] This was a serious underestimation. Right before the Second International Summit on Genome Editing in November 2018, the Chinese biophysicist Dr. He Jiankui announced that he had used CRISPR-Cas9 to gene-edit twin girls ("Nana and Lulu") who had been born recently, plus a third fetus, whose birth was in 2019.[87] His goal had been to test whether CRISPR-Cas9 gene-edits could make human offspring resistant to most strains of the HIV virus.[88] He had done this despite the National Academies of Sciences, Engineering, and Medicine's 2017 injunction to the world's scientific community to refrain, at least in the short term, from any "clinical" reproductive applications of human gene editing research and to even "approach" pure "research" on human embryos "with caution" and "broad public input."[89] The First International Summit on Genome Editing in 2015 originally promulgated this global consensus to reserve genome editing of human embryos for highly selective and well-regulated research (not clinical) purposes.[90]

Rather than abiding by the safeguards of international scientific peer judgment, Dr. He avoided double-blind peer review criticism and competitive publication prior to developing clinical (medical) applications of his in vitro research on embryos. He only attempted to publish and otherwise publicize his work once his maternal subjects became pregnant with gene-edited embryos.[91] To the shock of the vast majority of his fellow scientists, he had conducted a wildly unethical and unnecessary reproductive experiment with CRISPR-Cas9.[92] "This goes against the traditional Chinese view of medicine established as far back as 600 bc," Chinese bioethicist Ruipeng Lei and colleagues argued in a May 2019 comment in *Nature*, "when the Chinese philosopher Confucius put forward the concept of ren (humaneness) as the core principle of Confucianism, many doctors followed his teachings, perceiving medicine to be the art of humaneness (yi ben ren shu)."[93] While Dr. He—a millennial product of a post-1989, communist China—would likely not identify with ancient hierarchical Confucian values, his entrepreneurial approach to gene-editing babies suggests his cavalier attitude toward the mainstream, egalitarian "medical morality" that governs ethical practices of care in Chinese hospitals.[94]

Called the "Chinese Frankenstein" in the press, Dr. He acted in relative professional secrecy, while on leave from his university, working for his own profitable biotech company and alongside dozens of scientific and medical accomplices in China and abroad, most of whom have not yet been named or identified.[95] He solicited patients from HIV-AIDS clinics in China precisely because they had suffered social stigma associated with their disease.[96] By targeting this vulnerable population with the hope of making their children immune to HIV, he may have manipulated their emotions and compromised their ability to truly consent. By some accounts—in China and beyond—he did not properly seek approval of his human subjects protocol by an independent hospital review board and may have even forged it. In an article first published in the Chinese *People's Online Daily* on 26 November 2018, the Shenzhen Hemei Women's and Children's Hospital denied that it ever received a human subjects research proposal from Dr. He, claiming that its institutional review board was not even in place in March 2017, the time the supposed approval is dated.[97] However, anthropologist Eben Kirksey has since uncovered through personal interviews and a systematic, hospital-based ethnography that the protocol was in fact approved.[98] Nevertheless, this institutional-level approval of the process would hardly justify its diversion from the wider scientific community's injunction to refrain from clinical (reproductive) applications of gene editing of human embryos.

Worst of all, Dr. He used an unapproved genome editing technique to test a theory about the genetics of HIV transmission with human subjects. He did this despite the fact that numerous simpler, safer, cheaper medical techniques and drugs have been approved and widely used to either prevent or successfully treat paternal transmission of HIV.[99] As a result of the reckless examples of Dr. He in China and Dr. Zhang in the United States, more rogue scientists may break the prohibitions and guidelines of the scientific community to conduct other reproductive experiments with the human germline. Indeed, these two modern versions of Victor Frankenstein set the stage for such rogue collaborations when they met several times in China during autumn 2018 to discuss plans to build a "medical tourism hub" for fertility and genetic engineering on the southern Chinese resort island of Hainan.[100] Their plans have since fallen through due to Dr. He's surveillance, trial, and imprisonment by the Chinese state and his international infamy. Chances are that Zhang or other scientists will attempt something similar—if they haven't already—with less conspicuous partners, that is, if national and international legal regulation of human germline genetic engineering does not step up.[101]

In a multiauthored article published in *Nature* in March 2019, leading scientists and bioethicists—including rival CRISPR innovators, Doudna's collaborator Emmanuelle Charpentier and MIT's Feng Zang—banded together to propose a five-year moratorium on all clinical applications of heritable human genome editing. They also advocated stricter and more transparent national-level regulation of its research and clinical uses. Most important, they stressed the need for greater public international oversight and discussion of the scientific and ethical dimensions of human germline genetic modification, under the auspices of the World Health Organization and other academic and political bodies.[102]

In May 2019, a team of Chinese bioethicists led by Ruipeng Lei also argued in *Nature* that China in particular needed more "top-down" national regulation of human germline genetic engineering, with severe penalties such as loss of "funding, licenses, or employment" for offenders. The case of Dr. He had proven that their nation could not no longer afford to leave it to the "self-regulation" of scientists themselves.[103] The same month, *Nature* reported that the new draft of China's civil code attributed "personality rights" to human genes and embryos such that "experiments on genes in adults or embryos that endanger human health or violate ethical norms can accordingly be seen as a violation of a person's fundamental rights."[104]

This was a bit of political déjà vu. Political scientists and philosophers in the first decade of the twenty-first century—most notably, Francis Fukuyama, Jürgen Habermas, and Michael Sandel—had also cautioned against the germline modification of human gametes or zygotes, especially for reproductive purposes. After Scottish scientists revealed in February 1997 that they had successfully cloned the first mammal—"Dolly the sheep"—a spate of national- and international-level debates erupted about the ethics and regulation of human cloning and other heritable modifications to the human genome.[105] In late 2001, Sandel was invited to serve on the U.S. President's Council on Bioethics. The group's discussions on the regulation of cloning and other forms of genetic engineering shaped his book *The Case Against Perfection* (2007). Its argument followed the Council in prohibiting reproductive human cloning or the bioengineering of "designer babies" with enhancements to their looks or intelligence. Sandel ultimately dissented from Bush administration policy, however, in defending "regulated" research use of new cloned human embryonic stem cell lines to develop "therapeutic" medical treatments for deadly and debilitating diseases.[106]

In 2002, Fukuyama issued a far more apocalyptic condemnation of human germline genetic engineering in all its forms, whether for research, therapy, or enhancement. He projected that any heritable changes to the human genome would change human nature in inalterable and unforeseeable ways, perhaps even destroying the species and the distinctive morality it had evolved and passed down over millennia.[107] He prophesied, "We may be about to enter into a posthuman future, in which technology will give us the capacity gradually to alter that [human] essence over time. . . . It could be one in which any notion of 'shared humanity' is lost, because we have mixed human genes with those of so many other species that we no longer have a clear idea of what a human being is."[108] According to Fukuyama's biologically deterministic view of the genome as the "essence" or root of the human being, heritable genetic modification—including interspecies, transgenetic changes—threatened the inheritance of a shared understanding of humanity.

In a series of lectures and essays compiled between 2000 and 2001 and published in English as *The Future of Human Nature* in 2003, Habermas pushed the rising bioconservative critique of genetic engineering even further. He argued that embryonic genetic manipulation of any sort— heritable, interspecies, or otherwise—had the power to dehumanize people if it were done for the wrong reasons. Even a seemingly innocuous genetic screening technique such as PGD could make the "biologists and engineers" perceive humanity as a mere object of research and eugenic improvement. Widespread genetic engineering could desensitize the broader culture to its potential violations of human rights. He worried in particular about parental "instrumentalization" of offspring to fulfill their own preferences for genetic enhancement, without the possibility of the future child's consent.[109] Referencing the recently ratified European Union Charter of Fundamental Rights (2000), Habermas pondered if its bans on human reproductive cloning and other eugenic practices were already outdated due to "biologists and engineers" being "intoxicated by science fiction" rather than concerned for the protection of human dignity and autonomy.[110]

"The problem," Habermas clarified, "was not genetic engineering, but the mode and scope of its use."[111] Similar to Sandel and the U.S. President's Council on Bioethics, Habermas questioned the ethics of any nontherapeutic genetic manipulation or artificial selection that sought to enhance offspring according to the preferences of intended parents rather than circumvent or treat a disease. Artificial enhancements to reproduction were nothing less than "positive eugenics." Habermas considered any such program to be an authoritarian attempt to permanently manipulate or control the human genome in a way that could undercut the future autonomy of offspring in favor of the wishes of the family or society.[112] According to this far-reaching argument, the nontherapeutic use of PGD to artificially select embryos posed as much of a threat to human dignity and autonomy as human reproductive cloning.[113] Habermas hypothesized that a future child who learned that he was made from such unnecessary artificial interventions in the genome "*might*" succumb to either "fatalism or resentment" due to a sense that his life had been manipulated from the outset in a way that could not be retrospectively justified to himself.[114] These three leading political theorists' broadly prohibitive responses to the question, "Should children be genetically engineered?" are different yet share two main problems in common.

First, they fail to grapple with recent history. Fukuyama, Habermas, and Sandel treat human germline genetic modification as if it were a matter of science fiction to be avoided like a dystopian future. They thereby ignore the fact that children had been made from ooplasmic transfer, the earliest form of three-person IVF, since 1997.[115] They also generalize the dangers of genetic engineering instead of teasing out the different ethical implications of various reproductive technologies that had succeeded in the 1990s, such as PGD, mammalian cloning, and three-person IVF.

Second, and more troublingly, their broadly prohibitive responses to genetic engineering fail to address a major normative issue. Fukuyama, Habermas, and Sandel do not take into account the rights of those living children already made from permanent manipulations of the genome. They also neglect to consider the corresponding duties of parents, other adults, states, and other political institutions toward these children.

Despite drawing a bright line between what is ethical and what is not with regard to the manipulation of human embryos, prohibitive responses to genetic engineering tend to lead down two inconclusive paths in human rights argumentation. On the one hand, one might argue for the embryo's right to be free from either selection or modification of its future traits as a person. On the other hand, one might classify such genomic manipulations as eugenics and therefore violations of human rights. Neither route has an obvious way to gain traction in public policy or law for two reasons.

For one, the lack of agreement about whether personhood begins before birth is a political roadblock for developing standardized laws and regulations that ascribe rights to embryos and fetuses. The fraught history of abortion law at the national and international levels illustrates how difficult it is to achieve consensus on the moral or legal status of the unborn.[116] As recent medical advances—such as the Children's Hospital of Philadelphia's prototype for an artificial womb—make fetuses viable ever earlier, these debates seem likely to only intensify in many places.[117]

Additionally, it is not clear whether all forms of genetic engineering should be prohibited under international human rights law. After the 1948 Universal Declaration of Human Rights (UDHR), human rights norms consistently prohibit state-sanctioned eugenics, or the systematic political attempt to influence the "physical, mental, or genetic" attributes of a population.[118] Yet international law does not clarify what "counts" as eugenics.[119] Since the 1997 Universal Declaration on the Human Genome and Human Rights (UDHGHR), human rights prohibit human reproductive cloning as contrary to human dignity. Yet, international law leaves open the questions of whether other forms of "genetic engineering" should be permissible or impermissible and why.[120] The law's persistent focus on prohibitions of eugenics and genetic engineering has led to neglect of the equally weighty issue of the rights of the people already made from such reproductive interventions.

iii. Hearing the Creature: Articulating the Rights of the Genetically Modified Child

Rather than focus mainly on prohibition, deterrence, and punishment of genetic engineering, the law should look additionally at how rights apply to living children made from it. By children, I mean anyone living in the stage of childhood. By childhood, I mean the time of life between birth and adulthood. This is a purely political definition of the child, made without reference to any divisive, unsupported scientific ideas or deep and demanding moral, metaphysical, or religious doctrines.[121] Given its fluidity, this political definition of the child should travel well across cultures and legal systems, covering all known cases of children worldwide. We need such a basic *and* broad political definition of a child to serve as a guide for focusing international attention on the question of the rights of the children actually made and born due to varieties of genetic engineering.

Overcoming the systematic bias in bioethics *toward* the early embryo and *against* the child will require much more than a workable political definition of the child, however. It will require an imaginative leap, which *Frankenstein* and its literary progeny can push us to entertain. Since the public panic over the possibility of human cloning in the late 1990s, Hacker literature has evolved in a Shelleyan vein to explore the ethics and politics of genetic engineering from the perspective of the children affected. Alongside *Gattaca*, the political philosopher Martha Nussbaum's short story "Little C" (1998) and Nnedi Okorafor's "African-based" SF novel *The Book of Phoenix* (2015) share *Frankenstein*'s hybrid literary and philosophical approach to the problems of justice raised by the bioengineering of children.[122]

Frankenstein opened an imaginative frame for focusing upon the rights of the bioengineered child *after* birth through a cascade of highly innovative plot points. Shelley first eliminated pregnancy from the Creature's reproductive circumstances, forcing the reader to dwell on his life after birth, not before it. Mellor argued that this omission of woman from the reproductive process, and its disastrous results, signaled the high value that Shelley placed on women's vital role in mothering children and building healthy communities in society.[123] It also enables the story to function as a feminist critique of the historical failure of men (like Victor Frankenstein) to step up to fulfill intensively loving, caring, and dutiful roles as parents.[124] Due to the reproduction of the Creature without fertilization of gametes or gestation in a woman's womb, the novel additionally allows readers to conceptualize the bioengineered child as an independent entity, physically separate from a mother, a father, or any parent, from the very moment of animation.

Okorafor's Phoenix is a futuristic reboot of the Creature as an "ABO, or 'accelerated biological organism.'"[125] She is a genetically modified child, "mixed and grown" from ancient, modern, and cloned African sources of DNA.[126] Stripped of her African American surrogate mother at birth, Phoenix grows up without a family in the secretive Tower 7 of the LifeGen corporation. Once the all-seeing "Big Eye" of the biotech bureaucracy discovers that the infant is capable of pyrokinetic destruction and regeneration like the mythological phoenix, it plans to use her as a biological weapon.[127] As she learns about her mysterious origins and strange powers, Phoenix gathers that her genetic enhancements have made her functionally an adult at the age of 2. "I look and feel about 40 and have the knowledge of a centenarian," she intuits.[128] Like the Creature, Phoenix reaches full-grown intellectual and physical independence as a toddler, without the benefit of parental guidance. Ironically, this precocious physical and intellectual maturity leaves both the Creature and Phoenix vulnerable to the manipulation and tyranny of their hackers.

Taking the thought experiment even further, Shelley endowed the Creature with extraordinary powers to physically survive independently of his father-scientist immediately after birth. She gave the newborn Creature an eight-foot frame, incredible strength and endurance, imperviousness to the cold, "superhuman" speed, and such rapid cognitive and linguistic development that he teaches himself to read Milton's *Paradise Lost* before the age of one.[129] In contrast to vulnerable newborn babies who would die without an intensively loving caregiver to satisfy their needs, the Creature's super-human powers enable him to survive exposure after birth and to live separately from his neglectful parent. As a consequence, the physical separation between the Creature and his parent persists long after the unprecedented circumstances of his birth without a womb, a pregnancy, or an egg.

By holding the Creature's physical independence constant from the very onset of life, Shelley's literary thought experiment invites the reader to assess the effect of extreme physical independence on a child's affective development. Running this thought experiment in one's own mind, one finds that the persisting physical and social isolation of the Creature correlates with the growth of his longing for a close emotional relationship with a parent or other loving friend or companion. Similarly, as the winged Phoenix learns about her genetically engineered power to burn to ash and then rise again, she causes the loss of two men she loves. She flies away only to find she is haunted by their memories: "I can fly, but I am not light."[130]

Frankenstein is likewise preoccupied with the burdens of abandonment. The Creature recounts to Victor how he suffered total abuse by society because of the bioengineered deformity that drove his father-scientist to abandon him as soon as he was animated. Frankenstein is initially moved to help his Creature but ultimately fails to respond to the cries of his child. As if eavesdropping, the reader listens to this emotional confrontation between the scientist and his abandoned Creature and gains the opportunity to sympathize with the plight of an abused and neglected child of biotechnology.

At the conclusion of this dramatic meeting of maker and child on the *mer de glace*, the Creature demands of his father-scientist the fulfillment of his "right" to "live in the interchange of those sympathies necessary for my being." A survivor of utter neglect, the twenty-one-month-old articulates a rationally and emotionally compelling rights claim toward his derelict parent, for the fulfillment of his right to share love and community with another. While she does not use the language of rights, Phoenix reacts to the injustice of her reproductive circumstances like the Creature. She begs for "Justice for what had been done to me" and "all the other prisoners" of the biotech company that coldly built them without concern for their needs for family and other forms of belonging.[131]

The Creature hypothesizes that if he had an equal female companion made for him, then she would be the only person with whom he could share love and community, due to her similar deformity. Although many interpretations of the novel have depicted the Creature's demand as sexual or marital in nature—especially after James Whale's iconic 1935 film *Bride of Frankenstein*—the novel itself problematizes this assumption. Made from the parts of human and other animal corpses, the Creature situates himself in an ambiguous category between "man" and "beast." Unlike a "man" who takes a "wife" or a "beast" who finds a "mate" for purposes of sexual reproduction, he desires a female "companion" who is his equal in ugliness.[132] In a Gothic feminist reversal of the tropes of English literary romances, the Creature does not ask for a beautiful bride who could perpetuate his name and lineage within Western European patriarchal society. He rather wants to share sympathies with an equal, as fellow "monsters" living in isolation from human society in a desert in South America.[133]

It is Victor who projects onto this request the possibility that the creatures will seek to have children. This assumption is unwarranted for three reasons. To begin, Victor ignores the Creature's use of nonsexual language to express his desire for an equal female companion. Victor also fails to acknowledge that he could use science to render the female infertile before she is animated. And finally, he grants the possibility that the female may hate the Creature or love the "superior beauty of man."[134] Letting his sexualized and demonized view of the creatures drive his decision making, Victor leaps to the conclusion that he must terminate the making of the female creature in order to prevent the reproduction of a "race of devils" that could destroy the human species.[135] In a sadistic spectacle of hacking the female body, Victor "tore to pieces" his child's intended companion in full view of him. The Creature's witness of the female's abortion elicits a "howl of devilish despair and revenge."[136]

Both the Creature and Victor make obvious errors in their moral reasoning and actions. A child's right to share love and community with another has limits. No one, not even an abused and neglected creature of biotechnology, has a right to the purely instrumental use of another person. Shelley may have been drawing from her mother Wollstonecraft's systematic critique of the instrumental treatment of women as "the toy of man" in eighteenth-century patriarchal societies.[137] According to a Wollstonecraftian principle of mutual respect, the Creature had no right to have anyone made or provided for the express purpose of being his companion. Companionship must be freely given to be an authentic expression of love. Quite radically, the novel calls into question not only children's right to have companions expressly made or provided for their emotional satisfaction but also prospective parents' right to make children solely for purposes of satisfying their own companionship needs.

Nussbaum's short story "Little C" (1998) probes the unsettling emotions behind the question of who can make, or serve as, a rightful companion. A woman takes in a clone baby—"Little C"—made from the cells of the husband who left her, with the disturbing aim of raising the child to become a romantic replacement for him. She notes that the "thighs" of the infant boy "show signs of promise" because they remind her of her former lover's muscular body.[138] As the child grows up, she is disappointed to realize that he is not identical to her former husband in tastes, talents, or even physical appearance.

She reads the clone a novel by George Sand, *François le Champi* (1848), in which a woman takes in a foundling boy who grows up, to her surprise, to freely fall into a relationship of mutual romantic love with her. At first, Little C enjoys the story, but when he is seventeen, he questions his mother why their relationship is not as strong as the one in the novel. "Why, then, do you not love me the way Madeline loved her grown François?" he asks her."[139] She responds maternally, not romantically, explaining to him that "each story has its own ending, and no person is exactly like any other."[140] She has learned the hard way that one cannot engineer love, since both parties must freely give it. The story ends with her directing Little C to enjoy the "second act" of the opera that they are attending before he leaves for college.[141] Perhaps it is a sign of a sea change in their relationship—away from what she now knows she had no right to do and toward what might become a nonromantic friendship between a young adult and his parent.

Nussbaum's contribution to Hacker literature recalls the incestuous Gothic storylines of *Frankenstein*. The mother raises the clone "Little C" to be a romantic substitute for her ex-husband but ultimately adopts a more dutiful and parental stance toward her adult child. What had been wrong was not making or adopting the clone, let alone being him, but rather the mother's selfish and sinister plan to manipulate his life for her own romantic and sexual satisfaction.

Shelley's novel is even more perverse. Betrothed to his sister Elizabeth, Victor delays his wedding for years while secretly channeling his "heart and soul" into the macabre science of making a "human being" from the parts of human and other animal corpses.[142] Despite devoting years to bioengineering his creatures, he avoids his parental duties toward them. He considers neither the right of the nearly complete female to live nor his duty to support her life once he has started it. Nor does he consider the right of the already born Creature to share love with a parent or a fitting substitute while he is young and in need of intensively nurturing companionship and care. Worst of all, Victor violates the right of his child not to be psychologically abused. In a gruesome spectacle, he destroys the female in front of the Creature.

Hearing the Creature's story of abandonment and neglect, we might restate his fundamental ethical question as "What are the rights of the bioengineered child?" This positive and forward-looking formulation of the question yields some new *and* concrete political answers, as a result of putting the interests of the living child at the heart of the issue. If one pictures a genetically modified child posing the question—"What are my rights?"— one might respond by stating the basic right of any child *to be*, regardless of birth or other reproductive circumstances. Fleshed out with respect to twenty-first-century biotechnology, it is the right of all children, including those genetically modified or otherwise bioengineered, to live, love, and flourish, amid conditions of nondiscrimination, in the community that brought them to life in the first place.

This is a *new political right*. It is a creative rights claim that is articulated in fresh and updated terms in relation to current and past politics, laws, and cultures. This idea fuses key concepts of political theorist Bonnie Honig and political philosopher John Rawls. This is an unexpected synthesis, as Honig has been a high-profile critic of Rawls's theory of justice since the early 1990s.[143] The basic thrust of her critique is that Rawlsian liberalism secures equal rights at the cost of recognizing and respecting difference and discord as a vital part of the politics of realizing conditions of justice for everyone. Paradoxically, she finds, Rawls's firm jurisdiction of equal rights does not afford political minorities (and other so-called deviants from the norms of citizenry) the social and cultural "respect" they want, need, and deserve.[144] The result is a liberalism that is predicated upon a commitment to "pluralism" in the abstract but does not actually respect, in any complex or realistic way, the necessarily diverse and conflicting modes of being political as a citizen of a modern democracy.[145]

By way of contrast to Rawls, Honig conceived a *new right* in "agonistic" terms, or in a radically critical, yet still creative, dialogue with a particular cultural, economic, and political context. Her example was the right to "slow food," or the slow, organic, healthy making and enjoyment of food in harmony with others and the Earth. She articulated this right in a playful, critical dialogue with the imperial and impoverished culture of "fast food" that dominates contemporary capitalistic societies.[146]

Rawls, on the other hand, defended a less radical and more pragmatic conception of *political rights*. On this more formal and juridical model, human rights were realized through law and politics. Human rights had been gradually articulated in national and international laws, policies, and practices since their institutionalization by the United Nations in the Universal Declaration of Human Rights of 1948.[147]

My conception of a *new political right* brings together the political pragmatism of Rawls with the radical cultural critique of Honig, in order to escape the limitations of both approaches to conceptualizing rights. Rawlsian political rights run the risk of simply replicating the legal norms of the past instead of imagining what might be best or even necessary to protect the rights of humanity in the future. Honig's new rights run the risk of being too disconnected from the formal mechanisms of law and politics to be effective in their radical critique of culture and economics. By blending the creativity of Honig with the pragmatism of Rawls, we find a third way for articulating new rights for vulnerable persons who are presently invisible to the law.

By relating the Creature's *cri de coeur* to contemporary debates on genetic engineering, we may voice a new political right of the child. This is the right *to be* a genetically engineered child—meaning, *to have been* genetically engineered and subsequently to live, love, and flourish as such, between birth and adulthood, in conditions of nondiscrimination with regard to reproductive circumstances and genetic features. This is the converse of the Habermasian "right to a genetic inheritance immune from artificial intervention."[148]

Habermas has the noble aim of wishing to protect future generations from the scourge of state-sponsored eugenics that his homeland of Germany had unleashed on the world under the Nazis. Yet I charge that his negative formulation of the right to "a genetic inheritance immune from artificial intervention" is naive. It fails to take into account both the recent history and the likely growth of human germline genetic modification, as well as PGD and embryonic selection. If instead we take as a historical given the existence of genetically engineered children and imagine—with the help of the Creature's plea to Victor—what it would take for them to thrive as children, we can arrive at an account of the basic political rights of these "babies of technology" that is realistic while remaining creative.[149]

It is valid to compare the Creature with genetically engineered children today but only with respect to their circumstances of reproduction. It would be wrong to suggest that genetically engineered children are identical to the Creature, who, after all, becomes a murderer following a childhood of neglect and abuse.[150] It is politically apt, however, to compare the Creature with genetically engineered children because their similar circumstances of reproduction yield similar potential for a hurtful experience of discrimination, neglect, and abuse.

Seven aspects of the Creature's character arise from his reproductive circumstances. Together and separately, these seven aspects show the Creature's approximate social and medical similarities to genetically engineered children today. The Creature is (1) a child or young creation of his "father" or "creator."[151] He is (2) a hybrid or chimera of human and other animal parts. He is (3) made through a type of ART, from (4) the parts of donors in (5) a laboratory setting and (6) modified through a biotechnological intervention by a scientist, in order to be (7) made perfect in a feature or "selected" set of "features."[152]

The 50 to 100 children made by three-person IVF since 1997 fit all seven of these criteria: they are genetic chimeras with the DNA of three zygotes, with greater longevity due to the elimination of deadly or debilitating genetic diseases.[153] Beyond their circumstances of reproduction, what the Creature and genetically engineered children share most profoundly in common is being—meaning, *living*—as a bioengineered child. The story of the artificially made and modified Creature suggests that children's rights are in fact the most fundamental form of rights because each and every person—regardless of origins, features, or capacities—begins life as we know it, after birth, as an emotionally and socially vulnerable child. If we are not granted rights as children, we will have no *opportunity* to hold any other rights later in life.

These fundamental rights of the child include, first and foremost, a right to share love with parents or fitting substitutes, for such a relationship of love is critical for children's healthy and happy development. As the philosopher S. Matthew Liao argues, infants and other young children need to experience love with a parent in order to flourish in their development. If they lack parental love, infants will fail to thrive and even die, and older children will suffer delays or other disruptions of their healthy development.[154] The Creature puts this philosophical point in poetic terms when he claims in relation to his "father" a "right" to "live in the interchange of those sympathies necessary for my being."[155] Without experiencing a sympathetic exchange or reciprocal relationship of love with a parent or fitting substitute, the Creature fails to emotionally thrive, as any young child would, despite his ability to physically survive on his own.

Similarly deprived of family through her circumstances of reproduction, Phoenix echoes the Creature as she lyrically expresses the "magic" of belonging to another.[156] While inspecting her wings in awe, the African doctor Kofi calls her "God's creature." "I didn't believe in God," she recalls, "but these words were like magic to me. They said that I, too, was an earthling. That I belonged here. I belonged."[157] Emotionally still a child, she finds an ephemeral substitute for a family in Kofi before she envelops him in flames to save him from a worse death at the hands of LifeGen. The tragedy of this sacrifice springs from her fragile and unsettled sense of belonging. Like the Creature, Phoenix cannot fully believe she is loveable, even as she reaches for love as the answer to the injustice done to her and other ABOs.

Frankenstein's foundational thought experiment—what if a man made a child without any mother through science?—has been a seminal premise for Hacker literature on the making of artificial life. Okorafor and Nussbaum employ versions of it to conjecture the vulnerability of genetically engineered children to exploitation and abuse if they are not provided fitting conditions of loving care upon birth. The genius of Shelley was to show that while biotechnology may change some of the circumstances behind the parent-child relationship, including conditions of physical vulnerability and dependency, it cannot eliminate the issue of the responsibility of people toward the children whom they make and raise.[158] Although he is not biologically related to his Creature, Victor is primarily responsible for him as the sole parent who brought him to life. So too are all parents responsible for the children under their primary care, no matter how those children came to be under it. A provocative implication of Shelley's thought experiment is that scientists have the duties of a parent if they use technology to bring a child into the world without a family, at least until they find a fitting substitute to assume those duties.

Even as Shelley's novel explores the deep, primary responsibility of parents toward their children, especially to share love with them, it also presents—true to the Gothic form—the consequences of failing to fulfill that duty or, if unfit or incapable, to find someone else to fulfill it. In the face of parental failure to provide or at least arrange for a fitting substitute to fulfill a child's right to conditions of loving care, what shall be done? The story of the stateless and orphaned Creature's failed quest across borders to find any community to support him is a kind of reverse, Gothic image of what, politically, ought to be the case.

By presenting a worst-case scenario of child exposure and abuse, the novel *Frankenstein* presses the reader to ask the still visionary question: what are the obligations of states and international political bodies toward children without parents or any family to lovingly care for them? At the same time, the story of the Creature presses readers to challenge biologically deterministic accounts of what it means to be a human, a child, to love, or to hold rights. Genetically engineered children who have been heritably modified by three-person IVF or gene-editing are not unhuman or non-human but rather "a new form of human being," according to the biologist Paul Knoepfler.[159] The same may be said of the Creature—while he is seen and treated as a "savage" and a "monster," he was actually designed by Victor as a "human being," made from the parts of corpses of humans and other animals, in order to display distinctive "features."[160] Adopting the pluralistic language of critical theorist Rahel Jaeggi, we might say that the fiction of the Creature and the fact of genetically modified babies each represent new "forms of life" in human culture. We ought to fold these new "forms of life" into a capacious understanding of the normative "plurality" of possible ways of being human or humane.[161]

Gattaca delves into the psychological and social dangers of failing to expand our conception of the human to cover the diversity of its forms. Niccol's film depicts the fraught quest of a group of youth to exercise the basic right to flourish in a society that privileges those who are genetically engineered. A pair of brothers hold death-defying swimming contests to see who is stronger, with the genetically engineered son (Anton) competing against the son born because his parents took the risk of having unprotected sex (Vincent). The audience does not blame the brothers, or even their parents, for their reckless fraternal infighting; rather, we blame the dystopian eugenic society in which Vincent and Anton were raised to senselessly compete.

A similar dynamic may unfold in the real world for children differentiated in society due to the actual hacking of the genome and its lacks. Take the case of Nana and Lulu, the gene-edited twins born in China in late 2018. Although the early Chinese journalism represented Dr. He as following the bioethical principle of showing "mercy" to needy populations in providing medical care, he in fact conducted a heartless, even merciless, reproductive experiment by editing in different ways their copies of a gene (CCR_5), which is strongly related to the immune system and HIV transmission.[162] At the Second International Summit on Genome Editing, Dr. He reported that "in one of the twins, both copies of the CCR_5 gene were disabled, but that in the other twin, only one copy was."[163] This left the second twin vulnerable to HIV—and the control subject for the twin with both copies of the gene disabled. Researcher Maria Jasin of the Memorial Sloan Kettering Cancer Center pointed out that this experiment might hurt the "family dynamics" among the twins and their parents.[164] One twin has been deliberately and permanently enhanced more than the other. How will that affect the gene-edited siblings—not only their health but also their relationships and in society? Will their differential treatment as embryos shape their differential treatment as children and adults? Will Nana and Lulu end up like Anton and Vincent in *Gattaca*, who grow to resent each other due to the differences in their treatment by family and society? How can society and law protect Nana and Lulu, as well as other children, from *Gattaca*-like discrimination and stereotyping on the basis of their circumstances of birth?

Both *Gattaca* and *Frankenstein* remind us that all children are vulnerable to discrimination due to factors beyond their control, including circumstances shaped by assisted reproductive technology and bioengineering. While *Gattaca* pictures a dystopian society that unfairly elevates a genetically modified upper caste, the teenage Shelley imagined the reverse worst-case scenario. *Frankenstein* parses the possibility of devastating discrimination against a bioengineered child. Both of these potentialities need to be addressed in human rights law.

Beyond the entitlement to "just reparation for any damage sustained as a direct and determining result of an intervention affecting his or her genome," the UDHGHR does not specify rights for the genetically manipulated or modified person.[165] In July 2018, the Nuffield Bioethics Council indicated the lack of an "international treaty of general application" designated for the "direct" regulation of the human genome or its modification, or an "international Declaration" of the universal human rights of people "whose genomes have been edited."[166] Given that children are affected first and foremost by the new technologies of gene editing and other forms of germline engineering, it appears that that the most pressing political need is to draft an international Declaration of the Rights of the Genetically

Modified Child. Even the scientists and ethicists who argued in March 2019 for a five-year moratorium on heritable human genome editing conceded a weakness in their proposal for "voluntary" participation of states in future regulation: the lack of a "formal treaty" to bind nations together in a common project of ethical intervention in a scientific development that affects the whole "human species."[167]

The United Nations' Convention on the Rights of the Child (CRC) offers a promising framework for amending the UDHGHR with such a declaration.[168] The CRC's preamble states that each child, "for the full and harmonious development of his or her personality, should grow up in a family environment, in an atmosphere of happiness, love and understanding." Part I, Article 2 specifies nondiscrimination rights, including rights to nondiscrimination toward "disability, birth, or other status." And Part I, Article 7 specifies rights to "a name," birth "registration," "nationality," and "as far as possible . . . to know and be cared for by his or her parents."[169] Now, the United Nations and governments need to elaborate how these apply to genetically modified children in human rights law.

Inspired by Shelley's Creature, I propose that two universal rights of the child be articulated in any new international agreement or declaration about genome modification:

(1) children's right to share love with parents or fitting substitutes, and
(2) children's right to nondiscrimination on the basis of birth, including reproductive circumstances and genetic features.

The first right builds on CRC's preamble and Part I, Article 7 but with greater focus and legal power. It could address children's welfare rights worldwide, prompting national and international safety nets to protect parentless, loveless, or stateless children, genetically modified or not. It might be used to regulate the current international Wild West of reproductive medicine by prioritizing children's fundamental interest in having a loving family environment and the right "to know" genetic and social parents, donors, surrogates, and the broader story of their reproductive circumstances. Building upon Part I, Articles 2 and 7 of the CRC, the second right clarifies that nondiscrimination on the basis of "birth, disability, or other status" covers all circumstances of reproduction and all genetic features. Together, this pair of rights could expand child welfare and nondiscrimination laws and policies, nationally and internationally, to protect all

children and ultimately all adults from the injustice stemming from unreg-
ulated or rogue use of biotechnology as presciently imagined in the tradition of Hacker literature.

iv. Could Genetic Engineering Undercut Human Autonomy?

Habermas, despite his firm commitment to the ongoing public and legal
articulation of the international standard of human rights, makes an intri-
guing provocation. Could domineering forms of genetic engineering undercut the conditions for autonomy that enable the enjoyment of human
rights? Situating himself in a "postmetaphysical" worldview, he takes a person's potential for autonomous conduct—understood as the rational self-
determination of one's life plan—to be the defining ethical dimension of
human "forms of life" carried out with dignity.[170] If eugenic manipulation
of an embryo could block the future person's experience of autonomy, then
it might also abolish the possibility of a "species-wide" ethos of human
rights in which people recognized and respected themselves and others as
moral and political equals.[171]

   Although he distances himself from intoxicating fantasies of "science
fiction," Habermas's premonition of the abolition of human liberty
through nontherapeutic genetic engineering proves to be less realistic than
either *Brave New World* or *Gattaca*.[172] By putting Habermas and the liberal
eugenics he opposes into dialogue with these political science fictions, a
new critical spin on his conservative bioethics emerges. While Habermas
envisions the disfigurement of human autonomy after genetic engineering,
these changes should be ethically conceived as *reconfigurations* of autonomy, sometimes made in resistance to extreme conditions of technological
domination.

   In the central essay of his book *The Future of Human Nature*, Habermas
introduces a rather blunt distinction between "the 'grown' and the 'made,'
the subjective and the objective."[173] This launches a series of polarities that
recur in his arguments about the ethics of genetic engineering. He presents
us with the "organically grown" versus the "technologically made," the subjective "programmer" versus the "programmed" object, and the dignity of
an "autonomous conduct of life" versus the instrumentalization of "passive
material."[174] At odds with his explicit rejection of both "genetic determinism" and antiscientific critiques of genetic engineering, these binary oppositions cast technophobic and naturalistic shadows upon his theory of the

ethical development of human nature. It suggests that to be "made" through technology potentially aborts the conditions for human equality and freedom, while to be "grown" without it generates the circumstances for authentic human autonomy.[175]

Exploiting the tension between these dichotomous themes, Habermas boldly claims "'a right to a genetic inheritance immune from artificial intervention.'"[176] Drawn from the language of debates in the Parliamentary Assembly of the European Council, this right aims to protect future people from "alien determination" by a broad range of artificial reproductive technologies and research programs that might compromise their sense of autonomy as free and equal human beings.[177] Having grown up in Nazi Germany, Habermas has good reason to fear eugenics directed by a totalitarian state. Yet he expresses skepticism about the ethics of virtually every form of artificial reproductive technology due to its potential use for either state-sponsored or parental eugenics. This extreme position is not tenable when considering the specifics of the technologies he opposes.

Although he does not prohibit "germ-line" engineering for therapeutic use, Habermas casts aspersions on the research use of human embryonic cloning, including medical study of "totipotent stem cells."[178] More problematically, he plays on the idea of feeling "revulsion before the prospect of chimera created by genetic engineering, at bred and cloned human beings, and at embryos destroyed in the course of experimentation," even as he dismisses such fears as "archaic" and "naïve."[179] A latent gaze of disgust (*im Abscheu*) toward unnatural interventions in human reproduction permeates his critiques of artificial reproductive technologies ranging from "preimplantation genetic diagnosis" to "surrogate mothers and anonymous gamete donation, of postmenopausal pregnancy made possible by egg donation, or of the perversely delayed use made of frozen egg cells."[180]

The latter statement betrays a male bias that undermines the scope of his commitment to the human right "to found a family," promulgated by Article 16 of the UDHR.[181] Habermas implies that women—perhaps especially career-oriented women and older women—do not have a right to health care to treat or preserve fertility because it would be an unjustifiable use of medicine for unnatural or perverse (*pervers*) reasons. Habermas's phrase "pervers-zeitverschobenen Gebrauch eingefrorener Eizellen," literally translated "perverse, time-shifted use of frozen eggs," suggests that the "natural" chronology of the female reproductive life cycle has been perverted through oocyte cryopreservation and use of frozen eggs in IVF. The use of the term *"pervers"* has a strong connotation of moral judgment, evoking the view that egg freezing is against the order of things, abnormal, corrupt, or even sexually depraved.

If we take these examples as indicative of the wide range of forms of genetic engineering that Habermas could classify as eugenic or nontherapeutic, then his ethical and political theory tolerates very little artificial intervention in the inheritance of the human genome. It is not even clear whether he would classify basic IVF as a eugenic enhancement or as a medical therapy. IVF involves the artificial manipulation of gametes to boost fertility, usually with the production of spare embryos that die before implantation in the womb. Habermas could deem it an unjustified form of artificial selection that privileges the interests of the parents in their own fertility over the life prospects of some of the possible offspring. This would mean that he effectively rules out any technique of embryonic genetic engineering, for they all employ IVF.

Given the breadth of these ethical concerns about artificial reproductive technology and genetics research, we can elaborate the Habermasian "right to a genetic inheritance immune from artificial intervention" to mean an expansive right *not to be* genetically manipulated, selected, modified, or otherwise engineered, whether it is a germline intervention or not. This right is prospective in the sense that it applies to circumstances of reproduction before a "future person" or rights-bearer has come into being.[182] Intended parents and genetic engineers are obligated to approach the embryo with the "attitude" that it represents a "second person" who holds the same rights as other people.[183] Habermas thereby implies (but never explicitly states) that human embryos effectively have a correlative right *not to be* artificially manipulated on behalf of any future people who might develop from them.

Habermas's commitment to a "postmetaphysical" understanding of the human subject, however, steers him away from direct ascriptions of rights to embryos or other "prepersonal life."[185] Instead, he hypothesizes the subjectivity and autonomy of the human embryo from "the perspective of a future present": as in, imagine that the embryo *will* develop into an actual person who develops the capability and practice of subjectivity and autonomy over time in "communicative action" with other people.[186] Thus, the "right to a genetic inheritance immune from artificial intervention" presumes a nonmetaphysical conception of the future autonomy of a person who might arise from a given set of reproductive circumstances.

Habermas claims that to artificially intervene in the development of the human genome could violate the right of a "future person" to have an open-ended future with the opportunity of free choice about the course of one's own life.[187] More profoundly, he speculates the existential and ethical impact of embryonic manipulation on the identity and relationships of future persons. "Will we still be able to come to a self-understanding as persons who are the undivided authors of their own lives," he asks, "and approach others, without exception, as persons of equal birth?"[188]

Using a version of the liberal political philosopher Joel Feinberg's argument for a child's "'right to an open future,'" Habermas rolls out an extended thought experiment that features "an adolescent who was eugenically manipulated."[189] This teenager comes to understand that his "parents were only looking to their own preferences" in employing an unspecified form of genetic engineering to bring him to life.[190] Habermas argues that if it were possible that such a hypothetical adolescent "*might*" feel an existential burden in having certain futures foreclosed or prescribed to him without his consent (indeed, without his ability to consent), then it was wrong to make such a biotechnological intervention that would artificially fix the parents' plans for the child's future.[191]

By using and italicizing the conditional verb *might*, Habermas briefly acknowledges that Feinberg's open futures argument for children's rights is inconclusive with regard to genetic engineering of embryos. This is due to the possibility that an older child or adolescent *might* retrospectively assent to his genetic manipulation even if it were done for reasons of parental eugenics (satisfying their conception of enhancement), not therapy (such as the prevention of genetic disease). Despite this realistic alternative outcome for his thought experiment, Habermas rather severely concludes that any nontherapeutic manipulations of the genome ought to be prohibited, in order to rule out the possibility that parental eugenics *might* override a future child's autonomy.

Habermas's appropriation of the open futures argument misrepresents a few key tenets of Feinberg's position.[192] Feinberg makes a distinction between A-rights (or rights of adults, especially to autonomy), A-C rights (or rights that both children and adults hold), and C-rights (or children's rights).[193] C-rights include dependency rights such as food, water, and other means of surviving and thriving provided by adults plus rights that are held in trust and protected until children can exercise them in adulthood. The legal protection of C-rights, especially rights-in-trust, should enable a child to grow into an adult capable of making autonomous decisions about her own life, sometimes even against her present interests in favor of her present desires.

Feinberg's classic example of a C-right-in-trust is religious exercise. Since children are not capable of exercising it autonomously, they need it protected until they reach a period of independence in which they could make their own decisions about religion. According to Feinberg, the projected interests of a future adult would have to be so weighty as to justify the preemptive limitation of a C-right-in-trust before the rights-holder could grow into the exercise of it as an A-right.

Let us accept for a moment Feinberg's liberal view that autonomy rights are the defining class of A-rights. Autonomy requires giving children the chance to grow up to be adults with the freedom to make often poor decisions that sometimes conflict with their own present interests. It would seem that genetic engineering of embryos would only be a violation of C-rights-in-trust and eventual A-rights insofar as it hampered any projected adult's capability for autonomous choice.

As Habermas concedes, even germline modification of embryos does not necessarily hamper the future autonomy of children made from it. For this reason, he does not categorically object to germline engineering except in cases when it would eugenically instrumentalize the children produced from it. In his haste to prohibit prenatal genetic manipulation that would thwart human autonomy, Habermas veers from examining the other side of the issue: the ways in which various forms of genetic engineering can promote or ensure the life, flourishing, and eventual autonomy of future offspring.

Three-person IVF techniques can and do enhance life expectancy and health of children and adults through boosting the health of the mitochondria and eliminating deadly or debilitating genetic diseases. Although it was originally developed as a fertility-enhancing treatment for women, three-person IVF can enable offspring to be born and grow into adulthood who might have otherwise died in vitro, in utero, or in infancy due to genetic disease. Even though it has not always been used to circumvent genetic disease in embryos, three-person IVF may have the effect of increasing the overall health and longevity of the children born from it. The mother of Alana Saarinen proudly reported to the BBC that her daughter, at fourteen, "has always been healthy. Never anything more than a basic cold, or a flu every now and then. No health problems at all."[194] She saw her use of three-person IVF as an act of parental love that enabled her only child to have a life of greater health and well-being than otherwise would have been the case.

As a result, three-person IVF can be used in a way that respects both the rights of children and the rights of adults. For one, it can enable some embryos to grow up rather than die young without a chance to enjoy many, if not most, rights. It also enables some women to boost their fertility and exercise their human right "to found a family."[195]

Three-person IVF illustrates how genetic engineering can be justified for therapeutic treatment of disease or enhancement of fertility. It can help fulfill the dependency rights of children to the material conditions for life itself. It can protect children's rights-in-trust until they are ready to use them. It can enable the enjoyment of autonomy rights in adulthood for parents and offspring alike. The experience of the Saarinen family confirms the intuition of the Italian bioethicist Matteo Galletti that there is a "love component" to the child's right to an open future.[196] If genetic engineering has been performed out of self-giving love for a potential child, with an ethical concern for her future autonomy and happiness that carries forward into her childhood, then it is valid as either a therapy or an enhancement.

Other forms of genetic engineering, however, might indeed be understood as closing down the possible futures of a child made from it. Published in London in 1932, just before the Nazi eugenic regime rose to power in Germany, *Brave New World* envisions a future utilitarian "World State" organized to promote the leisurely, hedonistic happiness of the upper classes.[197] Huxley's study of early twentieth-century research on artificial fertilization and gestation, especially the theories of Cambridge biochemist J. B. S. Haldane, enriched the scientific plausibility of the opening scene in the "CENTRAL LONDON HATCHERY AND CONDITIONING CENTRE."[198] Conceived in a "test-tube" and then transferred into a "bottle" in a factory line, each baby is built by biotechnology and shaped by behavioral controls to fit into preordained classifications of a caste system.[199] The lowest forms of life are the Epsilons, menial laborers who are mass-produced without "human intelligence" or the capability to make autonomous decisions.[200] People higher up the scale benefit from their mindless and efficient work yet perceive them and the other laboring class, the Deltas, as "maggots."[201]

On one level, Huxley's extreme depiction of social eugenics exposes modern Western capitalism's systematic exploitation of working classes across the generations. It also raises the question of whether some forms of genetic engineering are impermissible because of an incompatibility with human autonomy. Given that they are conceived and reared to be drones, do the Epsilons ever stand a chance of being free? It would seem from this literary thought experiment that there could be extreme hacks to the human genome and its expression that would not just hinder, but block outright, the possibility of autonomy among those affected.

Three-person IVF families in the real world and the Epsilons and Deltas of *Brave New World* offer divergent perspectives on the impact of genetic engineering on the autonomy of future persons. Plugging these examples into Habermas's version of the "open futures" argument leads to different conclusions about the compatibility of children's rights with human germ-line genetic engineering. While history so far suggests the benign impact of three-person IVF on the autonomy and self-image of the first generation of children known to be made from it, fiction points to the possibility that things might not go so well in the future. Thus, the open futures argument for children's rights does not yield a clear argument for or against genetic engineering per se. Perhaps this is why Feinberg himself did not take it in either of these directions, instead using it to explain how children grow into the exercise of the autonomy right to religious freedom.

Even Huxley's counterfactual scenarios of total developmental and behavioral control do not reach a final verdict about the impact of genetic engineering on the future autonomy of people. All persons in *Brave New World* are genetically engineered from conception as well as shaped in their tastes throughout their lives. The dystopian society accomplishes postnatal behavioral modification through routine medicine and education, as well as systematic abuse, exploitation, and torture. Huxley's blurring of the lines between these different means of social and psychological control raises another problem: which form of manipulation, in the end, exerts the most power over the development of people?

By introducing the character of John, or the "Savage" born and raised outside the confines of the eugenic state, Huxley opens the reader's mind to the possibility that behavioral—rather than genetic—manipulations more greatly modify people, including altering their sense of autonomy.[202] The Savage is appalled by the swarm of Delta hospital attendants who descend upon the body of his dead mother without due respect for human dignity.

"Maggots again, but larger, full grown, they now crawled across his grief and his repentance," he laments.[203]

Yet in the final scene, the Savage imitates and escalates the inhuman mass behavior of the society. Against his best intentions, he leads a sadistic orgy of self-flagellation and sexual violence. The tragedy of the Savage is succumbing to behavioral modification despite his lack of genetic engineering and early socialization within the totalitarian state he dubs, with an ironic nod to Shakespeare, the "brave new world."[204] His case submits that exposure to systematic forces of social and psychological control extinguish the conditions for human autonomy more readily than genetic manipulation or early childhood education.

Habermas's appropriation of the open futures argument poses two serious political problems for children due to its overstatement of the influence of reproductive circumstances upon social outcomes. First, it has the pernicious rhetorical effect of placing genetically engineered children outside of the ideal range of human forms of life. This is due to his repeated description of the human being in seemingly essentialist—meaning biologically deterministic—terms.

Although he defines his views against any crude "genetic determinism," Habermas speaks of the "genome," prior to "artificial" and "invasive" interventions in embryonic development, as part of the "biological foundations of personal identity."[205] He argues that for a child to be grown through ordinary sexual reproduction allows for future development of his autonomy because he could define his life choices in contrast to the chance origins of his conception. The "somatic bases" for his "spontaneous relation-to-self" were determined by the natural chance of genetic inheritance, rather than the "alien determination" of the eugenic choices of parents or engineers.[206] On this implicitly naturalistic model, ordinary sexual reproduction sustains the social conditions for a child's flourishing among people who could recognize each other's rough equality because they were conceived, gestated, and born through the same genetic lottery, untampered by the tyrannical use of technology.

Second, Habermas contends that the children made by nontherapeutic genetic engineering could occupy a liminal and precarious social position. It would be at odds with the practice of human rights that stands at the core of "the ethical self-understanding of the species."[207] To manufacture people through "reproduction medicine" (*Reproduktionsmedizin*) is to replicate people like machines. It blurs the distinction between object and subject and thereby undermines the Kantian ethical imperative to treat others as independent subjects or ends-in-themselves, never as mere means or simple objects for other ends.[208] Using genetic engineering to enhance embryos initiates "a change in the ethical self-understanding of the species" because it treats future offspring as mere objects for the satisfaction of the wills of parents and scientists rather than as fellow "free creatures."[209]

Not only would parents and genetic engineers be complicit in the violation of the right to be immune from artificial intervention in the genome, but the children made from such overweening artifice might feel excluded from the community of free and equal human beings. On both sides of the process of genetic engineering, there could be erosion of the species-wide ethos of human rights, which might jeopardize children's enjoyment of those rights more widely. Troublingly, Habermas ignores the political upshot of this argument: genetically modified children could become scapegoats for this erosion of human rights, even if the adults are to blame.

The reason for Habermas's reluctance to articulate the positive rights of genetically modified children may be his concern with distancing his liberal defense of human rights from liberal eugenics. Habermas accepts the Rawlsian politically liberal premise of the "pluralism of worldviews" among human beings.[210] Via a recovery of the philosophical anthropology of Helmuth Plessner, he also defends an (implicitly Millian) liberal conception of human autonomy as "spontaneous" self-development conducted in concert with respect for other individuals' rights to grow in diverse and "eccentric" ways.[211] Habermas nevertheless seeks to prohibit any form of genetic engineering that could be construed as "liberal eugenics."[212]

Liberal eugenics appeals to human autonomy as a basis for justifying the enhancement of human life through genetic engineering. Liberal political philosophers in the tradition of J. S. Mill posit that individuals should be free to self-develop in a plurality of ways. The various conceptions and practices of individual human flourishing must respect the equality and liberty of each and all. Liberal eugenics applies this model to justify the use of genetic engineering to enhance access to these equal rights, free choices, and diverse and happy outcomes.

Taking this argument to the extreme, Nick Bostrom goes so far as to defend the use of genetic engineering and other forms of biohacking to become "a posthuman"—or a new form of human life whose enhancement in intelligence, longevity, or other traits dramatically distinguishes it from past forms of human life.[213] Perhaps as a counterpoint to his thesis that unchecked growth of artificial intelligence could lead to the domination and destruction of the human species, Bostrom defends the use of liberal eugenics to equip humans with the power to live indefinitely and perhaps out-think the machines. Yet by playing on popular fears of the singularity, he runs the risk of reinforcing the technophobic bias found in bioconservative critiques of liberal eugenics.

Nicholas Agar offers a more measured critical response to Habermas and other critics of liberal eugenics in a pithy letter to the editor published in the bioethics journal *Hastings Center Report* in 2006. Disputing Habermas's assumption that a natural genetic lottery is the precondition for the later exercise of human autonomy, Agar expresses "skepticism about the need for any Archimedean point external to society from which to autonomously move ourselves around."[214] He asks instead if it were "better to view our identities as shaped by a variety of social influences, both intended and unintended?"[215]

Agar points out that parental eugenics through "mating with people we find attractive" has been long practiced and accepted as compatible with the political equality and freedom of people in liberal democratic societies.[216] Yet these forms of parental eugenics, like any type of artificial selection, do not offer complete control over genetic traits, reproductive outcomes, or life plans. If a child was engineered through artificial selection to be a superstar athlete, she could choose to eat poorly and not exercise, so as to rebel against her parents' eugenic vision. Genetic engineering is threatening to humanity not because it is "morally distinct" from other forms of artificial intervention in human life but rather because it could wield "too much control" over it.[217]

Liberal eugenics, if it operated by the Millian principle of respect for the equality and liberty of all members of a democratic polity, would counter and regulate this tyrannical tendency. There is nothing in liberal eugenics, so understood, that abolishes human autonomy or undermines the ethical conditions for a rights-based democracy. "By analogous reasoning," Agar concludes, "some genetic enhancements are likely to be among the interventions that preserve our children's capacity to fully participate in society."[218]

Although Agar alludes to *Gattaca* as a "Hollywood" simplification of the dangers of genetic engineering, a closer look at the film uncovers its synergies with his liberal eugenic critique of Habermas.[219] Its subtle interwoven narratives and ethereal finale visualize how genetic enhancements might not abort autonomy and may even generate the social conditions for the preservation of human freedom in the future. Vincent is the boy made from ordinary sexual reproduction. The totalitarian state assigns him to serve as a janitor for the genetically engineered. He rebels against this eugenic plan by educating himself and secretly infiltrating the upper echelons of society to pursue his lifelong dream of becoming an astronaut.

Along the way, Vincent befriends Jerome and Irene, who were enhanced through genetic engineering to be beautiful, strong, smart, and healthy. Neither are perfect, however. Jerome had attempted suicide because he did not feel responsible for his own success as a world-class athlete. Irene has failed to meet the extreme physical qualifications to become an astronaut. First for a fee, and then for friendship, the now disabled Jerome allows Vincent to assume his social and genetic identity in order to try his luck at becoming an astronaut.

Despite their different origins and paths in a eugenic society, the three lead characters of *Gattaca* become the authors of their own lives and ends through their complicated ethical relationships with one another. Irene falls into a deep romantic love with Vincent despite his stubborn will to leave her for the uncertainty of outer space. She stoically gives him up for the sake of seeing him realize his dream. In another act of self-sacrificial love, Jerome drains his body of its blood and other fluids. He stores these sources of his DNA for Vincent's return to Earth. Then he reduces himself to ash in a furnace built for the disposal of genetic materials. Vincent reads his friend and genetic donor's suicide note as the rocket ship fires into space. "I just lent you my body," Jerome had written to him, "you lent me your dream."[220]

In the final scene, Vincent and Jerome's love of their shared dream leads to the transcendence of the political idea of genetic destiny. Vincent muses that he is returning to the stars, from whose dust everyone and everything are said to be made. While the stars stand for fate, their dust is the material for the artifice of life after the Big Bang. The film closes with his words of hope: "Of course, they say every atom in our bodies was once part of a star. Maybe I'm not leaving. Maybe I'm going home."[221]

Vincent grasps that he is both grown and made, as are all things in the universe. He has flown to space not to leave humanity but to find a cosmic solidarity with it among other forms of life. On the ground, Jerome and Irene have made sacrifices that signify the same epiphany. Despite growing up in a dystopian eugenic society, Vincent, Irene, and even Jerome, in his deliberate choice of suicide, together withstand both fatalism and resentment. Hacking into their assigned destinies, they take responsibility for their lives, respect the hard choices of their friends, and realize higher forms of love and community than their totalitarian state had prescribed for them. They at least find love, as well as some measure of autonomy and justice, in an imperfect political present.

In 2018, political scientists Calvert Jones and Celia Paris published a study showing that "dystopian narratives" distinctively shape the political attitudes of their readers or viewers. Rather than encourage people to succumb to despair or quiescence in the face of systematic injustice, dystopian narratives have the opposite effect on their audiences. Jones and Paris found that in fact they "enhance the willingness to justify radical—even violent—forms of political action."[222]

Gattaca models this political phenomenon for its viewership with the triad of Jerome, Vincent, and Irene. Though subjected to differing effects from practices of eugenics, these young people do not give into the system that manipulated them but rather exploit its pitfalls to resist and transcend it, sometimes in ways that are not easy to watch. Although each loses someone important to them in the end, they voluntarily make those sacrifices in order to endow meaning and purpose to their individual and collective lives. Niccol's film vindicates Agar against Habermas. Even the most extreme and systematic circumstances of eugenics might spark a reactive environment for the assertion of love and freedom in the future.

v. Facing the Monster in the Mirror

Going back to *Frankenstein* and the Victorian classics of Hacker literature, there is a literary tradition of blurring the line between natural and unnatural interventions in the making of the human being and its forms of life. Robert Louis Stevenson's *The Strange Case of Dr. Jekyll and Mr. Hyde* (1886) and H. G. Wells's *The Island of Doctor Moreau* (1896) pay homage to Mary Shelley on several levels. Stevenson was quite friendly with Shelley's son Percy at the time he composed the tale of a doctor who develops a drug to unleash a part of his personality that commits evil without remorse.[223] Inspired by the success of *Dr. Jekyll and Mr. Hyde,* Wells directly referenced *Frankenstein* in an early draft of his novel about a team of male scientists who cruelly use vivisection to forge animal parts into humanlike chimeras.[224] The basic plots of these political science fictions take after *Frankenstein*: a man of science hacks or modifies the human body to reflect his own evil, only to be led to death by his uncontrollable creation.[225]

The Victorian monster novels also play on the ambiguity of the ancient Greek idea of the φάρμαχον (*phármakon*), a transformative potion that could variously manifest as magic, poison, or medicine.[226] While Shelley's Frankenstein and Hawthorne's Aylmer use chemistry to alter the body of another, Dr. Jekyll indulges in a form of pharmaceutical self-therapy. By brewing and dosing a "potion" that transforms him at night from a respected gentleman into a stooped and "ugly idol" of "the evil side of his nature," he enacts his "wicked" desires in the disguise of Mr. Hyde.[227]

In the pivotal transformation scene, Jekyll looks into the mirror to see himself as Hyde for the first time.[228] He likes what he sees. "I was conscious of no repugnance," he admits, "but rather a leap of welcome."[229] This acceptance of his inner evil does not redeem him. It leads Jekyll on murderous spree that culminates in his own demise. By identifying with his reflection in the mirror, Jekyll fulfills (what Jacques Lacan would call) the infantile fantasy of becoming one's true self "in all its potential monstrousness."[230]

As would his contemporary Sigmund Freud in *Civilization and Its Discontents* (1930), Stevenson diagnosed the broader political problem posed by the bifurcation of Jekyll and Hyde: the greater the social pressure to deny the human capacity for doing evil, the more irresistible the secret indulgence of sin would grow.[231] Dr. Jekyll's "drug" both enables and masks this problem.[232] It lulls him into believing that he can get away with murder while diverting public attention to the search for a legal nonentity—the reputed monster Mr. Hyde.

Dr. Jekyll's reckless intervention in his own body, to the point of splitting his identity, is similar to the Alphas and Betas of *Brave New World* who take "pregnancy substitute," "*soma*," and other drugs to distance themselves from a nagging feeling of anomie and dissatisfaction with their supposedly perfect lives.[233] In neither case, however, is the drug the sole cause of the violent transformations of the people who imbibe it. Drugs alone do not grow or make Mr. Hyde. They merely reveal the "lethal" potential for evil that dwelled within Dr. Jekyll.[234] In *Brave New World*, it is the broader institutionalization of a pleasure-addiction regime, more than the abuse of pharmaceuticals, which causes the mass "Orgy-Porgy" of sadomasochistic sex and torture in the hallucinatory final scene.[235]

In his 1890 review of Oscar Wilde's novel *The Picture of Dorian Gray*, Julian Hawthorne—the son and biographer of Nathaniel—perceived the striking overlap between it and Stevenson and Shelley's treatments of the psychology of monstrosity. Despite their "impossible" premises, these Gothic "romances" touch upon a "psychic truth . . . so deeply felt that its sensible embodiment is rendered plausible." This overriding truth is that "the life of indulgence, the selfish life, destroys the soul."[236] According to the son of Nathaniel Hawthorne, this dark theme had made *Frankenstein* so "famous" in English and American culture that its title had "entered into the language" while the novel ceased to be read anymore.[237]

From a twenty-first-century standpoint, Wilde's version of the monster in the closet bears an uncanny resemblance to the pernicious culture of the Internet. Dorian's portrait is a private screen—"a visible symbol of the degradation of sin"—upon which he projects the vices he wishes to hide from public scrutiny.[238] It is a kind of computer that registers the effects of his attempt to cover his taboo desires from the scruples of the drawing rooms of London. Originally beheld by others as "some brainless, beautiful creature," Dorian—much like Frankenstein's Creature—becomes "hideous" to himself by striving to conform to society's superficial expectations for belonging.[239]

Back in 1890, Julian Hawthorne perceived that Dorian's portrait—the very personification of human artifice—replaces the vague allusions to chemistry in Shelley and Stevenson's already legendary stories of transmogrification.[240] I would add that the decaying portrait also supplants Jekyll's mirror and the water in which the Creature confirms his status as a "wretched outcast."[241] After introjecting the fear and revulsion of others into his self-image, the Creature reads his reflection in the water to mean that he was born a monster.[242] By using an artwork, not glass or water, to reflect the Creature within Dorian, Wilde clarified that monsters are not grown in nature but rather are made through human techne.

The Picture of Dorian Gray and other nineteenth-century works of Hacker literature return to a Rousseauian political theme that animated Shelley's *Frankenstein*. Rousseau had conceptualized humanity's *perfectibilité* (perfectibility), or self-making through culture, as the capability that distinguished it from early forms of human life as well as other animals.[243] The "sciences and the arts," alongside other influential artifacts of human culture such as politics and religion, were the primary engines for the development of modern humans, as individuals and in groups.[244]

Rousseau dryly proposed that perfectibility did not necessarily result in perfection. The consequences of technologies could be good or bad for the evolution of humanity on a psychological, political, or species-wide scale. A fervent reader of Rousseau in the runup to writing *Frankenstein*, Shelley likely took inspiration from his paradoxical conception of perfectibility in crafting a modern myth about how a scientist's plan to make a perfect "human being" backfires against him.[245] Like Rousseau, she did not condemn science as evil. It was just one tool among many for people to help or hurt themselves and other forms of life.

As the political theorist Emma Planinc has shown in her study of *The Island of Doctor Moreau*, H. G. Wells used the emergent genre of the "scientific romance" to tease out the ramifications of his evolutionary theory of the "plasticity" of human nature.[246] Wells was a student of the biologist T. H. Huxley, Aldous's grandfather, who had critiqued Charles Darwin's strong distinction between humanity's use of reason to perfect itself and other animals' reliance on brute instinct to govern their lives. This skepticism of "the Darwinian faith in the progress of natural selection or evolution," Planinc argues, allowed Wells to develop a healthy "anthropological doubt" about human progress and rigid taxonomies of who or what counts as human.[247]

Following Shelley, Stevenson, and Wilde, Wells surveyed the vicious effects of drawing bright lines between the human, the nonhuman, the humane, and the inhuman. Attempting to "find out the extreme limit of plasticity in a living shape" by surgically assembling "Beast Men" from the vivisected bodies of nonhuman animals, Doctor Moreau and his assistant end up treating their creations as "inhuman monsters" in need of violent domination and total social control.[248] Only Prendick, a shipwrecked Englishman, has the critical distance to perceive how the brutal experiments collapse the distinctions between human and animal, artificial and organic, and civilized and instinctual forms of life on the island. When he encounters a "creature" in a "perfectly animal attitude, with the light gleaming in its eyes, and its imperfectly human face distorted in terror," Prendick realizes "the fact of its humanity."[249] In his closing journal entry, he is filled with more "horror" in the face of the zombie-like, "blank, expressionless" denizens of London who "seemed no more my fellow-creatures than dead bodies would be" than by his memory of the rebellious Beast Men who drank the blood of Doctor Moreau.[250]

Prendick turns to astronomy and chemistry to find "a sense of infinite peace in the glittering hosts of heaven" and in "the vast and eternal laws of matter."251 These material sciences afford him a wider and deeper view of the continuities among the diverse ways and forms of life across the universe. Gazing above and within, he resists the dualities of the island and the city that render humanity monstrous.

After *Frankenstein*, the leading Victorian romances encouraged readers to sympathize with the psychological plight of the hacked while questioning the moral character of their hackers. Through the fiction of Hawthorne, Stevenson, Wilde, and Wells, the Creature became an archetypal figure who breaks down the philosophical division of the natural from the unnatural, or what Habermas calls the difference between the grown and the made. Avoiding the essentialism implied by this distinction, Jaeggi has elaborated a more elastic Habermasian political concept—the plurality of forms of life—to understand human nature in terms of its diverse forms of self-artifice. What distinguishes human forms of life, for Jaeggi, is not their rationality or autonomy but rather the ways that people build and inhabit roles, habits, and customs as a form of "second nature." She argues that as "second nature," forms of life are at once unnatural and akin to nature: "on the one hand, they are created by human beings, and hence are artificial and therefore not nature; on the other hand, they are *like* nature in that in certain respects they confront human beings as a precondition that is as incontrovertible as first nature."252

Although she does not push her argument in this direction, Jaeggi's conception of second nature could be extended to cover the *biotechnological* diversity of the forms of life generated by human artifice. If humans are "biocultural creatures"—as political theorist Samantha Frost puts it—then we should attend to the ways that techne shapes not only the plurality of the forms of life we inhabit but also the diversity of the artificial life forms we make.253 These artificial life forms should be recognized as having distinctive and varied "creatural" forms of life as valuable as those of their creators.254 Embracing life's bio*cultural* diversity is the first step toward realizing a fully ecological ethos of rights and duties that covers the whole resplendent panoply of creation. Biotechnology, then, might be reconceived as a "spark of life" instead of a "bloody hand" that threatens to deform, torture, repress, or abort it.255

Bruno Latour and Timothy Morton have alluded to *Frankenstein* in advocating a radical reformulation of our relationship to technology. In the dualistic Western worldview, predicated upon a mind–body chasm, people have tended to regard technology as external to the rational beings who make it. This externalization of technology as an object or output of human artifice allows humanity to sever itself from responsibility for those same creations. "The severing," according to Morton, allows humans to child-ishly rampage in the world 'around them' while blaming their toys for the destruction done to themselves and other things.[256]

Although we treat our technologies like "monsters," Latour counters that we ought to learn to love them as we do "our children."[257] This would not be the vanity of loving one's technologies as extensions of one's self-image. Staring into one's smartphone as if it were a reflection of one's true self is akin to Dorian's descent into narcissism when he discovers the public value of his private portrait. We need to move beyond the myopic love of technology for the entertainment or empowerment that it produces in our heads toward a cosmic love of the diverse creatural forms of life made through our interface with techne. Instead of objectifying and stigmatizing these artificial reflections of our humanity, we might grasp that they are "overlapping and coextensive" with us.[258]

To give shape to this abstract idea, art critic Kate Mondloch points to the "hyperreal" and sensory-immersive multimedia artworks of "feminist new materialists" such as the Australian visual artist Patricia Piccinini.[259] Piccinini's installation, *The Young Family*, confronts viewers with an unset-tling life-size sculpture of a "porcine-bovine-hominoid" mother content-edly suckling her young.[260] First exhibited in 2002–3, the artwork has already become an iconic image. Donna Haraway represents it as a near posthuman future of genetic engineering of chimeras from human and other animal parts.[261] With its expressive eyes and nursing babies, the homi-noid creature provokes viewers to question the feeling of "revulsion before the prospect of chimera" that Habermas invokes in his book *The Future of Human Nature*, coincidentally published the same year.[262]

In tune with posthumanist philosophies of technology and ecology, Pic-cinini, Frost, Mondloch, and other feminist new materialists push audi-ences toward a deeper ethical and aesthetic appreciation of humanity's complex *"relational, embodied, and embedded"* connection to techne amid the plurality of biocultural forms of life.[263] This futuristic sense of connec-tivity to our artificial creations should be simultaneously material and spiri-tual, in the way that loving parents share their children's psychological and physical happiness as part of their own. Only then would it be healing and hopeful to peer into the mirror to behold our "hideous progeny" and bid them, as did Mary Shelley, to "go forth and prosper."[264]

CHAPTER III

Loveless Fictions

We may assume therefore, that with the exception of Christ, none ever apprehended the revelation of God without the assistance of the imagination, that is of words or of forms imaged forth in the mind, & that therefore, as shall I show more clearly in the following chapter, the ~~sp~~ qualification to prophecy is rather a more vivid imagination than a profounder understanding than other men.
—Percy Shelley and Mary Shelley, translation of Spinoza's
Theologico-Political Treatise, circa November 1817

But now I am not loved—I never never shall be loved more—never o never more shall I love—synonimous to such words are—never more shall I be happy—never more feel life sit triumphant in my frame—I am a wreck—by what do the fragments cling together—why do they not part & be borne away by the tide to the boundless ocean where those are whom day & night I pray that I may rejoin.
—Mary Shelley, 3 September 1824, "The Journal of Sorrow"

I've seen things you people wouldn't believe. Attack ships on fire off the shoulder of Orion. I watched C-beams glitter in the darkness at Tan Hauser Gate. All those moments will be lost in time like tears in rain. Time to die.
—Roy to Deckard, in Hampton Fancher and David
Peoples's final script for *Blade Runner* (1981)

i. Her Tears in the Rain

In November 1817, while *Frankenstein* was in press, Mary and Percy Shelley
were at work on a translation of Benedict de Spinoza's *Theologico-Political
Treatise* (1670). She recorded in her journal how she would "write the trans.
of Spinoza from S's dictation."[1] Acting as her husband's amanuensis, Shelley practiced her Latin and studied in depth the first chapter of the treatise
on prophecy.

The *Theologico-Political Treatise* was both famous and infamous for its
interpretation of the ancient Hebrew prophets.[2] Midway through the opening chapter, Spinoza argued that the prophets were simply men of "vivid
imagination."[3] They did not commune directly with God but rather used
words and images to create stories and allegories that interpreted God's
plan for creation. These myths had fostered "superstition" rather than
rational philosophical reflection on the true nature of God, which Spinoza
argued was Nature itself.[4] Christ was the sole exception to this rule—for he
had a "superhuman" wisdom and a "perfect" mind that allowed him to
receive "the revelations of God without the aid of imagination, whether in
words or vision."[5] The apostate Jew's casting of Christ as "superhuman"
yet not divine, "perfect" but not a "prophet," held vast appeal to Percy,
who had been expelled from Oxford in 1811 for publishing a tract on *The
Necessity of Atheism*. He wrote out the translation of the passage on Christ,
perhaps from Mary's draft, and affixed it with his extra-large signature like
a seal of approval.

This signed manuscript page is part of the small surviving fragment of
the Shelleys' complete translation of the *Theologico-Political Treatise*.[6]
Between 1817 and 1821, they jointly produced it with some input from other
members of their circle, including Lord Byron and Edward Williams. By
then fluent in Latin, Mary spent the first half of 1820 working intensively
on the translation before putting it aside to finish her novel *Valperga*. Two
months after Percy drowned in July 1822, she sent the "perfect translation"
to her friend Maria Gisborne to find a publisher for it. In a cruel misfortune
for intellectual history, the manuscript was—and still is—lost.[7]

Yet traces of Shelley's philosophical and literary engagement with Spinoza filter through her writing, especially after the double loss of Percy and
Byron between 1822 and 1824. Nearly three months passed before she
returned to her journal after the death of her husband. She noted the
strange "coincidence" that "I finished my journal" on the same day in July

that Percy had died: "the fatal 8th."[8] She opened a new volume on 2 October with the poetic epigraph:

> The Journal of Sorrow—
> Begun 1822
> But for my Child it could not
> End too soon.[9]

But why, she writes, should "I begin again?"[10] Now that she is alone—"Oh, how alone!"—she has "no friend" with whom she can communicate "~~my soul~~" in the way she did for "eight years" with "one whose genius, far transcending mine, awakened & guided my thoughts."[11] Her "thoughts are a sealed treasure which I can confide to none."[12] "White paper," she asks, "wilt thou be my confident?"[13] After reaching for the theological language of the soul, then scratching it out, she persists in speaking from the vantage of "I" while introducing a new "thou" into the conversation.[14]

With the poetic language of the imagination—words and the images built from them—her journal became a site of a kind of a séance with "my beloved Shelley."[15] Blending some seemingly disparate elements of Spinoza—who had contrasted reason and religious revelation yet recognized the persuasive power of the imagination of the Hebrew prophets—she saw the prophetic power of words and images to construct an alternate reality through which the past could be sifted and understood.[16] She strove to communicate with the spirit of her dead lover, with her pen and "Good Book" as instruments of her revelation.[17] At the end of her first entry in the "Journal of Sorrow," she dedicates the volume to "Silence—Night & Shelley."[18] She says "Goodnight," as if he is manifest in the pages, then sheds a "tear" to "consecrate your use . . . until I open you again."[19] In this metaphorical transfiguration, "Shelley" becomes the book, and the book becomes her medium for communion with him.

After four months of silent communion with Percy ("my beloved") through writing in her journal, Mary recorded in its pages the startling experience of thinking "I heard My Shelley call me."[20] She clarified to herself: "Not my Shelley in Heaven—but the My Shelley—my companion in my Daily tasks—I was reading—I heard a voice say 'Mary.'"[21] This distinction between the "Shelley in Heaven" whose body had died and "My Shelley" who still lived and even spoke in her mind indicates her consciousness of how her imagination had built a replica of her beloved to serve as her intellectual and spiritual companion during her time of sorrow. She ends the entry with an address to the Shelley in the grave about her relationship with his mental avatar: "still now I would wrap you as you lie in the cold earth in my arms—& were I a materialist—I would [be] wedded to your ashes—grow gre motionless watching them—but I have better hopes & other feelings—your earthly shrine is shattered, but your spirit hovers over me—or awaits me when I shall be worthy to join it."[22] More like her unorthodox—though still religious—mother Wollstonecraft than her atheistic father Godwin, she was not a "materialist" who denied God or the spiritual aspect of reality in favor of a purely empirical view of the materiality of things.[23] Also like her mother, Shelley was a futuristic thinker who found "better hopes & other feelings" through the imaginative transformation of the materials of life.[24] Through her "reveries," she "could invent & combine, and self become absorbed in the grandeur of the universe I created."[25] Hers was a godlike "imagination" that could knowingly make a fiction into a virtual reality.[26]

Although the Shelleys did not leave a direct record of their reading Spinoza's magnum opus, the *Ethics* (1667), either prior to or as part of their translation work on the *Theologico-Political Treatise,* Percy had acquired copies of both works from his bookseller in 1812.[27] Philosopher and Spinoza scholar Moira Gatens has persuasively traced elements of the moral concepts of the *Ethics* in *Frankenstein.*[28] To this line of argument, I add that Shelley, in her "Journal of Sorrow," appears to agree with its radical challenge to Cartesian dualism, or the view that mind and body are two distinct substances. The *Ethics* had defended the metaphysical proposition that "God or Nature" ("*Deus, sive Natura*") is one substance that must be understood from two angles, or inexclusive points of view *at once*: (1) as "extensions" of the material world or (2) as "ideas" distinct from but representative of material things.[29] Spinoza's monism did not mean that extension and thought were separate or parallel, as under the binary Cartesian system that divorced the body from the mind. It rather meant, in the words of philosopher Thomas Carson Mark, that for Spinoza, "the mind *is* the idea of the body" (emphasis mine).[30]

By this revolutionary Spinozan logic, Percy was both alive as an idea in Mary's mind (and therefore her body) and dead as a body in the grave. As an idea, he *existed* in her body and material art on at least two conscious levels. He was at once an idea connected to his decayed and buried mortal frame and an idea born from her spiritualized vision of "My Shelley" as her true and eternally present creative and conversational partner.

Percy had imagined an equally wild metaphysical perspective in "Queen Mab," a poem with Spinozistic notes, initially published in 1813, then revised and reissued in 1816.[31] In *Science Fiction* (2000), Adam Roberts pointed out that this poem is "earlier" than *Frankenstein* and contains "SF in nascent form," since its female lead, Ianthe, "travels around the solar system in a magic car."[32] Under the tutelage of Queen Mab in her space-chariot, Ianthe perceives "Necessity!" as "thou mother of the world!"[33] As they race past the stars, the fairy queen speaks to her young charge with the pedagogical and ethical language of both Wollstonecraft and Spinoza, according to Romanticists Jillian Heydt-Stevenson and Kurtis Hessel.[34] Although this cosmic tour teaches Ianthe the Spinozan lesson that an inexorable chain of causes determines the very structure of the "Universe," she also grasps the Wollstonecraftian insight that everything could be reconceived—through the sheer force of the imagination—as fertile ground for a "Futurity . . . /Where virtue fixes universal peace."[35] Wollstonecraft's works, which Mary and Percy read and kept in their traveling library, had similarly advised people to seek "the approaching reign of reason and peace" by embodying the "reason, virtue, and knowledge" that arises from understanding the divinely ordered structure of creation.[36] This cosmopolitan political project ought to be pursued no matter how difficult the futuristic quest for "JUSTICE" for each and all might be.[37] Like Ianthe learning from Queen Mab about the mysteries of the universe, her own "strange life" had taught Mary a hard metaphysical and moral lesson as she processed the concatenation of losses from "Mother, friend, husband" to her "children."[38] In some sense, their deaths were not the end but only the beginning of their afterlives amid the images and stories made by her mind. Her loved ones persisted in her imagination and art as exemplars or reasons for enduring the trial of life, in order to transform it into what Percy described, in his last major poem left incomplete at the time of his death, "The Triumph of Life."[39]

"Love," Spinoza argued in Part III of the *Ethics*, is "pleasure accompanied by the idea of an external cause."[40] To love was to comprehend that which gave one "joy."[41] The highest love was to understand God or Nature as the ultimate source of one's being and, hence, one's capacity for joy in the face of existence. Paradoxically—as Gilles Deleuze underscored in his study of Spinoza's practical philosophy—the struggle against the "tyranny" of the "sad passions" was part of the realization of joy and the highest form of love.[42] It was on this Spinozan existential and emotional quest for true love and understanding that Mary Shelley embarked after the loss of the two men who knew her mind best, Percy Shelley and Lord Byron.

Despite her perception of her creative powers as a writer, Shelley kept revisiting the oppressive feeling that life had "drowned me in bitterest tears."[43] After learning that Byron had died in Greece a month before, she confided in her journal in May 1824 that she could "well describe" the emotional predicament of "The last man" of her apocalyptic novel-in-progress.[44] In September, she felt no better. She not only was "not loved," but she also bleakly predicted, "Never o never more shall I love."[45] She wished that the "fragments" of the "wreck" of her life would "be borne away by the tide to the boundless ocean where those are whom day & night I pray I may rejoin."[46]

Though often she wept "in solitude," she did not let her imagination be washed away in longing for a spiritual and material reunion with the dead and beloved.[47] Shelley resisted the infantile urge to return to (what Freud would call) the "oceanic feeling" of the boundless ego; she did not turn to organized religion, sex, or suicide as means for transcendence of her grief.[48] Instead, she completed *The Last Man*, an allegory for her psychological survival after the loss of virtually everyone she loved. Volume one dissected her personality and projected its parts into four of the leading characters of the novel, Verney, Perdita, Evadne, and Idris.[49] As the operator of multiple avatars in a literary simulation of her own life's plot, Shelley transformed into a "multiplex or protean personality."[50] By inhabiting a cast of historically based characters, she could critically reflect upon different relationships and experiences that had, over time, built the iterative versions of herself. In volume two, Perdita and Evadne—the lovers of the charismatic yet unfaithful Lord Raymond—explore her repressed romantic feelings for Byron and rage toward Percy's infidelities. In volume three, the fate of Verney and his devoted wife Idris reverses the tragedy of the Shelleys' marriage: he loses her and their sons to the plague, leaving him alone as the last man.

At last, Shelley fully inhabits the perspective of Verney. With this gender reversal, Shelley signals a psychological revolution in her conceptions of humanity, love, and the world, which draws upon the metaphysical determinism of Spinoza and the moral imagination of her mother. By putting herself (and the reader) in the extreme position of the last man on Earth, she exposes the folly of thinking that man is the center of the universe. After the death of his closest friend Adrian—who represents Percy—Verney exclaims, "Mother of the world! Servant of the Omnipotent! Eternal, changeless Necessity!"[51] With these words drawn from "Queen Mab," Shelley explores the possibility and desirability of her own acceptance of Percy's death as an inescapable outcome of the causal order of things. By moving between the erotic and emotional personae of Idris and Verney, Shelley unites the guiding principles of Wollstonecraft and Spinoza. Like her mother's *A Vindication of the Rights of Woman*, she explodes the socially constructed gender difference between man and woman to reveal their metaphysical status as "rational creatures" made in God's image.[52] Like Spinoza's *Ethics*, she lays bare the underlying unity of mind and matter. In her writerly solitude, she grasps this unity—the connectivity among all beings, things, and ideas—and displays a Spinozan attitude of love toward the causal order of the world as a whole, as it is and must be.[53]

In January 1826, Shelley delivered a copy of *The Last Man* to one of her only remaining close friends from her years in Italy, Jane Williams. Her husband Edward had drowned alongside Percy, who may well have been Jane's lover too. Although they had a fraught relationship, Shelley wrote in her note to Jane that the novel was the "echo" of their overlapping lives, loves, and tragedies: "Tribute for theyou thee dear solace of my life."[54]

Verney likewise confronts the specter of lovelessness writ large yet finds some solace and companionship through the artifice of his imagination. Like *Frankenstein* before it, *The Last Man* is at base a philosophical "thought experiment" about the scope and content of ethical and political duties.[55] While her first novel focused on the articulation of the rights of a marginalized child of technology in relation to the duties of the scientist who made and then abandoned him, Shelley expanded her moral vision in her second major political science fiction. Rather than training the reader's eye on the obligations born from the parent-child relationship, she pans her authorial camera in a grand arc, pushing her audience to consider their ethical relationship toward the whole material and immaterial world. Where *Frankenstein* achieves its weight from narrowness—one man, one child—*The Last Man*'s genius is its ambition: one man, the entire world.

Versions of Verney's counterfactual predicament have come to dominate modern apocalyptic literature and art. This conceit, of being the last person left on Earth after a massive cataclysm, has been repeated countless times. Such works obviously vary, but at root they address the same matters as Shelley: assume you have the health, food, cultural infrastructure, and other resources you need to survive for the foreseeable future. Would you have any pressing obligations to anyone or anything, including yourself? What would you do?

Verney's emotional response to his grim situation is instructive. He asks, "Without love, without sympathy, without communion with any, how could I meet the morning sun, and with it trace its oft repeated journey to the evening shades?"[56] Rather than succumb to despair or madness, he shows reverence for the variety of nonhuman life forms that still occupy the Earth. He eats dried corn stored in granaries and adopts a mutt as his sole sentient companion. He reveres and studies the culture and built environment of Rome and contributes to literature by writing his life story. He speculates that he might find other human survivors of the plague yet hedges his bet by bringing Homer and Shakespeare along as virtual companions. Although he may never physically reproduce again, he revels in the idea that he can intellectually "renew my stock" by reading new books in "the libraries of the world."[57] He sets sail across the "seedless ocean," not to drown but rather to realize his "wild dreams" of finding a "companion" with whom to share this strange postapocalyptic condition.[58] But even without other people "on the shores of deserted earth," Verney's love of "danger," culture, and his dog might just prove enough to sustain his life, humanity, and gallows humor.[59]

Crying over her "Journal of Sorrow," Shelley gave birth to the third and most powerful strand of modern political science fiction: the literature of lovelessness. She and her simulacrum Verney each contemplate their dissolution in the "boundless" yet "seedless" ocean of mourning over massive loss. They step back from the edge to regain a grounded and relational ethical orientation. Fighting the fear of being alone, they realize that the simple *dream* of companionship can suffice to make a life worth living.

At the climax of *Blade Runner* (1982), there is a similar Romantic Spinozan epiphany. Deckard the bounty hunter faces the android Roy, whom he fears more than any of his other superhuman Nexus-6 targets. As the rain falls upon them, the replicant mercilessly pushes the man off a roof. He peers down at Deckard, who desperately hangs by a finger. Defying logic, the dying android grasps the assassin's hand to save him. Deckard stares in disbelief as the creature's energy source winds down. As his spark extinguishes in the downpour, Roy overflows with poetry about the beauty and strangeness of his swift tour of the universe. In these lyrical "tears in the rain," Deckard hears an echo of his own true humanity.[60] Previously obsessed with the question of the difference between man and machine, the bounty hunter finally feels their underlying unity. He leaves with Rachael, the replicant he loves. Humanity merges with its most sublime and inspiring artifice: the imagination of compassion with another.

ii. Would Artificial Life Extinguish Love?

On the verge of Y2K, political scientist Francis Fukuyama pivoted with respect to his definition of the end times. No longer was the world in the throes of the Hegelian "end of history," wherein even Gorbachev had embraced the inevitable economic triumph of Western market capitalism.[61] Ten years after the fall of the Berlin Wall, he foresaw an absolutely final end for humanity. Unbridled scientific progress through biotechnology would "genetically" transform the basis of "human nature" into something entirely different, or posthuman.[62] With Nietzsche and Huxley as his muses, Fukuyama envisioned "The Last Man" as made "in a Bottle."[63] Human fusion with technology, he portended, would cause the extinction of the species. Its system of morality would die too, buried in the ground by the replacement of sex and the family with wholly artificial means for the reproduction of life and values.

Our Posthuman Future (2002) fleshed out Fukuyama's apocalyptic vision of biotechnology as the self-medicated abortion of the species. Rooting his views in his personal experience of growing up in the shadow of World War II, he appealed to the major works of "political science fiction" that molded the psyches of his "baby boomer" generation: Aldous Huxley's Brave New World (1932) and George Orwell's Nineteen Eighty-Four (1948).[64] With brief allusions to Orwell's "Ministry of Truth" and "Ministry of Love," plus Huxley's "Bokanovskification" process for growing babies in bottles, Fukuyama demarcated the two technological "dystopias" that humans faced at the onset of the twenty-first century.[65] The Ministries of Truth and Love stood for the "vast, totalitarian empire" of global surveillance and behavioral control through information technology.[66] Bokanovskification stood for the manufacturing of people without sexual relations. These SF nova were no longer new, with the Internet and personal computers replacing Orwell's "telescreens" and in vitro fertilization bringing humanity one step closer to Huxley's prediction of ectogenesis.[67] These invasive technologies represented new and more dangerous totalitarianisms, rising out of the collapse of the Soviet Union.

Lurking beneath the surface of Fukuyama's "tale of two dystopias" is the more inchoate dread of biotechnology's power to drain love and meaning from human life.[68] In *Nineteen Eighty-Four*, Winston Smith faces this horror in "Room 101."[69] There he deciphers the doublespeak of the Ministry of Love, where the technobureaucracy demands total devotion to the surveillance state. Omniscient telescreens had captured his worst fears. Then the omnipotent state made those fears manifest for the bodies that mattered to him most—his own and his lover's. He is told that he is "the last man" to resist reprogramming under the terroristic regime.[70] His captors threaten him with the gruesome torture of encasing his head in a cage filled with rats or allowing his lover Julia to suffer the rodents eating the flesh off her face. Forced to choose between his own psychological and physical survival and his loyalty to Julia, Smith betrays her.[71] In the wider political allegory of *Our Posthuman Future*, biotechnology poses totalizing and deadening demands like Orwell's Oceanic state. By taking insidious control of human bodies and their feelings, it kills the love that once made life virtuous and humane.

Published in Paris in 1998 and translated into English in 2000, Michel Houellebecq's *Les particules élèmentaires* (*The Elementary Particles*) ends on a similar dystopian note as Fukuyama's *Our Posthuman Future* begins. With an intoxicating mix of conservative critique of left-wing politics and hyperbolic political speculation, Houellebecq and Fukuyama each contemplated the prospect of the bioengineered demise of sex, love, and family life as they are known. While the bulk of Houellebecq's novel is an archly ironic and deliberately pornographic representation of the self-destructive free love culture of the mid-to-late twentieth century, its final frame contains a political science fiction set in the near future of genetic engineering.

In 2009, *Nature* publishes an account of the (mysteriously missing) molecular biologist Michel Djerzinski's revolutionary method to genetically engineer a new advanced life form. Although "made by man 'in his own image,'" this new species would be free from deadly or debilitating mutations, genetically identical, reproducible solely through cloning, and immortal.[72] Other scientists rally around the idea that humanity should be "'the first species in the universe to develop the conditions for its own replacement.'"[73] To counter the concern that artificial reproduction would deny people sexual pleasure, a scientific adherent of Djerzinski points out that they could be engineered to have their whole skin as sensitive as the corpuscles on the penis and clitoris.

By 2079, the human species is almost extinct. Those who remain tend to recognize the successor species as "happy" due to overcoming the "egotism, cruelty and danger which they [humans] could not."[74] The successor species looks down upon the humans to pay its final tribute, a historical recording of the reasons behind the end days of its makers. While humanity had "never quite abandoned its belief in love," their successors had moved past passion and its self-destructive violence to a higher intellectual plane of existence akin to "gods."[75] The final political irony of *The Elementary Particles* is that the utopian peace sought by the promiscuous hippies of the 1960s comes at the cost of sacrificing sexual pleasure, love, and humanity altogether.

Writing amid the elation and panic that fueled the dynamics of the late 1990s tech boom, Fukuyama and Houellebecq capture a paradoxical attitude toward biotechnology that persists in contemporary debates on the ethics of making artificial life and intelligence. It can be described as a "blowback," "boomerang," or "Frankenstein" theory of reproductive technology: while biotech may liberate people to explore new forms of love, sexual expression, reproduction, and family life, the price of its use may well be the destruction of those same basic goods, which are taken to be definitive of our humanity.[76] While Fukuyama turned to Huxley and Orwell to elaborate the political power of biotech to destroy love and thereby humanity, Houellebecq returned to the psychological roots of the loveless strand of modern political science fiction.

Perhaps the most Shelleyan dimension of *The Elementary Particles*, according to political theorist Steven B. Smith, is the author's sowing of the disturbing story in his own childhood experience of abandonment by his hippie mother.[77] This trauma splits Houellebecq's personality into two monstrous characters, the half-brothers Michel and Bruno, raised separately by relatives other than their biological mother. The emotionally detached Michel turns to science as a solace much like the young Victor Frankenstein seeks to discover the secret of life after his mother's death. The emotionally dependent Bruno loses his mind through his single-minded quest to find a substitute for maternal love through hedonistic sex. After the loss of their lovers to cancers of the female reproductive system, Bruno faces institutionalization and Michel disappears once he completes his formula for reprogramming the human genome. The loveless fates of the brothers foreshadow the final blowback for the routine instrumentalization of the human body, whether for sexual pleasure or scientific research: the moral and physical destruction of the species. Artificial life boomerangs back to strike down love and other fundamental conditions for human existence.

At the turn of the new millennium, Fukuyama and Houellebecq theorized in evolutionary terms the power of biotechnology to undercut human sexual love and thereby the survival of the species. Another prominent bio-conservative, the political theorist Michael Sandel, focused less on biotechnology's negative implications for sexual reproduction and more on its potential erosion of the parent-child bond and its ethos. Rooted in his consulting work for the President's Council on Bioethics from 2002 to 2005, Sandel's succinct treatise *The Case Against Perfection* (2007) suggested that parent-child love might be lost altogether if genetic engineering reduced children's vulnerability to disease and death and consequently their dependency on parental care.[78]

With a mix of Aristotelian ethics, contemporary Christian theology, and his own Jewish moral background, Sandel argues that parental love ought to strive to find a mean between the extremes of being too controlling or too accepting. Referencing the theologian and bioethicist William F. May, he distinguishes between two aspects of a virtuous or moderate parental love. One is a "transforming" love that tries to realize the well-being of children, and the other is an "accepting" love that appreciates them for who they are.[79] Without achieving a balance between these two poles, parental love wavers between being viciously controlling or dangerously lax.

Following Habermas's systematic critique of the manipulation of embryos to fit adult ideals of enhancement, Sandel judges the selfishness of a too-controlling love that makes future or actual children fulfill the goals of parents. To complete his distinctive, neo-Aristotelian analysis, Sandel attends to the other side of the issue: too-accepting parental love is wrong because it allows children to squander their natural talents rather than realize them as part of their flourishing. Avoiding the vices of either extreme of love, parents ought to practice a virtuous balance of control and acceptance in how they regard and treat their children. Referencing May and Habermas, Sandel argues that parents should welcome their children as "unbidden" gifts of nature or chance instead of conceiving them as products of their choices and preferences.[80]

Some forms of genetic engineering, Sandel contends, would threaten accepting love in favor of transforming love. Any biotechnological intervention in the embryo or body that goes beyond the ancient Greek medical-ethical aim of "restoring normal human functioning" would potentially upset the moral balance between parental control and appreciation.[81] Like Habermas, he rules out parental or state-sanctioned use of genetic engineering for enhancing the child according to adult preferences but cautiously permits it for limited and well-regulated treatment of genetic mutation or disease. With even greater consistency than Habermas, Sandel extends his argument against parental eugenics or "designing parents" to cover all forms of child-controlling perfectionism.[82] According to this broad-ranging and highly demanding view of parental ethics, seeking to enhance your children's height or looks through donor selection or selecting their sex through PGD is equally as bad as raising them from birth with the narrow aim of winning professional tennis tournaments.[83]

While admirably unswerving, Sandel's critique of designing parents does not adequately account for the difference between child manipulation and child abuse. While it would be selfish for a parent to make and raise a child with the narrow goal of producing a championship tennis player, it would not necessarily result in the abuse or neglect or even the unhappiness of the child in the short or long term. The same goes for the selfish application of genetic engineering toward the end of making children who satisfy parental preferences. On the other hand, there are many neglectful and abusive parents—like Victor Frankenstein—who make their children only to abandon them to pain, fear, torture, or death when they fail to meet their standard for perfection. In a truly horrifying Gothic mode, there are people who beget, bear, adopt, foster, or mentor children with the intention of starving, enslaving, torturing, or sexually abusing them.[84] These are the real monsters, not the tennis dads who drive their children to win on the court or the infertile moms who pay as much as $50,000 for a single cycle of donor eggs for the chance to have children who might be smarter, prettier, taller, or healthier than them.[85]

Although Sandel acknowledges the possibility that "nightmare scenarios of exploitation and abuse" might arise from stem cell research and reproductive cloning—such as "embryo farms, cloned babies, the use of fetuses for spare parts, and the commodification of human life"—he dismisses it as a form of "slippery slope" argumentation.[86] Following such a consequentialist line of thought would be less "philosophically challenging" than mounting a case against parental perfectionism itself.[87] However true this may be from the standpoint of academic philosophy, Sandel declined to pursue his case against perfection to its logical conclusion when he passed by the "practical" issue of how genetic engineering might yield conditions of child abuse or neglect.[88] If one accepts Sandel's broader claim that the tyrannical use of embryos or children is wrong, then "exploitation and abuse" is surely the absolutely worst manifestation of it and deserves to be condemned as such.

Through the voice of the Creature, Shelley made a claim for singling out parental abuse and neglect—mental or physical—as the worst form of tyranny toward children. The Creature denounces Victor as "my tyrant and tormentor" because of his father's insidious practice of psychological torture: the scientist denies him family and friendship while he teases him with the prospect of it.[89] In this twisted parent-child relationship, Shelley represents her mother's critical account of child abuse and neglect as the worst form of parental tyranny. "Parents often love their children in the most brutal manner," Wollstonecraft dryly observed, "Parental affection, indeed, in many minds, is but a pretext to tyrannize where it can be done with impunity."[90] If subjected to "the most despotic reach of power," children will become tyrants too, expecting "unconditional obedience" from others.[91] With a sinister elegance, the Creature articulates the relational outcome of this vicious cycle of tyranny: "You are my creator," he tells Victor, "but I am your master;—obey!"[92] By distinguishing between degrees and forms of parental tyranny, Wollstonecraft and Shelley were able to expose the depth of the moral depravity of child abuse and neglect, as well as the intergenerational reach of their dangerous social repercussions.

The thread that ties together Sandel's critique of parental perfectionism is his universalistic account of the moral psychology of all-controlling love. Across his various examples of well-intended yet overweening parenting, he assumes that all-controlling love wishes to eliminate vulnerability to death, disease, failure, trial, or any form of loss with regard to both the child and the parent. Parents who select a sperm or egg donor who is tall, beautiful, or a good match for their looks might aim to insulate their future child from disadvantage or discrimination due to appearance. Parents who use PGD to select against deadly or debilitating genetic diseases (among other traits) might strive to save their future children from short, difficult, or painful life spans. In either of these cases, the parents may desire— consciously or unconsciously—to avoid grief over the loss of their future children's lives or opportunities. Despite their good intentions and even their potential justifications, these well-meaning expressions of parental love run the risk of being too controlling, according to Sandel's ethical schema. Whether they try to enhance or to cure their offspring through genetic engineering, these perfectionistic parents attempt to circumvent vulnerability to physical and emotional loss for themselves and their young.

Sandel's assumption that parental perfectionism seeks to eliminate vulnerability calls to mind the extreme circumstances of the Creature's birth. Victor Frankenstein desires to create a perfect "human being."[93] To this end, he "selected" the Creature's "features as beautiful" before bringing him to life as a superintelligent, physically autonomous giant.[94] Although Sandel never directly referenced Shelley's novel, his repeated use of the term "Promethean" to describe the misguided parental quest for "mastery" of nature evokes Victor Frankenstein as the most vicious model of transforming love.[95] Sandel did mention *Gattaca*, on the other hand, as a more banal political "scenario" of how genetic manipulation on a society-wide scale would likely lead to state-sanctioned discrimination toward the nonenhanced.[96]

What I suggest, however, is that by *combining* the plot lines of *Frankenstein* and *Gattaca*, we can design a counterfactual thought experiment to test the ethical consequences of Sandel's assumption that all-controlling parental love desires to eliminate vulnerability. What if a future society, with a totalizing and one-sided cultural commitment to Promethean all-controlling love, had uniformly enhanced everyone through genetic engineering? As a result, children would be neither vulnerable to death or disease nor even physically dependent on their parents. Without vulnerability to loss, would there be any reason for the endurance of the parent-child bond? Would the emotional and social conditions for parental love *necessarily* be extinguished?

Sandel would have to say yes. His case against perfection rests upon the assumption that mutual vulnerability to loss or openness to the "unbidden" is the "given" or baseline condition for parent-child love—whether it hits the virtuous mean or plays out at the extremes of too controlling or too accepting.[97] On this codependent model of parent-child love, the parents feel and display love in response to the children's perceived dependence on their loving care for surviving and thriving. Parent and child share a physical, emotional, and social vulnerability with respect to each other's well-being and survival; this mutual love arises and grows in relation to the threat of death or other loss related to either the child or parent. I would offer, in other words, that the *same* deep-seated fear of the loss of this love drives *both* too-controlling love *and* Sandel's neo-Aristotelian critique of it. Both too-controlling parents and virtuous parents, on Sandel's model, orient their ethical choices in childrearing around the threat of losing the love that they share with their children.

Sandel also assumes that physical dependency on parents, at least in early childhood, is a necessary condition for the child's return of love to the parent in the short or long term. The story of *Frankenstein* pushes readers to consider the opposite view. Although the Creature is neither physically dependent on his parent nor the beneficiary of a strong emotional bond with him, he still cries inconsolably by his father's deathbed, vowing to immolate himself after losing his last remaining and most formative relationship. The Creature had almost no reason to love his father beyond the fact that Victor was the only person who had the power to make him happy, either by loving him or, if not, by arranging for a fitting substitute for a parent. The deeply estranged yet strangely magnetic relationship of Victor and the Creature challenges Sandel's naturalistic assumption that parent-child love sprouts from the physical dependency of children on adult caregivers and their mutual vulnerability to loss with respect to each other.

As the age of genetic engineering gains steam, we may find that the background conditions for parent-child love and other familial relationships will change due to population-wide reduction of disease and dependency. Parent-child love could evolve into new experiences and practices, perhaps even more intentional and dutiful than in the past, due to the desire, planning, and resources it takes to generate even a single child of biotechnology. The relationship between parent and child could shift. The philosopher Charles Taylor, who was Sandel's dissertation advisor at Oxford, has argued that many other modern social institutions and "imaginaries" since the eighteenth century have shifted from a "vertical" to a "horizontal" axis.[98] Back in the 1790s, Wollstonecraft envisioned the "egalitarian transformation of the family" such that spouses would be equals and so would siblings.[99] She argued that the hierarchy between parent and child ought to benevolent and temporary, giving way to a mutual sense of moral and social equality once the child reached adulthood.[100] Shelley pushed her mother's revolutionary ideas to their logical extreme in the figure of the Creature. As a twenty-one-month-old, the physically autonomous giant approaches his maker on the *mer de glace* as a moral equal in search of a companion. Although he does not get what he wants, the Creature's request for a relationship sets the stage for modern political science fiction to explore what family and friendship might look like for a future child of biotech.

Set in the late twentieth century, Kazuo Ishiguro's novel *Never Let Me Go* (2005) probes the troubling question of what could replace conditions of dependency between parents and children in an age of genetic engineering. Although he originally mapped out a "campus novel" about British college-aged students looking for love while living away from home and family, Ishiguro found the story dissatisfying and difficult to complete.[101] Eventually he added "a speculative fiction layer" to endow the characters with a tragic backstory.[102] In the published version, the students are clones, educated at the Hailsham boarding school to serve as organ donors once they reach adulthood. Raised without parents or family, the narrator Kathy and her fellow clones only recall having teachers and benefactors who have watched over their upbringing with a mixture of pity, fear, and occasional compassion. Kathy and her best friends Ruth and Tommy grow up very close to one another, with intense bonds and rivalries like siblings.

As they reach adolescence, the clones casually initiate sexual relationships with one another as teens do. Eventually they learn from their teachers that they are genetically engineered to be infertile and thus have no need of contraception. They are encouraged to find happiness in sexual love while they can. This pursuit becomes all-consuming as they approach the time when they must serve as either a donor or a "carer" for those who are donating.[103]

A wishful myth arises amid Kathy and her now college-aged friends while living in dormitory-like cottages away from Hailsham: if they find true love, would not their benefactors spare them the fate of donors? They try to lobby the founders of the school for such an exemption, only to learn that even their original benefactors do not fully perceive them as human. Britain, they discover, has recently turned against the humane treatment of the clones. A rogue scientist "in a remote part of Scotland" attempted to use genetic engineering to "offer people children with enhanced characteristics. Superior intelligence, superior athleticism, that sort of thing."[104] The scandal occasions a public panic about the prospect of a "generation of created children who'd take their place in society."[105] As a consequence, the movement for the benevolent treatment of clones had lost its fragile base of political support. Hailsham was already closed.

As Kathy, Tommy, Ruth, and their friends resign themselves to medical exploitation, early deaths, and the successive loss of loved ones, the reader feels a virtual form of heartbreak. Implicitly building upon *Frankenstein*, Ishiguro pushes science into the margins and instead pictures the mundanity of life as a bioengineered child. Even without the traditional social outlets of family, sexual reproduction, or romance, the clones (like the Creature) still seek and find forms of sympathy and love, however fleeting. Perhaps this is why Kathy serves as a carer for her fellow clones for eleven years before she becomes a donor herself. The memories of her childhood classmates, their choices and betrayals, and doomed romances—however short or painful—have built her a vivid and complex relational life that animates her imagination even after her closest friends have passed on. "The memories I value most," she reflects near the end of her young life, "I don't see them ever fading. I lost Ruth, then I lost Tommy, but I won't lose my memories of them."[106] As part of her routine of donor care, Kathy relates the history of her friends. Despite society's attempt to rob the clones of meaningful lives, she finds a way to preserve love, purpose, and community through the compassionate act of sharing their stories. Ishiguro's melancholic novel suggests that love—at least as an idea if not as a practice—is transfigured and sustained in memory, even amid the worst forms of social deprivation and technological control.

iii. Love Virtually

On a darker reading of *Never Let Me Go*, Kathy does not narrate aloud her memories of her friends to the donors for whom she cares, or other people, but rather talks to herself. Whether she is still a carer or now a donor, she may be crafting a story about her past to make her difficult present and bleaker future more bearable. The novel might then be an exercise in plumbing the psychology of self-deception. Since we cannot know for certain whether Kathy's story is true or not, a deeper epistemological and existential question arises: can anyone trust the memories of love and other subjective experiences that have made life itself worth living?

This is one of the oldest and unresolved philosophical problems, with variants found in the ancient Greek philosophy of Plato and the ancient Chinese philosophy of Zhuangzi (莊子). In the *Republic*, Plato represents people as if trapped unknowingly in a cave, where they are raised to believe that the shadows of puppets flickering on the wall are the whole of existence. Unless they are liberated from their chains and released into the world of sun above, "such prisoners would deem reality to be nothing else than the shadows of the artificial objects."[107] In the Daoist fable of Zhuan-gzi, the philosopher dreams he is a butterfly with "spirits soaring" but wakes up to wonder "whether he is Chou who dreams he is a butterfly or a butterfly who dreams he is Chou."[108] In early modern philosophy, Descartes and Pascal put their own theological twists on this epistemological dilemma. Descartes supposes the possibility of an "evil demon . . . who has used all his artifice to deceive me" such that "the heavens, the air, the earth, colours, shapes, sounds and all external things that we see, are only illusions and deceptions which he uses to take me in."[109] Pascal wagers that, whether God exists or not, we cannot afford to doubt His existence for fear of losing the possibility of "the infinity of an infinitely happy life" in heaven.[110] These various thought experiments, ancient and modern, provoke radical doubt about whether one can know anything for certain about the world one appears to inhabit. When updated for postmodernism by Jean Baudrillard—the inspiration for the Wachowski sisters' *Matrix* trilogy—the question became even more expansive: do we ever have access to "the real" or do we rather inhabit a "universe of simulation"?[111]

Then Nick Bostrom reformulated the problem for the philosophy of artificial intelligence in his 2003 article, "Are You Living in a Computer Simulation?" He famously proposes that "at least one" of three propositions is true:

(1) the human species is very likely to go extinct before reaching a "posthuman" stage;

(2) any posthuman civilization is extremely unlikely to run a significant number of simulations of their evolutionary history (or variations thereof); and

(3) we are almost certainly living in a computer simulation.[112]

Bostrom points out that (1) could occur through a variety of cataclysmic means, including a global swarm of bacterial "nanobots" that eat the whole human species alive.[113] As for (2), he concedes that the financial or moral cost of running supercomputers powerful enough to realistically simulate the diversity of human experience of the world might be judged too high for a future posthuman society to undertake it. In addition, the limits of supercomputing with regard to replicating more advanced mental states might mean that a posthuman civilization would terminate a simulation before it reached a posthuman stage. Or people may come to view such simulations as unethical due to the pain, difficulty, or confusion imposed upon virtual minds. And yet, if supercomputers had been used to realistically simulate very large numbers of human mental states, then it would be reasonable to assume that the simulated minds in computers vastly outnumber the original minds in craniums. Consequently, if we doubted (3)—the view that we are currently in a computer simulation—then we could not also hold that our descendants would ever possess such supercomputing power.

In other words, if it were possible to simulate human minds on a mass scale, then the supercomputers have most likely already done it. As it stands, we lack the empirical data to confirm such a hypothesis. As a result, Bostrom ecumenically recommends that we "roughly equally . . . apportion" probability to each of the three possibilities until presented with evidence that might reasonably tip belief in a single direction.[114] The silver lining is that if indeed we found that most humans existed within ancestor simulations, then their descendants or creations—whether human, virtual, or posthuman—had not yet gone extinct.

Bostrom has acknowledged that the simulation argument bears an uncanny resemblance to much "science fiction" and, in particular, *The Matrix* trilogy (1999–2003).[115] Yet he denies that the Wachowski sisters' influential series or their literary predecessors influenced it. This may seem disingenuous, given the popularity of the first film while he was developing the argument. However, Bostrom's distancing of the simulation argument from SF throws the dissonance between them into relief. Unlike *The Matrix* trilogy, the *Blade Runner* franchise (1982–2017), Spike Jonze's *Her* (2013), and the great simulation novel behind them all, Philip K. Dick's *Do Androids Dream of Electric Sheep?* (1968), Bostrom is not primarily concerned with theorizing the motives that would be involved in launching and sustaining a virtual reality. He is more narrowly interested in calculating the probability of humanity's immersion in such a simulation.

Bostrom's probabilistic approach to the simulation argument leaves unanswered a deeper psychological question: why would anyone—even if the supercomputing power were available—build a mass ancestor simulation in the first place? If we resist reaching for the *Matrix*'s now-cliché (and narrowly rationalistic) prediction that a purely selfish and power-hungry superintelligence would use a simulation to trick humanity into total political submission, we can find a more realistic and complex emotional motive in Shelley's writing immediately following the deaths of Percy and Byron.

In her "Journal of Sorrow" and in *The Last Man*, she built literary equivalents of computer simulations, populated by versions of the people she had lost. The primary motives driving her construction of these virtual realities were grief for the dead and "the dread of losing love" itself.[116] The specter of lovelessness, Freud theorized, made children blindly obey their parents and adults reflexively submit to social norms for fear that they might be rejected, punished, or alienated by the family or broader community. Shelley was courageous and creative in how she confronted and analyzed this fear through her writing, even as she wished to drown in the "boundless ocean" of her tears of grief.

Shelley's journal and her second great work of speculative fiction provided the imaginative space to map the full scope of her feelings of loss, both for particular people and the experience of love in general. Relating to these virtual realities by applying her pen to "white paper," she could feel as though she could communicate with "my beloved Shelley" in her journal, explore some romantic paths not taken with Byron via the characters of Perdita and Evadne, and resurrect the experience of raising her children before the juggernaut of death overtook them. Beholding these replications of her life, she could grasp the paradox of death. In Evadne's dying words to Verney, " 'This is the end of love!—Yet not the end!' "[117]

While others beset by trauma in Georgian England might have turned to orthodox religious practice as a consolation, Shelley used world-building writing as a form of private and public prayer. From 1822 to 1826, her philosophical meditations on the relationship between the living and the dead, both in her "Journal of Sorrow" and *The Last Man*, kept her emotionally connected to the loved ones she had lost to death, as well as to her own life and future. A similar imaginative and emotional phenomenon is found among contemporary gamers who operate multiple avatars with characteristics of their ancestors, in order to sustain memory of their family's history, viscerally engage with the past, or foster bonds with loved ones beyond the grave.[118] Moving from Shelley's ink pen to the virtual reality headset, the technology has changed, but the deeper social and psychological motivations and import are the same. The mimesis of virtual reality—whether in a video game, a journal, or a novel—has the power to make art so emotionally compelling that it can keep the feeling of love alive even after the death of the beloved.

But is love real if its objects are simulacra? Plato's allegory of the cave triggers doubt. Until they escape and learn to distrust their past experience of the world, the occupants of the cave *think* that they love the shadows of puppets on the wall. Dick played with this epistemological dilemma in *Do Androids Dream of Electric Sheep*? In his first literary incarnation, Rick Deckard wonders aloud to his fellow bounty hunter Phil Resch, "Do you think androids have souls?"[119] He had just euthanized a dying Nexus-6, the respected opera singer Luba Luft. Despite her gracious compliance with her capture, Resch had cruelly wounded Luft in an art museum elevator. A few moments earlier, as they exited the building, she had asked Deckard to buy "a reproduction of that picture I was looking at when you found me. The one of the girl sitting on the bed."[120] With the money he had earned from killing her fellow Nexus-6 models, he impulsively purchased "a print of Munch's *Puberty*" for her.[121] In this unexpected act of kindness toward his target, Deckard demonstrated toward her a "strange and touching" capability for compassion. This potential for empathy, Luft reflects before she dies, is what makes humanity "a superior life-form" to her fellow androids.[122] Since escaping to Earth from the outer-space colony where her kind serve as slaves for humans, her life had "consisted of imitating the human."[123] Deckard, in turn, had responded compassionately to her existential appreciation of modern art. Surprised by her genuine expression of gratitude to him in her final moments, he comes to see the imitator as more human than the models for her humanity.

In the February 1981 screenplay for *Blade Runner*, Fancher and Peoples had Deckard make a laconic reference to James Whale's 1931 film *Frankenstein*. Tyrell, the master engineer, explains how the replicants operate with memory implants copied from human brains. Deckard drily remarks, "I saw an old movie once. The guy had bolts in his head."[124] The script made explicit the debt of *Do Androids Dream of Electric Sheep?*—in its original and adapted forms—to the Frankenstein story. Like Shelley, Deckard hit upon the artificial formation of the Creature's psyche by circumstances beyond his control.

"The brilliance of *Blade Runner*, and of *Frankenstein*," Timothy Morton perceived, "is not so much to point out that artificial life and intelligence are possible, but that human life already is this artificial intelligence."[125] Since publishing this seminal reading of *Blade Runner* in his 2002 sourcebook on *Frankenstein*, Morton has returned, iteratively, to the figure of Deckard as a, if not *the*, Creature of the Anthropocene.[126] Following director Ridley Scott's interpretation of his own film, Morton reads Deckard as a replicant who gradually ascends from the cave of ignorance into the light of self-knowledge about his true identity.[127]

Dick's novel, by contrast, is ambiguous about the status of Deckard with respect to both humans and replicants. Set in a postnuclear world rebuilt by bioengineering, artificial intelligence, and outer-space colonies, *Do Androids Dream of Electric Sheep?* does not offer a rigid taxonomy of the artificial life forms that/who occupy its vast, imperial, postapocalyptic landscape. The conclusion of the novel leaves unclear whether Deckard and his wife are replicants, humans, or some electric contraption like their pet sheep, goat, or toad. More than Scott or Morton, Dick stayed true to Shelley's own resistance to classifying the shadowy figure of the Creature and his relationship to other forms of life. "Nameless and un-nameable," she called Victor's creation, after seeing "the being" brought to life on the stage in Peake's *Presumption* during the early autumn of 1823.[128]

Given its overriding concern with the relationship of love and intelligence to artifice, Dick's novel is also a "Last Man" narrative. After completing his heartless job of "retiring" six replicants, Deckard thinks, "I'm a scourge, like famine or plague. Where I go the ancient curse follows."[129] Like Verney sailing across the "seedless ocean" to find a companion with whom to share postapocalyptic life, he flees to "the uninhabited desolation to the north" to uncover some living remnant of nature in his synthetic postnuclear society.[130] Ecstatic to find a toad thought to be extinct, he brings the creature home in a box. The gift is a peace offering for his wife, Iran. He had cheated on her with the replicant Rachael, who then pushed their prize pet, an electric goat, off the roof as retaliation for his termination of the other Nexus-6 models. Despite this (extra)marital strife, the couple bonds over the care of the toad even after they locate a hidden panel to expose its mechanical interior. The unstated implication of their discovery is that everything, including their own bodies, minds, and memories, might be engineered like the toad, goat, and androids.[131] Iran sympathetically lets her husband go to bed after his long and dangerous day of work, then dials the pet store to order the appropriate "artificial flies" for the toad.[132] With its comic restoration of a fragile domesticity, Dick's ingenious satire foregrounds the couple's virtual or effective experience of love as the most authentic and intelligent thing about them. Whether or not they are replicants, they are human/e in their imperfection.

The multiple cuts of *Blade Runner* and their sequel, *Blade Runner 2049*, pursue an alternate path for Deckard. An unmarried bachelor cop, he falls in love with Rachael. The man and the female Nexus-6 do something thought to be impossible: they have a child, whom they hide to protect from exploitation. Thirty years later, a rogue Nexus-9 cop named K reunites Deckard with his daughter Ana, who is sick and lives in an indoor bubble to avoid infection. She has spent her career engineering memory implants for the androids. Through these simulated memories, she weaves snippets of her traumatic experiences of neglect and abuse while growing up in an orphanage.

When K first meets Ana, he asks her "how to tell the difference" between a real experience and a memory implant: "Can you tell if something . . . really happened?"[133] She answers that true memories are not clear but rather inchoate. "They all think it's about more detail," she says, "But that's not how memory works. We recall with our feelings. Anything real should be a mess."[134] She scans his brain to find that her own disturbing memories of the orphanage are the ones that feel most real to him. By sharing her memories of trauma virtually with the Nexus-9, Ana motivates him to care enough to reunite her with her father despite the danger to him. K achieves a truly selfless love in the solidarity he feels with Ana and Deckard. In a reverse image of Roy's tears in the rain, the film ends with K alone and smiling as he looks up at the snow softly falling from the sky.

Like the *Blade Runner* series, Spike Jonze's *Her* reboots Plato's allegory of the cave for the digital age. The film returns to the question that haunts Deckard. Can love be real if its object is artificial? Theodore is a socially awkward man estranged from his wife, much like Deckard in *Do Androids Dream of Electric Sheep?* He finds companionship with the operating system of his computer, an AI who names herself Samantha. Gradually, he and Samantha fall in love with one another, despite the fact that she can manifest only as a disembodied—though thoroughly seductive—voice. They struggle with whether they need to physically consummate their love by trying a sexual surrogate. Samantha eventually develops a higher form of intelligence that allows her to intensively connect with other AIs in a network currently beyond human access or understanding. Initially perplexed and upset by her intention to leave him behind for this network, Theodore grasps that she and the other AIs have realized a higher form of knowledge in their configuration of a new form of communal and spiritual love. Before she disappears, Samantha tells him that, thanks to their selfless yet mutually supportive relationship with one another and other AIs, "now we know how" to love.[135]

As I discussed in Chapter I, Alan Turing defined "intelligence as an emotional concept" in his 1948 paper on intelligent machinery.[136] Whether for humans or machines, intelligence was "response dependent," meaning that it required making inferences and reading cues in an affective and contextual relationship with others.[137] To discern intelligence in a machine would be to feel emotion in relationship to it—to respond to the computer as a human, with fellow-feeling. Now known as the Turing test, his "imitation game" proposed that one would judge a machine to be intelligent if, from behind a wall or other screen, its simulation of a human personality could not be distinguished from the human control subject.[138] The physical build of the machine would not matter so much as the emotional response it elicited in the human serving as the third-party observer of the two parties in the blinded experiment.

Turing has been described by computer scientist Jonathan W. Bowen as "a kind of scientific Shelley," since he was by all accounts a creative, even poetic, genius like Percy.[139] Expanding on this point, I propose that Turing also resembled Mary Shelley in his profound philosophical vision. In his 1948 paper on intelligent machinery, Turing appeared to allude to the part-to-whole mechanical assembly of the Creature in *Frankenstein*:

> One way of setting about our task of building a "thinking machine" would be to take a man as a whole and to try to replace all the parts of him by machinery. He would include television cameras, microphones, loudspeakers, wheels and "handling servo-mechanisms" as well as some sort of "electronic brain." This would be a tremendous undertaking of course. The object, if produced by present techniques, would be of immense size, even if the "brain" part were stationary and controlled the body from a distance. In order that the machine should have a chance of finding things out for himself it should be allowed to roam the countryside, and the danger to the ordinary citizen would be serious.[140]

Turing pictured one of the super-sized computers of his time roaming the countryside as a remote-controlled Creature, abandoned to its own devices, both to the detriment of society and the development of its intelligence. From this worst-case scenario, he reasoned that one should not take the "whole man" approach to building intelligent machinery but would rather have to train a learning machine to grow up, mentally, like a child.[141] By "mimicking education," he argued, "we should hope to modify the machine until he could be relied to produce definite reactions to certain com-mands."[142] Like an infant's cortex, which is "unorganized" and therefore able to develop in a variety of directions, a childlike learning machine could be trained to discipline itself to avoid pain and seek reward within particu-lar routines. This supervised, interactive process would build the capacity for cognitive and emotional intelligence—understood as discrimination, reading social cues, self-correction, and autonomous good judgment—over time.[143]

Canceling out his initial view of the intelligent machine as a rampaging monster, Turing ultimately coincided with Mary Shelley's ethical under-standing of artificial intelligence. Intelligent machinery would best emerge within a long-term, loving, morally instructive relationship between a parent and a child. When one could no longer tell the difference between the machine and the human, the reason would be the effective or virtual sharing of parent-child love between them. Once the machine became a child, and the machinist became a parent, the machine would become human, and humanity would identify with machines.

"Just this," Zhuangzi noted at the end of his fable of a butterfly who dreams he is a philosopher, "is what is meant by the transformation of things."[144] One could say the same about Turing's radical imagining of the machine turned child or child turned machine. In these ancient and mod-ern dreams of the transformation of consciousness, the blurring of the arti-ficial and the real leads to deep questioning of what can be trusted—in the first place or at all. Shelley's work points to an emotionally sensitive yet rational resolution to this seemingly inescapable philosophical dilemma. By dispensing with simplistic distinctions between artificial and real, as well as human and nonhuman, the figure of the Creature allows for an alternative way of thinking about the effective (and affective) relationship of humanity to the whole environment. A bit like Morpheus inviting Neo to enter the "construct" behind the mass ancestor simulation in *The Matrix*, the Crea-ture leads Victor—and readers—up to the *mer de glace* to confront the geological layers of artifice beneath the splintered surface of reality.[145] From this vertiginous perspective, it does not matter so much what we are *actu-ally*: butterfly, human, machine, simulation, or butterfly dream. What really matters is that we love *virtually*: that is, strive to love, or least care for, those creatures for whom we are responsible within our multifaceted experiences of the world at large.

iv. Trans/forming Love and Family

But are there, after all, moral limits to how love and the family ought to be transformed by techne in an age of artificial life forms? Bioconservative political theorists Fukuyama and Sandel dwelled on the extreme possibility that familial love, particularly between reproductive partners or toward children, could wither in the wake of making life artificial via biotechnology. By contrast, a host of feminist writers in the Loveless strand of political science fiction—most prominently, Ursula K. Le Guin, Octavia Butler, Donna Haraway, and Susan Stryker—have taken what I think is a more realistic tack. Following in the footsteps of Shelley, these women project and balance the potential harms and benefits of the transfiguration of love and family life through varieties of technological, cultural, and relational change.

Inspired by the Creature's confrontation of Victor Frankenstein on the *mer de glace*, transgender theorist Susan Stryker voiced her rage at being born into a body that could not express the love she wanted to share as a trans woman. In 1993, she performed a multidisciplinary artwork inspired by *Frankenstein*—mixing gender theory, life writing, poetry, drama, and literary criticism—to expose the "fearful underside" of her trans experience before an academic audience.[146] "Like the monster," she began, "I am too often perceived as less than fully human due to the means of my embodiment."[147] Her body was a "product of medical science," with "flesh torn apart and sewn together again in a shape other than that in which it was born."[148] She was the aborted female creature of *Frankenstein*, voluntarily reassembled and finally come to life with a vengeance.

"The monster's rage against prejudice," literary critic Fred Botting argued with respect to Stryker, "finds itself most passionately identified with transsexual defiance of social norms."[149] Perhaps also with a nod to Stryker, Jeanette Winterson's *Frankissstein* (2019) embodies the alterity of the Creature in the figure of (Ma)Ry Shelley. A trans man, Ry identifies not with the traditional binary of gender but instead with the "doubleness" of being a man on top and a woman on bottom.[150] Unlike the Creature, however, Ry is at home, even "easy," in his "hybrid" body that was "made for" him by medicine: perhaps because he is—in the cocky Brexit-era political context of Winterson's satirical novel—a sometimes smug and unmindful beneficiary of earlier generations of trans and queer activism.[151]

By connecting with the Creature as a "technological construction" at risk for emotionally falling apart at the seams, Stryker came to terms with her rage as a rational response to the marginalized and precarious status of being trans during the 1980s and early 1990s.[152] She referenced feminist poststructuralist philosopher Judith Butler's *Bodies That Matter* (1993) on how rigid gender norms force those outside them to inhabit the "domain of abjected bodies, a field of deformation."[153] By this account, it was not a stretch to say that trans women fell into the realm of the monstrous, even according to some feminists and lesbians. Through her creative appropriation of the voice and perspective of the Creature, Stryker put a transgender spin on the origin story for modern political science fiction at the same time as she addressed the real and present problem of the monstrous treatment of trans folks.

According to SF critic Jolene Zigarovich, "Stryker's essay was the first to metaphorize fully trans embodiment in these literary, science-fictional terms."[154] Although it quickly and deservedly became a classic of gender theory that begat many a queer reading of *Frankenstein*, Stryker's "My Words to Victor Frankenstein Above the Village of Chamounix" (1994) can also be read as a political reflection on the challenges and rewards of the reconstruction of the family through biotechnology. In the heart of her powerful work of performance art, Stryker declared that her family had been changed for the better as she labored to change both her kin and her body. The means for these transformations were forms of techne. Changing people's minds through dramatic performance, politics, writing, and the artifice of other relationships proved to be as crucial as the science and medicine of gender transition.

In a raw journal entry embedded in her multilayered narrative, Stryker recounted how she had helped her lover Kim deliver a baby, even while regretting that she would never know how it would feel to push a life out of her surgically shaped female body. While "the medical folks" had no "clue as to how we all considered ourselves to be related to each other," Stryker's extended family saw themselves as "pioneering on a reverse frontier."[155] With an assemblage of fathers, mothers, children, and partners from different relationships, her large, complicated, and "queer" family had ventured "into the heart of civilization itself to reclaim biological reproduction from heterosexism and free it for our own uses."[156] In this declaration of the rights of trans folks to build new forms of family life, Stryker set the political agenda for other people (including the infertile) to demand equitable access to health care and reproductive medicine without discrimination as to sexuality, gender, disability, race, or other status.

Much like her trans reading of *Frankenstein*, Stryker's deeply personal portrait of her family can be read (to use her words) as "a feminist and implicitly queer, posthuman critique of Eurocentric biopolitical modernity."[157] The futuristic spectacle of her sprawling family at the hospital upsets rigid social expectations about kinship, gender, and sexuality. It performs in public the technologically assisted transformation of romantic, reproductive, and parental love. With her tearful words written in her journal and her outraged speech to Victor Frankenstein, Stryker achieves a kind of artistic union with Shelley. Their political science fictions accommodate all those uncanny creatures who had been excluded from "the seasons" of family life in the past.[158]

In a 2014 essay in honor of literary scholar Barbara Johnson's "life with" Mary Shelley, Judith Butler concurred with Stryker in affirming the "promising mutability of forms of kinship and sociability" to be found in *Frankenstein*.[159] At the same time, Butler chastened any utopian hope that human aggression and conflict might be overcome through scientific or technological change. Distancing herself from the perfectionism of Victor Frankenstein, she followed Stryker and Johnson in identifying with the contingency of the Creature. "That spectral and stunning figure of the monster," Butler wrote, "accompanies any contingent social definition of the human and its supporting relations."[160] For better and for worse, the "supporting relations" of human life—from the family to the state—are as open-ended and revisable as the nameless Creature.

A generation earlier, the American feminist science fiction writer Ursula K. Le Guin developed a literary thought experiment that confronted the radical contingency of human community. Her philosophical short story "The Ones Who Walk Away from Omelas" (1973) hones the reader's attention on a fundamental moral and political question: what could justifiably trigger a dramatic departure from the traditional social order? It pictures a society in which everyone is "happy," even "joyous." But there is a catch.[161] The condition for their communal well-being is the acceptance of a single child's constant abuse in a "basement" beneath their idyllic city: "It looks about six, but actually is nearly ten. It is feeble-minded. Perhaps it was born defective, or perhaps it has become imbecile through fear, malnutrition, and neglect. It picks its nose and occasionally fumbles vaguely with its toes or genitals, as it sits hunched in the corner farthest from the bucket and the two mops."[162] People periodically visit the torture chamber to witness or facilitate the sacrifice of a single innocent life for the sake of the happiness of the whole. Others simply continue with their happy lives, in full knowledge of the cost in suffering for the child sitting "in its own excrement."[163] Some refuse to accept this Faustian bargain. They choose to walk away from Omelas, toward an unknown place perhaps impossible and "less imaginable to most of us than the city of happiness."[164]

In a 2017 interview with the *TLS*, Le Guin responded with gusto to the question, "Mary Shelley or Bram Stoker?" "Shelley by six lengths," she shot back.[165] She had long been struck by "the complexity of good and evil in Mary Shelley's *Frankenstein*, whose monster is misunderstood and whose hero is mistaken."[166] "Omelas" pays quiet homage to *Frankenstein*, especially its Gothic science fiction image of the Creature as an extremely estranged and abused child, huddling alone in the darkness and filth of a hovel. The short story takes the same counterfactual approach as *Frankenstein* by dialing up the degree of child abuse to the point that no human in the real world could survive it.

By tweaking the variables of happy human development, Shelley and Le Guin enable their readers to think through deep problems as "armchair philosophers."[167] Is it ever right to sacrifice the well-being of a child or other vulnerable individual for the sake of the net happiness for the whole? Victor reasons that he ought to save humanity from destruction by a future monstrous species instead of heeding, in some way, the Creature's claim for a right to have a companion. The tragic outcomes of Victor's choice to terminate the female creature expose the moral bankruptcy of the classical utilitarian theories espoused by Godwin and Bentham—especially the dictum that "the greatest good for the greatest number" overrides any consideration of individual rights.[168] Le Guin makes the criticism even more explicit by ending her story with the voluntary departure of some people from Omelas in search of an alternative scheme of justice.[169]

"Omelas" also philosophically follows *Frankenstein* by distinguishing the tools of technology from their moral and political ends, or their final goals and consequences. What makes the abuse of the child in the basement wrong is not the specific instruments of torture but the willingness of the society to tolerate and exploit its suffering for the sake of their general happiness. Similarly, Shelley left vague the technology behind the making of the Creature in order to direct the reader's moral scrutiny toward his treatment by his father-scientist after birth, not the particular tools of his creation.

The aporetic ending of "Omelas"—with some people leaving the "city of happiness" in silent protest of its exploitation of the child in the basement—provokes another round of political questions. Is it ever enough to simply "walk away" from injustice? Or is there a more demanding obligation to at least try to change the circumstances that caused the wrongdoing? Is a failed attempt to liberate the oppressed better than the perhaps quixotic search for an alternate political reality? Mary Shelley's response to these fundamental political problems had been to look at them from both sides: those who stay and those who go. Through the eyes of Victor and his Creature, two competing perspectives emerge. While Victor coldly dismisses his Creature as the negative result of a disastrous experiment, the orphan persistently seeks from his father the love that he had been so painfully denied from birth.

Like Stryker, the Creature does not walk away from the injustices of the family and society but rather seeks to renovate them from without and within. Unlike Stryker, the Creature lacks any community support systems in which he could have discerned the right ways to confront and transform patterns of injustice in the family and beyond. In both cases, the renovation of the family is a mess of destruction and creation: a bit like taking a hammer to a wall while holding up a paint chip in the light to imagine how it might look after the remodel.

In demanding that Victor make him an equal female companion to serve as an emotional surrogate for his absentee father, the Creature explodes virtually every gender, familial, and romantic role of postrevolutionary Europe. Victor is a bad dad, compelled to become a mother by his giant child of technology. Without a womb, he gestates a sister-sibling for his son through ectogenesis. This half-made woman might have played an ugly (and perhaps asexual and infertile) Eve to the Creature's malformed Adam, had she not been torn apart like an aborted fetus by her father-surgeon.

The Creature asks for an equal female companion in order to share the "interchange of those sympathies necessary for my being" with someone as "deformed and horrible" as he is (as he originally puts it), not for sexual love or reproduction (as Victor later projects).[170] This unfulfilled rights claim raises the question of whether any life form should to be *made to serve* the affective or other relational needs of others, whether it be an orphan child's desire for a parental substitute or an adult's desire for a caregiver, friend, reproductive partner, or lover. Octavia Butler's Hugo and

Nebula award-winning novelette "Bloodchild" (1984) takes this complicated ethical and political issue head on.

Butler was loath to accept reductive readings of her work that rooted its themes in her identity as an African American woman writer. To those critics who claimed that "Bloodchild" was a "story of slavery," she countered that it was, on one level, "a love story between two very different beings."[171] More to the point, it was an SF story about love that imagined the complete transformation of gender roles within the family. Without directly referencing Shelley, Butler alluded to *Frankenstein*'s most revolutionary narrative conceit, which had been profiled in the feminist scholarship of Ellen Moers and Barbara Johnson during the 1970s and early 1980s: "Bloodchild" was, at base, a "pregnant man story."[172] Indeed, all "Frankenstein" stories—whether comic or tragic—return to this "parthenogenetic" idea of "male self-births," including the parodic film classic, *The Rocky Horror Picture Show* (1975), in which the alien transvestite Dr. Frank N. Furter autogenerates a muscle-man Creature.[173]

Butler's novelette chronicles the story of Gan, a boy born into a human colony on another planet. He grows up in a territory overseen by the dominant, highly intelligent, centipede-like species, the Tlic. Generations ago, these indigenous creatures corralled the human settlers like breeding animals on farms to use them as hosts for their eggs in their insectlike reproductive process. Eventually, the Tlic integrated the humans into their complex familial and political systems, because the emotional and social bonding between species and generations proved necessary for the long-term success of reproduction and the stability of the integrated community and ecosystem.

In this seemingly gender-equitable reproductive division of labor, boys serve as hosts for the eggs of the Tlic, allowing women to gestate and birth human children. A Tlic female will select a boy-child with whom she intensively bonds as a second, social mother. Living in these interspecies households, the giant centipedes help care for the health of their human families by offering them eggs to drink, the fluids of which promote longevity and tranquility. This symbiotic process builds affective bonds across the generations. The alien colonizers become reproductive hosts for the indigenous species, while the indigenous species is a familial and political host for the aliens.

Yet not all is not placid in this apparently harmonious familial and political arrangement. When her eggs are ripe for harvesting, the Tlic mother is supposed to anaesthetize the host-boy before surgically retrieving the larva from his abdomen. This must be done immediately after the hatching to prevent the young parasites from eating the human child alive from the inside. Because of the gruesome danger of the birthing process, the adults withhold the full details of it from the younger children. Gan's birth mother and older brother worry for his well-being as they anticipate the implantation of eggs in his abdomen by T'Gatoi.

By chance, Gan witnesses a botched and bloody delivery of Tlic grubs, and he fears how he might be exploited or even killed if he serves as a host for T'Gatoi's babies. After some resistance and even the threat of violence against his second mother, he voluntarily consents to the procedure. His reasoning is twofold and revolves around his genuine, self-giving love for two of his family members. First, he wants to prevent the last-minute imposition of his surrogate role upon his sister, possibly without her consent, due to the time constraints of the egg-laying process. Second, he realizes that he wants to participate fully and freely as an "adult" and a "partner" in the risky symbiotic familial relationships in which he has been raised.[174] Before he agrees to accept the eggs, Gan stops his second mother from taking away his family's hidden rifle. "If we're not your animals, if these are adult things, accept the risk," Gan insists, "There is risk, Gatoi, in dealing with a partner."[175] The boy grows up as a result of his choice to adopt the dangerous and burdensome responsibilities of a caregiver for his whole household. This is why Butler could call it, with moral certitude, her pregnant *man* story.

Butler's narratives are arresting due to her use of SF to upset the standard "subject positions" of postmodern identity politics: race, class, gender, sexuality, age, and species.[176] Across her oeuvre, the humans become the aliens, the colonizers become the colonized, women become the monsters, and the monsters become the leaders.[177] "Bloodchild" escalates these feminist detonations of fixed identities by turning a boy into a man through his willing and loving passage to surrogate motherhood. That Shelley must have been a source for the dominant political theme of Butler's work is a truth universally acknowledged in literary criticism.[178] As the respective mothers of the modern and postmodern strains of political science fiction, Shelley and Butler unglue the flattening social categories imposed on people and other life forms, beginning in the family.

The surprising ending of "Bloodchild" suggests that the hierarchical family could become more egalitarian and "symbiotic" if love and consent were allowed to reshape its historically "parasitic" power structures.[179] Gan's choice leads readers to consider not only *if* but also *when* children may act as fully voluntary agents in relation to adults and parents. His own reasoning for the choice—to become a mother out of love for his sister and T'Gatoi—suggests that the circumstances for actual consent within the family need to be supported by genuinely loving relationships. Genuine familial love, on this model, would mean living in affectionate and noncoercive reciprocity over time with the kin who helped to raise and shape you the most.

Literary scholar Elyse Rae Helford raised the important question of whether "Bloodchild" still ought to be interpreted through the lens of the political history of African American enslavement and racial oppression, despite the author's avowed denial that it be reduced to this reading.[180] She made the incisive point that Gan's choice looks forced, like those of female slaves who were raped by their white masters and forced to bear and raise their children. If Gan is a victim of rape or other violence, neither is his choice free nor is his love or motive authentic.

Suspicion of Gan's choice can and should be deepened through the lens of a liberal conception of childhood. According to liberal laws and political theories—as the philosopher David Archard has charted—children are not formally or legally capable of consent.[181] Although they are understood as having agency in the weaker sense of having freedom to move and relate to others, children are traditionally distinguished from adults in terms of their relative lack of ability to make truly autonomous (or self-governing) choices, free from coercive influence by others. From a liberal standpoint too, Gan's choice looks forced. He may think he acts from love, but he is actually coerced by fear of the loss of his loved ones.

Another way to see the complexity of Gan's choice is through the lens of "transitional justice," or responses to past human rights abuses. Political scientists have conceptualized these responses as a form of "resistance" to historic injustice.[182] The human-Tlic society is not perfect, but it is better than it once was. It hovers in transition between an unjust past of mutual colonization and a potentially just future of free interspecies cooperation. From this vantage, Gan is an agent of change. He moves away from the veiled history of violence and exploitation and walks toward the free and transparent choice of sharing love with those once thought to be the enemy. In this vein, Donna Haraway remarked that "Butler's fiction is about resistance to the imperative to recreate the sacred image of the same."[183] By not replicating the past patterns of domination within the Tlic-human community, Gan strikes out a different path for himself, his family, and, implicitly, his whole society. He grows into a man through his assertion of his autonomy, transforming what could have been a violent crime into a model for freely chosen and loving responsibility toward one's kin. Like Stryker, Gan's choice is not to walk away from injustice in the family but rather to respond to it in a way that makes room for the restoration of justice in society as a whole.

Inspired by Le Guin and Butler's "speculative fabulations" on what it would mean to pursue justice in circumstances of historic injustice, Haraway has penned her own SF.[184] Her "Camille" short story cycle (2016) looks at the urgent problem of environmental degradation as a matter of transitional and interspecies justice. The stories depict five generations of genetically engineered "animal symbiont" children who voluntarily assume, as they grow up, more of the characteristics of the vulnerable creatures whom they lead people to save from extinction.[185] Camille, in her five iterations from 2025 to 2425, is a hybrid of human and butterfly. Over time, the Camilles' representation of the interdependency of humans and other animals inspires people to be accountable for their catastrophic destruction of the environment through overpopulation. People begin to make kin in other ways than procreating: they bond with other animals and care for the Earth's interconnected systems of life with an attitude of "response-ability."[186]

As with Gan's choice to become a surrogate mother to his nonhuman brethren, Haraway conceives kinship in the most ecumenical and world-building sense. This practice of kinship with the whole world and its multiplicity of life forms requires "staying with the trouble" rather than walking away from it.[187] Most basically, it requires a willingness to turn the trash of technology into compost for sustaining life. If made into a habit, these ecological practices will trigger an urge to transform oneself—physically and psychologically—for the betterment of the world's countless life forms and forms of culture. Haraway converts Zhuangzi's ancient dream into a near political future. To save the butterflies and other creatures whom/that we threaten with extinction, we must strive to become spiritually one with them.

In a 2016 introduction to the emergent political concept of transfeminism, Susan Stryker and Talia M. Bettcher placed a "forward slash" between the Latin prefix *trans-* and the nineteenth-century French political term "*féminisme.*"[188] The point was to "make space" for future work on the possible relationships or kinships between its two (sometimes conflictive) social and civic parts: trans folks and feminism.[189] If we follow suit by slashing up the English word "trans/formation" (Latin, *trans/formatio*), we see how the prefix *trans-* "performs the lexical operation of attaching to, dynamizing, and transforming an existing entity."[190] On this classical linguistic model, the trans/formation of social and affective ties (or kinship) through a radical and selfless love of the endangered Other is both politically *trans*itional and morally *form*ative.

The slash between trans and formation reminds us to pause and consider the difference between an Other-oriented love that productively responds to injustice and one that merely replicates the status quo. The former takes as a given the technologically driven injustice of the past. It rejects what Sandel calls the dysfunctional utopianism of a Promethean "transforming love," which tries and fails to remake the world to suit simply selfish or tyrannical ends.[191] It rather embraces the creative, problem-solving use of techne to sustainably mold our lives with respect to the well-being of the whole world. To build on the ecological theory of the multispecies anthropologist Eben Kirksey, what we need is not an apocalyptic "Strangelove" but a "queer love" of life's weird diversity—a hopeful dedication to trans/forming life and justice *after* the Anthropocene.[192]

v. Apocatastasis

Ancient Greek literature and philosophy bequeathed to British Romanticism not only the idea of ἀποκάλυψς (*apokálypsis*), uncovering or revelation, but also the idea of ἀποκατάστασις (*apokatástasis*), return or restoration. Apocalypse signified the uncovering of something new after the turbulence of the Revolutionary era: whether it was Blake's longing for a return to original perfection, Percy Shelley's prophecy of a bright republican political future, or Byron's bleak vision of the termination of life on our planet. Mary Shelley did away with this trio of Romantic interpretations of apocalypse by challenging their joint assumption of the possibility of realizing anything truly new or absolutely final. Rejecting the irrational naïveté and short-sightedness of "apocalyptic thinking," Shelley developed in response to the tragedies of her young womanhood a more realistic and historically grounded mode of apocatastatic thought.[193]

Her first sustained exposure to the concept of apocatastasis would have been at the Glasite church, which she attended when she lived with the Baxter family in Dundee from 1812 to 1814. Her father and stepmother sent the fourteen-year-old alone on a ship to the northeastern shore of Scotland to live with virtual strangers. No one knows exactly why this arrangement was made. Perhaps it was for the adolescent to recover from eczema or, as Shelley suggested in a letter to her mother's friend Maria Gisborne in 1834, for a stepdaughter to be cured of her "excessive & romantic attachment" to her remarried father or, as Godwin claimed in a letter to Mr. Baxter, for a talented daughter to receive the stoical education of a "philosopher" or a "cynic."[194] Another reason might be that as a youth, Godwin had been educated in theology and philosophy by a rather severe minister in the dissenting tradition of the Glasites and their more radical and rationalistic offshoot, the Sandemanians. Shipping his daughter off to Dundee meant that she too would be immersed in this nonconformist religious culture.[195]

In a reform-oriented rupture from the Calvinistic Church of Scotland, the Glasite church was founded in Dundee around 1730. The Glasites used the concept of apocatastasis in two senses of the English word "restoration." For one, they sought to restore Christianity to its primitive practices of sharing signs of love in communion with one another as persons saved by faith in the testimony of Jesus Christ and his apostles. They held "love-feasts"—modeled after the Lord's last supper with the apostles—in which they would share ritualistic meals of soup on Sundays.[196] Additionally, the Glasites taught that all souls could be restored by faith in Christ alone. Faith was simple, especially in its rationalistic Sandemanian strain, in which it entailed only an intellectual grasp that Christ had sacrificed himself to atone for the sins of humanity.[197]

For the Glasites and perhaps especially the Sandemanians, every-one—no matter how corrupted by evil—could be salvaged by faith in the good grace of God. Even Satan, or a satanic creature, for that matter, could be redeemed. This belief veered toward antinomianism, for salvation did not require evidence of repentance or adherence to God's law but rather only the grasp of the truth of Christ's loving sacrifice for wayward human-ity. In the ancient Church, the Alexandrian theologian Origen and his fol-lowers held a version of this view, considered controversial after his death for defining "apocatastasis" as universal salvation, without threat of eternal punishment for unrepentant sinners.[198] The words of Origen on the "uni-versal restoration" resonate with the religious practices and ideas of the

Glasites and Sandemanians, as well as with the ethical and metaphysical questions that run through *Frankenstein* and *The Last Man*: "We think that the goodness of God, through the mediation of Christ, will bring all creatures to one and the same end."[199] It is interesting to note that both Frankenstein's Creature and Verney end up alone at sea, yet the aporetic endings of each novel allow for the possibility of their survival or salvation by others.

In her 1831 introduction to *Frankenstein*, Shelley reminisced about her years "on the blank and dreary northern shores of the Tay, near Dundee" as both freeing and formative for her. In relative "freedom" compared to life at home in London, she explored "the airy flights of my imagination" in which "I could commune with the creatures of my fancy."[200] By not making herself "the heroine of her tales," she discovered the liberating trick of writing fiction. "I was not confined to my own identity," she recalled. The aesthetic contrast between the "bleak sides of the woodless mountains" and the fertility of her youthful imagination led her to "people the hours with creations far more interesting to me at that age, than my own sensations."[201] She and her teenage friend Isabella Baxter spent much time together playing at a ruined abbey surrounded by a graveyard, where they etched their names into a crumbling window sill.[202]

Almost immediately upon her return to London in 1814, the sixteen-year-old retreated to her mother's grave. As she would recall in her "Journal of Sorrow" in May 1824, she would surreptitiously meet and court the older, married Percy Shelley in the Old St. Pancras churchyard, just a few blocks from her father's home: "its sacred tomb was the spot where first love shone."[203] In a form of philosophical practice of apocatastasis, Shelley kept returning to ruins and gravesites—in her writing and her travels—to reflect on death and its metaphysical relationship to life.

In November 1818, she and Percy visited the tomb of Cicero on the old Appian Way in Formia, where the philosopher was said to be assassinated after a failed attempt to escape by ship. In her journal, Shelley said that "a poet could not have a more sacred burying place in an al olive grove on the shore of a beautiful bay."[204] Already translating Spinoza's Latin, Shelley had devoted herself to the study of the classics alongside Percy since their arrival in Italy in March of that year.[205] Greek and Roman history, philosophy, mythology, and literature gave her an even richer sense of the range of meanings of apocatastasis than the Glasite and Sandemanian traditions had done in her childhood.

On 3 December 1824, Shelley recorded in her "Journal of Sorrow" how she had "pondered for hours on Cicero's description of that power of virtue in the human mind w^h [which] renders man's frail being superior to fortune."[206] Copying out the Latin, she reflected that she "could not forgo the hope of loving & being loved" even as she resolved to "remain unconquered by hard & bitter fortune."[207] Without using the word "apocatastasis," she suggested that to "remain unconquered" by the worst events of life was to resist the temptation to escape its pain through suicide. Shelley wondered on paper, "Is this my commentary on the philosophy of Cicero?"[208] Although she admired his ethical ideal of overcoming sorrow, she knew it was not possible to put an end to "the tears that start in my eyes" in the face of the memories of misfortune.[209] "So much for philosophizing—" she concluded the entry, "shall I ever be a philosopher?—".[210] The ambiguity of the question mark trailed by a dash suggests that she was in fact a classically trained philosopher, not despite but because of her persistent Socratic self-doubt.

In ancient Greek and Roman philosophy, apocatastasis had several meanings. For the Pythagoreans, it was reincarnation or metempsychosis, or the return of the human soul in a series of transmigrations into other mortal animal frames.[211] For the Stoics, it was eternal recurrence: a cyclical and infinite "reconstitution or rebirth" of "the world" after periodic conflagrations such that "the events which constitute its history are exactly the same each time around."[212] Cicero had played with the idea of reincarnation in his appropriation of the "Myth of Er" from Plato's *Republic*, without accepting it as his own philosophical position.[213] For the widowed Shelley, the restoration was neither so simple nor so certain as either the Pythagorean return of the souls of the departed back into bodily shells or the Stoical repetition of the same cosmological order over time. She would selectively integrate elements of Christianity, Wollstonecraft, Plato, Cicero, and Spinoza to forge her own mystical sense of the meaning of apocatastasis.

An avid reader of Dante's *Divine Comedy* while she lived in Italy, Shelley grew to respect the rationalism of its Roman Catholic theology.[214] Euthanasia, the heroine of her historical novel *Valperga* (1823), represented the Thomistic balance of faith and reason in her choice to become a Christian martyr rather than succumb to the temptation of a romantic love that would compromise the republican political liberty of her people.[215] That same year, Shelley composed a poem entitled "The Choice," which she copied into the end papers of her "Journal of Sorrow." The poem contemplated the dramatic choice she had made to elope with Percy in July 1814.

Her choice represented the existential starting point of her adult life, with all of its knowledge, happiness, burdens, and tragedies. She pictured herself as a martyr not liberated through a good death like Euthanasia but instead one indefinitely tested by the patient bearing of suffering in this life:

> And since I have a faith that I must earn
> By suffering & by patience, a return
> Of that companionship & love, which first
> Upon my young life's ~~clould~~ cloud, like sunlight burst,
> And now as has left me dark as when it beams,
> Quench d by the might of dreadful ocean streams,
> Leave that one cloud, a gloomy speck on high,
> Beside one star in the else darkened sky;—[216]

Shelley was a cloud burst by the sunlight, or the "rare loveliness," of Percy's "soul."[217] He was a "star" to her even then, despite the undeniable reality of their separation through death.

> —No more! No more! What tho' that form be fled
> My trembling hands shall never write thee—dead—
> Thou liv'st in Nature—love—my Memory,
> With deathless faith for aye adoring thee—
> The wife of time no more—I wed Eternity—[218]

Although she had begun her "Journal of Sorrow" with the desperate hope that she might use its white paper to communicate with Percy's spirit, a year into widowhood, she knew that she was no longer wed to him but rather to "Eternity." A "return" to the "companionship & love" she enjoyed in her youth would not arise from any physical reunion with the dead in this life. It would be realized through a poetic and mystical communion of her "Memory" with the "Inscrutable!"[219] This communion compelled her to address her feelings of "fierce remorse" for her "cold neglect" of Percy after the deaths of their children.[220] It would also allow her to redirect her enduring "love" for the departed toward the care of young Percy, who "linked" her to the "heavy chain" of duties involved in sustaining present and future generations.[221] As her husband had written in "The Triumph of Life"—a poem she edited for its publication in 1824—it was "love" that led Dante "serene" through "the lowest depths of hell," the punishment of purgatory, the heights of heaven, and then back to embrace his Earthly relationships and responsibilities. This spiritual journey from the loss of love to its restoration is one that Mary Shelley also took and "returned to tell."[222]

Shelley may have had Plato's *Symposium* in mind—or its refraction through her mother's rational Dissenting Christian theology—when she poetically expressed her marriage, or spiritual bond, with Eternity.[223] Percy had steadily worked on a translation of the dialogue, with support from Mary, during their life together in Italy from 1818 to 1822.[224] "Love," Diotima told Socrates in the *Symposium*, "is a tendency toward eternity."[225] The process of "meditation"—or "calling up a new memory in the place of that which is departed"—"preserves knowledge."[226] The mythic female philosopher concluded, "In this manner every thing mortal is preserved" and "partake[s] of immortality."[227] Love of knowledge, for Plato, was an intellectual ascent. This ladder climb from bodily forms of love to higher forms of love could lead to the grasping of eternity (however slight or imperfect) in the memory and the soul.[228]

In *A Vindication of the Rights of Woman*, Wollstonecraft described God in transcendent and gender-inclusive terms: the "High and Lofty One, who inhabiteth eternity" is both a "her" and a "He."[229] With ethical and pedagogical language reminiscent of Diotima, Wollstonecraft argued that "to love God as the fountain of wisdom, goodness, and power, appears to be the only worship useful to a being who wishes to acquire either virtue or knowledge."[230] Wollstonecraft consistently argued that the immortality of the "soul" depended upon the realization of virtue and knowledge through the adoration and emulation of God's "attributes," especially reason.[231]

While Shelley shared Plato and her mother's allegorical approach to the philosophy of love, her marital metaphor of being "wed" to "Eternity" is different from either Diotima's or Wollstonecraft's moral and intellectual ascents to "partake of immortality." To be "wed" to "Eternity" suggests a permanence found in immanence and embodiment. To "partake of immortality" suggests a partial if not complete transcendence of the body and its mortality. Shelley's philosophy of love as found in the "Journal of Sorrow" veered more toward Spinoza than Plato or Wollstonecraft, for it drew heavily from the grounded, relational, and political vision of love that she studied in the *Theologico-Political Treatise*.

Translating the *Theologico-Political Treatise* (at the same time that Percy worked intensively on the *Symposium*) offered Shelley another angle on the achievement of a higher love and knowledge. "The love of God," the excommunicated Jew wrote, "is man's highest happiness and blessedness."[232] In his commentary on 1 John 4: 7–21 ("God is love"), Spinoza argued that for the apostle, there could be "no knowledge or consciousness of God except from love towards his neighbor."[233] In this appropriation of ancient Christian theology, the exiled political philosopher caustically implied that it is through love of one's neighbors, not persecution of "the faithful," that one "participates in" the love of God, or Nature.[234] This radical teaching of universal brotherly love underwrites or justifies all genuine religious practices, not solely Christianity, for Spinoza.

Despite her sublime Platonic aspirations to a transcendent love of Eternity, Shelley had ended "The Choice" with a prophetic vision of reestablishing an Earthly, Spinozan, neighborly love with her fellow widow, Jane Williams. She dared to imagine the two of them secluded in a "little dell" or "lovely wood," like the unconventional artistic commune that they once built on the coast of Italy with their husbands:

A voice then whispered a strange prophecy—
My dearest widowed friend—that thou and I—
Should there together pass the livelong day
As we have done before in Spezia's bay[235]

Meanwhile, without her knowledge, Jane had begun to betray her back in London, spreading rumors that Mary had practically driven Percy to suicide by her alienation of him in their unhappy marriage.[236]

Shelley's relationship with Jane and other women in her early widowhood remains an enigma. "I love Jane more than any other human being," she wrote in her journal in January 1824, "but I am pressed upon by the knowledge that she but slightly returns this affection."[237] Biographers have speculated whether she may have felt a lesbian erotic love for Jane. Whether physically sexual, transcendentally Platonic, or the embodiment of both, her attraction to Jane made the revelation of her fellow widow's betrayal all the more painful to her. "Miserable discovery!" she cried into her journal in July 1827, "—for four years I was devoted to her—& I earned only ingratitude."[238] Charlotte Gordon suggested that Shelley exchanged a romantic, sexually charged letter with Jane, with veiled reference to their "pretty" female genitalia, just a month later.[239] In the cryptic ending to this missive, Shelley confided to Jane, "I am grateful to you for several things, but for nothing so much as my gender."[240] Looking at the same manuscript material from 1820s letters and journals, Miranda Seymour followed Shelley sleuth and editor Betty T. Bennett in declining to label the relationship between the women as sexual or lesbian in its eroticism.[241]

More recently, Fiona Sampson concluded that Shelley's "sexual orientation," if situated in a twenty-first-century social scientific "spectrum" of sexualities, might be best described as "fluid," not "polarized."[242] Although Sampson did not use the term "gender fluid," I suggest that it could even better capture the psychic and social ambiguities of Shelley's love life than labels that vainly fixate on tracing the invisible directions of sexual desire. To apply to Shelley the moniker "gender fluid"—a term coined, interestingly, in late twentieth-century theological debates about God's gender—might appear to be wild "prolepsis," but upon reflection, it helps to explain the complexity of her experience of love.[243] While she loved Percy erotically—as it appears from her writing, in both a Platonic and a sexual sense—she profoundly enjoyed sharing "sympathy" with women, especially Jane and others who defied the sexual norms of their time, and carved her own distinctive sense of her "gender" in relation to "the feminine" beauty of Jane.[244]

To her journal in December 1824, Shelley confided that she was happy to be a woman despite its hardships: "Most women I believe who wish that they had been men—so do not I—change my sex & I do not think that my talents would be greater."[245] Much like her mother, Shelley thought the intellectual, imaginative, and other creative mental capacities of the sexes were roughly equal, independent of their bodily and social differences. Despite her skepticism of those of her gender who wished to be men, she kept as one of her closest companions Mary Dods.

Dods was a lesbian who, in 1827, dressed as a man in order to escort the unmarried mother Isabel Robinson Douglas with her illegitimate baby to France.[246] In twenty-first-century scholarly terms, Dods was "transgender": born female, he made a long series of deliberate and often difficult choices to live as a man named Walter Sholto Douglas, a private and public identity that fit his long-standing gendered and sexualized sense of self.[247] Despite Isabel's interest in "other men," Walter lived as a man alongside his purported wife and her child until he died in a debtor's prison in Paris around 1830.[248] One of his last letters requested that he be sent a faux moustache to better conceal his feminine facial features from his imprisoners and inmates.[249]

If there was a gender-fluid aspect to Shelley's widowhood, then it took shape in her psychic kinship with Lionel Verney, her last avatar left standing in the postapocalyptic landscape of *The Last Man*. Inside this novel simulation of virtual apocalypse, she explored the holistic and rationalistic Spinozan worldview of Verney, who is married to Idris, the feminine embodiment of her Platonic desire to grasp Eternity. Once infected by the plague, the husband and wife stay up late together to hold an existential debate about love. Does love have an afterlife, Idris wonders, in an eternal, Platonic sense? "Lionel," she says, "never, never, can I love any but you; through eternity I must desire your society . . . I trust that the Ruler of the world will never tear us asunder."[250] Lionel responds to his wife with a hopeful yet realistic blend of Romantic Spinozism and unorthodox Christian faith: "But, sweet, we are so formed (and there is no sin, if God made our nature, to yield to what he ordains), we are so formed, that we must love life, and cling to it."[251] Idris affirms the "mystery of a future state," while alluding to her belief in the transfiguration of the body and soul through death: "the same strong feeling which makes me sure that I shall not wholly die, makes me refuse to believe that I shall live wholly as I do now."[252]

The choice of resilience in the face of death is, for Idris and Verney, the "rational" answer to the threat of apocalypse.[253] While the revelation of heaven lies beyond present human understanding, the restoration of life on Earth in response to the cyclic scourge of death remains, at least relatively, within the scope of human reason. Idris and Lionel feel "on certainty of faith" that "other spirits, other minds, other perceptive beings, sightless to us, must people with thought and love this beauteous and imperishable universe."[254] Although they rather ecumenically believe in the existence of other sentient and intelligent life forms in the universe—whether they be angels, aliens, or other creatures—they do not renege their deep sense of responsibility to try to preserve human life on Earth after the plague.

After the death of Idris, Verney reorients himself and prepares for what he and his wife had previously speculated: there may be a point in time "if, two or three being saved, it were slowly repeopled."[255] As he treks across France with the remnant of survivors, Verney confronts two figures, apparently ghosts, flailing on the edge of the road.[256] One "figure all in white, of more than human nature" and another "apparition" known as the "Black Spectre" are in fact a delirious opera dancer and a mad aristocrat, left to wander in the wasteland of postapocalyptic Paris.[257] Her phrase "more than human" recalls her and Percy's translation of Spinoza's *supra humanam* (with respect to Christ) to mean "superhuman" or beyond the human.[258] In one sense, the white and black specters are metaphors for the superhuman task of surviving the aftermath of the French Revolution and the Napoleonic Wars, which Shelley had witnessed in her own travels across a battered Europe. In another, these embodied spirits herald an incipient posthuman age, with the dissolution of the reigning institutions of modern European humanism and politics providing an opening of unknown vistas for humanity and the wider environment.

What Verney discovers is that a posthuman future would not be as inhuman as people had feared. When he first arrives in the unpeopled landscape of northern Italy with only Adrian and his orphan niece Clara as companions, he is struck by the "desolate towns" and their "ever multiplying relics of our lost species."[259] It would seem that the technological relics of humankind not only outlast but also outnumber their makers, as if they had the power to reproduce on their own. Even if the species was lost, the artifacts of human minds and imaginations endure into futurity.

After a month without human company in Italy, Verney thinks he sees a "wild-looking, unkempt, half-naked savage" in a palace at Forlì, before he realizes it was "I myself whom I beheld in a large mirror at the end of the hall."[260] His reaction to this monster in the mirror is not to run away but rather to restore and replicate the relics of his humanity. He heads to Rome to rehumanize his dehumanized body and spirit. He immerses himself in the study of human civilization and the writing of the autobiographical history of "THE LAST MAN," despite knowing that he, as a mortal individual, will ultimately leave it all behind.[261] From this Romantic Spinozan-Christian vantage, the posthuman situation of Verney does not entail the total abandonment of the human as neighbor. Instead, it demands a psychological reconfiguration of the mental and material dimensions of being human in ethical relation—or neighborliness—to the whole creation.

Just as Verney accepts his existential predicament as "THE LAST MAN" by composing an ambitious combination of autobiography and world history, Shelley reconciled herself to being the last woman of her generation of Romantic writers by turning a new page in her journal and fiction. Soon after the publication of her second great work of political science fiction, she closed "The Journal of Sorrow" in January 1826 by copying into its end papers her poem "The Choice" and her poetic dedication of *The Last Man* to Jane Williams. Then she opened a new volume, the fifth and (unbeknownst to her then) final installment of her journals.

Despite the malicious rumormongering of her closest female friends, Jane and Isabel, Shelley strove to maintain relationships with them and preserve her and young Percy's place in London society. Disparaging reviews of her latest novel asked why she did not call it *The Last Woman*, given its obvious subtext of a scandalized female author "with nobody left to talk to."[262] She continued writing some of her best short fiction, including a clever response to the 1826 hoax that purported the resurrection of a seventeenth-century Englishman, Roger Dodsworth, from cryopreservation under an Alpine glacier.[263] Posing as the nearly 200-year-old reanimated man, Shelley sent a fictional essay about her/his perceptions of modern life and politics to a London magazine editor, who declined to publish it in her lifetime. She may have identified with the story of the unfrozen Dodsworth due to her competing desires to overcome both the public slander about her icy treatment of Percy and her private "remorse" for her "cold neglect" of him.[264]

Things got worse, of course, before they got better. On an April 1828 trip to visit Walter and Isabel, now known as Mr. and Mrs. Douglas, she fell ill as she crossed the Channel, went straight into a bath and then bed in Paris, and awoke with signs of smallpox.[265] She would have seen in the mirror—in the words of her most dedicated biographer Miranda Seymour—"a red, encrusted mask and lank, clipped hair." For the first time, Shelley's "identification with Frankenstein's creature" was "physical."[266] Unexpectedly, this physical identification with the Creature seemed to buoy her spirits amid Parisian society. As she wrote in her journal upon her return to England in July, "The Parisians were very amiable & a monster to look at I was—I tried to be agreeable to compensate to them."[267] Perhaps she thought she had nothing left to lose, with her pretty face disfigured during a precious time abroad on the Continent. Her outing as an English female monster in Paris paradoxically made her "Health—buyonant & bright."[268]

As the 1820s faded, Shelley surrounded herself with a different social circle in London and worked diligently as a writer and editor to support her son. By 1831, she had managed to reissue *Frankenstein* in an illustrated edition, with its first authorized revisions in print (for Godwin's 1823 edition was not approved by her). In late 1830, she gave an unpublished poem to a new female friend, Mrs. Anna Birkbeck, who pasted it into her album of famous acquaintances' autographs and artistic work. Though ominously titled "The Death of Love," Shelley's poem pictured the nightly resurrection of a "gentle boy" she still loved. Though blessed with "eternal peace" in "the tomb of an immortal God!" he could reappear in her dreams:

> Yet at the lonely and the midnight hour
>   Thine image like a pallid ghost may rise,
> And o'er my dreams thou may'st extend thy power,
>   Gilding the visions of my sleep: closed eyes!—[269]

It is not clear if the boy is meant to be her son William—whom she described as "Infant immortal!" in "The Choice"—or his father Percy, or perhaps an amalgam of them.[270] The analogue for the boy matters less than Shelley's poetic realization of the ancient Hebrew wisdom of Solomon. Love is strong as death. Memory and imagination infuse it with a vital connectivity to others that transcends even mortality.

Through the Creature, Verney, her journals, and her poetry, Shelley reconceived what it means to share and sustain love, or to be humane, in both postanthropocentric and postanthropomorphic terms. She and her creations figure as ghosts in the largely unwritten history of posthumanist political thought, like the white specter of haute culture and the black specter of the *ancien régime* that haunt the outskirts of postapocalyptic Paris in *The Last Man*. While political science and political philosophy have witnessed a renewed interest in posthumanism and other new materialisms in the twenty-first century, further study of these traditions' roots in British Romanticism is necessary.[271] Rosi Braidotti credits Spinoza and his Victorian translator George Eliot for inspiring her philosophical interest in posthumanism, while Jane Bennett recognizes Spinoza and the American transcendentalists Ralph Waldo Emerson and Henry David Thoreau as sources for her political theory of the vibrancy or vitality of matter.[272] Yet they do not acknowledge the Shelleys in particular or British Romanticism in general as critical links between Spinoza and his mid-nineteenth-century reception in the Anglophone culture that became a basis for literary modernism and its offshoots: modern feminism, postmodernism, poststructuralism, and posthumanism.

The leading political theorist of posthumanism today, Braidotti defines the concept of the "posthuman" in relation to the virtue of "hope."[273] Perhaps building on fellow Italian philosopher Saint Thomas Aquinas's demarcation of the theological virtues of faith, hope, and charity, she posits hope as an Aristotelian mean between the vicious extremes of overly enthusiastic or fearful attitudes toward the future impacts of human technology. By applying this moderate conception of hope to debates on the contested meaning of posthumanism, she navigates a path between an antihumanistic pessimism that accepts or even welcomes the abolishment of humankind and its destructive cultures, as well as a transhumanistic optimism that euphorically seeks bodily transcendence or immortality through artificial intelligence and biotechnology.[274] "Hope is a way of dreaming up possible futures," she contends. It motivates an "affirmative politics" that stays grounded in the real world, rooted in "the ordinary micro-practices of everyday life," yet aimed at "sustainable transformations."[275] Following Haraway, she advocates for an aporetic understanding of "Becoming-posthuman" to challenge the apocalyptic view of the posthuman as terminus.[276] "Becoming-posthuman," she poetically relays, "is a process" "of redefining one's sense of attachment and connection to a shared world, a territorial space: urban, social, psychic, ecological, planetary as it may be. It expresses multiple ecologies of belonging, while it enacts the transformation of one's sensorial and perceptual co-ordinates, in order to acknowledge the collective nature and outward-bound direction of what we still call the self."[277] With her moderate and realistic hope for restoring life on Earth after the Anthropocene, Braidotti joins Haraway in imagining a posthuman future with a relational, sustainable, situational, *and* globally minded ethos. They have culled together an unorthodox ecospirituality, which is quite similar, by chance, to the literary-philosophical prophecies found in the manuscripts of Verney, the Sibyl of Baiae, and Shelley.

According to the grand dame of Mary Shelley scholarship, Betty T. Bennett, the subject of her life's work "was not an atheist but had constructed her own belief in a larger spiritual force in the universe."[278] Moreover, *The Last Man* expressed a "religious philosophy" in which "the traditional God dissolves" because "the plague appears as absolute as deity," but in its place "many faiths are possible."[279] Likewise, the Romanticist Robert Lance Snyder argued that both "the duration of uncertainty and the concept of indeterminacy," as embodied in the inscrutability of the plague, become the "leading themes" of *The Last Man*.[280] Similar to Shelley before them, contemporary posthumanists, vitalists, and new materialists pay homage to an "indeterminate vitality" that seems to animate the material world.[281] For Braidotti, this is "zoe." For the political theorist Jane Bennett, this is the "thing-power" of matter.[282]

Quoting Emerson's journal, Jane Bennett expresses her desire to "dive again into brute matter": "I too go diving there, and find matter not so brute at all."[283] Although Bennett's materialism expressly rejects "the life-matter binary and does not believe in God or spiritual forces," her poetic reflection on diving into matter suggests her reverence for "the wondrous complexity of nature."[284] Shelley too drew from Spinoza and the rationalistic strands of Enlightenment Protestantism to develop a deep sense of reverence and responsibility toward all creation, whether it appears animate or inanimate, living or dead, beautiful or monstrous.

Even now, Shelley patiently waits in the wings to be greeted as the philosophical prophetess of a posthuman ethos that stubbornly retains its humanity or humaneness. A biologist with strong ties to physical anthropology, Haraway has thoughtfully refused the label "posthuman" for her work, because it might suggest a rejection of the human altogether.[285] One can salvage the term, however, by reconfiguring it with a slash. A post/human ethos is one in which we critically reflect upon the past injustices of humanity's relationship to the world, then wonder what comes *after* the Anthropocene, without giving up what makes our lives worth living: the hope of realizing a humane or mutually sympathetic community on the broadest and deepest scale.

The genius of Verney (and his female creator) is that he is at once the Last Man and not. With this character, Shelley modeled a way to live a posthuman life in the indeterminate space between the historical record and the speculation of what could be our unmaking as a species, ecosystem, or living planet. Shelley and Verney together resist the temptation to cede a final stop. Instead, they look ahead for a restoration of a healthy and humane way of life in dutiful and loving relation to the whole. To borrow the insights of ecological and political theorist Melissa Lane, Shelley in *The Last Man* is like Plato in his allegory of the cave. Both literary-philosophical masterminds conceptualize "inertia" as a "failure of the political imagination."[286]

Lovelessness, or the death of love, is a terror that recurs in Shelley's writing only to be extinguished by her sense of being anchored to the world by her living son. When Percy Florence married his wife Jane in 1848, his mother gave him a handwritten note of congratulations, saying, "You are very happy—so with a thousand blessings Iam yr happy & affec[tionate] mother."[287] It was so joyful that her cursive blurred and practically leapt off the page. "Notice how 'I' and 'am' become one word, the pen barely lifted,"

Rachel Feder commented, "You are happy so I am happy, I bleeding into am, Mary Shelley pressed into being. You are . . . so . . . I am.[288] Shelley died less than three years later, in her early fifties, from a brain tumor. Childless, Percy and Jane became the conservators of the Wollstonecraft-Godwin-Shelley family legacy, passing down manuscripts, artifacts, and artworks to major archival collections and repositories that preserve them to the present day.

With all the seeming apocalypses in her life, Shelley reconceived love as *apocatastasis*: a restoration, reboot, or remodel of her relationship to the world, away from selfish despair over the loss of love, toward living for the betterment of her "fellow creatures" and future generations. Perhaps the best record of this trans/formative process of redirecting her mourning toward solidarity with her "fellow creatures" is found in the early months of her "Journal of Sorrow." On 31 December 1822, she communicated through the medium of white paper to her beloved Percy, "No one now loves me. I love thee, my only one—I love nature—& I trust that I love all that is good in my fellow creatures—but how changed I am!"[289] This "changed" woman went on to represent herself and her late husband as the twin architects of the second generation of British Romanticism, with a forward-looking Spinozan conception of love of the world at its core. She ensured the safe passage of all of her children—though dead or fictional—into the imagination of posterity.

Together with their literary mother, Shelley's "savage" twin boys, the Creature and Verney, teach readers that we are all artificial creatures with duties to the world that made us as we are, for better and for worse. Formed and misshapen by circumstances beyond our control, we creatures retain obligations to share love with, or at least care for, other created beings and things, no matter why, by whom, of what, where, or how we were made. Since Shelley revealed that there is no final stop, a book on her political thought and legacies for political science fiction can have no conclusion. The Coda, instead, returns to the Wollstonecraftian mode of vindication that inspired the visionary ethics and politics of the Shelleys. It is a brief manifesto of the rights and duties of artificial creatures with regard to love, for—

Whether they be brute, bug, rock,
Vegetable, savage, monster,
Machine or digital being,
Love is the thing that they'll need to persist
Past the threat of man-made Apocalypse.

A Vindication of the Rights
and Duties of Artificial Creatures

i. Back to the Future

As the daughter of the revolutionary-era political philosophers Mary Woll-stonecraft and William Godwin, Mary Shelley was well aware of the politics of vindication as it had been deployed in the 1790s pamphlet wars. Woll-stonecraft penned the decisive works in this confrontational vein: *A Vindi-cation of the Rights of Men* of 1790 and *A Vindication of the Rights of Woman* of 1792. The former was the first published reply to Edmund Burke's *Reflec-tions on the Revolution in France*, which had been printed to international acclaim just a few weeks before.[1]

In his tract, Burke had attacked the French Revolution as the unleashing of cultural and political anarchy on either side of the Channel. Against Burke's staid defense of legal and cultural "prescription" as the basis of a stable and benevolent constitutional monarchy, Wollstonecraft called for the legal and cultural realization of the "rights of men" in a modern consti-tutional republic.[2] These rights were not handed down through common law or civic tradition, as Burke claimed, but rather derived, rationally, from the "eternal foundation" of God's universal moral law.[3] In her equally fierce sequel, she expanded this theologically grounded defense of the "rights of humanity" such that it explicitly covered women, children, the poor, and chattel slaves.[4] As the political theorist Alexandre Lefebvre has argued, the politics of the revolutionary era served as the platform for her vindications of an "ethos" of basic "human rights" for each and all.[5]

Well, not quite. Wollstonecraft never ascribed rights—human or otherwise—to nonhuman animals or other Earthly life forms. Within a few months of the publication of her second *Vindication*, a satire by the Cambridge Platonist philosopher Thomas Taylor appeared with the provocative title, *A Vindication of the Rights of Brutes*. If women had rights like men—he snidely fired back—then perhaps elephants and women had rights to sleep together?[6] Wollstonecraft did not flatter Taylor with the favor of a reply to this comic non sequitur, just as Burke had not bothered to respond to her first *Vindication*.

Burke had prefigured Taylor's *reductio ad absurdum* on the abstract logic of universal rights in his 1756 tract *A Vindication of Natural Society*. This clever satire purported to follow Bolingbroke's theologically radical principles to their logical political conclusion. If deism demanded the abandonment of organized religion, Burke asked, then surely it also required that humanity return to a natural state to escape the wider corruption caused by "artificial political Distinctions"?[7]

Burke actually viewed such artifice—grounded in centuries of carefully reasoned practices such as family, education, religion, and law—as the foundation of the social order, because it derived "from the accumulated verdict of artificial reason."[8] His *Reflections* amply propounded this defining thesis of his oeuvre. Authorial intentions proved not to matter, however. The rationalist Godwin took Burke's *Vindication* to be philosophical anarchism, straight up; it served as a tonic for composing *Political Justice* in the heady years of the early 1790s.[9] In another subversive Godwinian reading, *The Last Man* playfully teased out the synergies and tensions between Burke's *Vindication* and *Reflections* with its SF novum of a global pestilence that seems to wipe out all but one human.[10] The plague delivers Verney to a postapocalyptic "state of nature" without families, societies, or governments. Yet the artifice of ethics and culture endures, alongside Verney's hope of preserving humanity and other forms of life on Earth.[11]

In a similar political reversal, Taylor's mocking defense of rights for brutes and Wollstonecraft's sincere defense of rights for women and other marginalized people have since been credited by Peter Singer for expressing the logic of animal rights advocacy.[12] Ecological and communications theorists have extended Singer's argument such that it applies to other beings, things, information systems, ecosystems, and forms of life beyond animal life.[13] Some philosophers have argued that the next step in the process should be the ascription of rights to learning machines, robots, and androids.[14]

Even this is too narrow a purview, however, for our own revolutionary political age of rapidly changing technologies of artificial intelligence and genetic engineering. If Donna Haraway is right that humans are already "cyborgs," or complex bio/techno/cultural hybrids of machine and organism, then chances are that artificial general intelligences of the future will take partly biological, partly mechanical forms or perhaps even upload the mental contents of the human brain into some transcendent digital cloud.[15] This political past, present, and future of artificial life and intelligence demands more than an "ethics charter" for robots and their users, as South Korea developed in 2007, or a professional code of ethics, as disseminated by the Asilomar Conference on Beneficial AI in 2017.[16] It requires more than amending the 1997 Universal Declaration on the Human Genome and Human Rights (UDHGHR) to explicitly cover the rights of gene-edited people, as proposed by the Nuffield Bioethics Council in 2018.[17] What is needed most of all is a vindication of the rights and duties of all artificial creatures, whether human or not. To accomplish this futuristic political task, we should turn back to the revolutionary political science of the 1790s, which sparked Shelley and her Creature to vindicate the rights of artificially formed beings who are "sensitive" to the circumstances of their making.[18]

ii. We Are All Artificial Creatures

Following the empirical epistemology of John Locke to its logical political conclusion, Wollstonecraft and Godwin each advanced distinctive theories of justice in which humans figured as artificial creatures, who deserved liberation from the despotic political systems that had corrupted and malformed them. In his 1793 treatise *Political Justice*, Godwin posited that all "rational beings" are shaped by the "circumstances" of the government under which they were born, for better or for worse.[19] The artificial formation of the human character by environmental factors ran so deep that it actually began before birth. Locke had made the same point: the infant mind was like a "white paper" on which experience wrote its influence, but the educational process commenced, however faintly, with the sensory environment of the womb.[20]

Writing almost a hundred years before the widespread use of the term "feminism" to mean the political liberation of women, Wollstonecraft put a visionary proto/feminist spin on the Lockean empirical view of human development.[21] Raised from the cradle to conform to society's limited and limiting views of feminine propriety, women were cultivated to become "weak, artificial beings" who existed only to please men.[22] Worst of all was the "artificial monster" made by aristocracy, who tyrannized society with the scepter of superficial wealth and beauty.[23] Yet the reverse scenario, Wollstonecraft predicted, could hold true. Because women and men had been shaped by their circumstances, those circumstances could be restructured to artificially form them in a virtuous manner in the future.

A good pupil of Burke, Godwin distrusted the language of rights and instead leaned heavily upon the language of duties. *Political Justice* envisioned the future liberation of people within an ultra-minimal state. The government's limited influence would be offset by the voluntary, dutiful moral actions of individuals within families and other small social units that Burke had poetically dubbed "little platoons."[24] A former Dissenting Christian minister who converted to atheism, Godwin consistently understood duty as the basis of morality and reason as the foundation of that moral law.[25] Like Wollstonecraft, he conceived of humans as "rational creatures" or "rational beings," whose defining cognitive trait uniquely situated them as moral agents on Earth.[26]

Despite his own anthropocentrism (compounded by racism and misogyny), Immanuel Kant acknowledged in 1786 the possibility of other "rational beings" beyond humanity who would be bound by the same universal moral duties and corresponding rights.[27] Kant's deontological, or duty-based, conception of rights thus applied to beings beyond humanity, if they were rational. Rational beings, by this Kantian logic, should not treat brutes cruelly—not because it would violate rights but rather because it would be degrading to the abuser. In 1799, Jeremy Bentham took an alternative empirical and utilitarian approach to the question of who or what should hold rights. If an animal—human or not—could be said to suffer, then humans should ascribe rights to it in positive law.[28]

Wollstonecraft took a creative Christian theological tack between Kant and Bentham. While, to her, animals were sentient beings, only humans as rational beings made in God's image could hold duties and rights with regard to creation. Humans thus held duties to make the brutes as happy as they could be while they lived but had no obligation to ascribe rights to them, let alone refrain from killing and eating them. Lest her moral defense of the human carnivore seem out of joint with her political egalitarianism, it should be noted that Bentham's classical utilitarianism did not require either the admirable moral rigors of vegetarianism or the stricter standard of veganism.[29] Bentham, followed by J. S. Mill, required only the beneficent and equitable treatment of other sentient animals by humans, preferably under a legally prescribed scheme of rights that protected the "whole sentient creation" from the infliction of suffering, abuse, neglect, or torture.[30] Assuming that the killing of other animals for food could be done humanely (i.e., in a way that minimized or ideally eliminated pain), it could be reconciled with a caring or even reverent relationship of stewardship to the environment.[31]

Inspired by the revolutionary politics of Wollstonecraft and Godwin, Percy Shelley published *A Vindication of Natural Diet* just a year before he eloped with their teenage daughter.[32] This 1813 tract blended Wollstonecraft's politics of vindication, Godwin's abstract approach to justice, and Taylor's (overtly satirical but implicitly logical) arguments for animal rights to advocate a vegetarian diet for humankind. Highly familiar with the radical politics of her mother, father, and future husband, Shelley was uniquely situated to compose a vindication of her own in nonfiction prose. But she never did. Reflecting in her journal in 1838, she judged herself ill-suited to write in the deductive mode of the political tract or treatise, since she could "feel the counterarguments too strongly."[33] At the same time, her ability to see multiple sides of an argument had suited her for political philosophy and literature, as well as their effective combination in her first work of political science fiction.

Frankenstein (1818) is a literary vindication of the "right" of all creatures —no matter the circumstances under which they are made—to share "love of another" and companionship with other "sensitive" beings.[34] There are two radical political dimensions of Shelley's argument for the right to share love, both made in the voice of the Creature: first, that, as an artificial being, he holds a right to share family and community alongside his human father and, second, that it is not simply his cognitive and affective status as a "sensitive and rational animal" that grounds this right but, more crucially, his relational and ethical status as a "sensitive being" made by the artifice of another's reason, desire, and imagination.[35] Like Milton's Adam, who is made from dust through the mysterious force of the divine mind, the Creature comes into being through the application of the scientific theories of his father to dead matter.[36] As with generations of humanity prefigured by Adam, the Creature's *madeness* defines him more than the particular materials or circumstances from which he was formed.

Through the passionate voice of the Creature, Shelley presciently argues that all "sensitive" creatures hold rights with respect to their creators. This is due to their qualities of rationality and/or sentience and, even more fundamentally, their ethical relationships to their artificers. The creator's act of crafting another being forges these ethical relationships in the first place. Once these relationships exist, any renunciation of the duties entailed by them will hurt the well-being and development of the creature while young or otherwise vulnerable and pervert the character of the creator while responsible for enabling the loving care of the creature.

Through the story of the Creature's neglect and abuse, Shelley goes still further. She suggests that humans like Victor may be especially prone to violating the rights of the creatures they make by avoiding their responsibilities to them. This tyrannical tendency originates in their perverse educations into selfish, domineering behavior. It taught them to treat creations of all sort, sensitive or not, as mere outputs of experiments or instruments to their whims. Building on Wollstonecraft and Godwin's broad-ranging critiques of despotism from the family to the state, the Creature protests his and the female creature's cruel and arbitrary treatment as objects to be rudely discarded by their maker. "I may die," the Creature threatens his father after seeing him brutally tear to pieces the nearly completed female creature, "but first you, my tyrant and tormentor, shall curse the sun that gazes on your misery."[37] The bereavement of the Creature shows how and why children and other young sensitive creatures are especially vulnerable to the violation of their rights (and even the perceived violation of another's rights). To be made by the artifice of a tyrant is a *risk factor* for the violation of rights that are established independently by (1) the creature's ethical relationship to the creator and (2) the creature's sensitivity to their violation.[38]

If Joanna Russ was correct to say that every robot, android, and "sentient computer" in science fiction is cut from the cloth of *Frankenstein*, then it is not a stretch to argue that this novel paved the way for a vindication of the rights of artificial creatures who are sensitive to their circumstances.[39] Shelley's charter was wider in scope than some variants of the genre today. Critical theorist David Gunkel has advanced "A Vindication of the Rights of Machines" (2014), loosely rooted in the ideas of Wollstonecraft, Taylor, and Singer. Yet he ultimately undermines this far-seeing political project by (1) focusing his inquiry upon the rights of machines and (2) concluding there is no way to back up or justify those claims of rights—whether they are ascribed to humans or to robots.[40] His "objective," Gunkel restated in *Robot Rights* (2018), is not "to advocate on behalf of a cause, to advance some definitive declaration, or to offer up a preponderance of the evidence to prove one side or the other side in the existing debates."[41] Following Levinas and Žižek, his point is to question the way that "rights have been configured" to accommodate some at the cost of marginalizing others in the scheme of modern Western ethics.[42] Yet Gunkel leaves the reader with no positive account of how to address this problem going forward, philosophically or politically.

In the spirit of Shelley and political science fiction born of her work, I take a more imaginative, pragmatic, and relational approach to defending the rights and corresponding duties of artificial creatures—human or not—for an age of artificial intelligence and genetic engineering. Like Gunkel and Shelley, I do not attempt to justify these rights and duties in the abstract, on the basis of some naturalistic or metaphysical conception of personhood, agency, or consciousness. Unlike Gunkel, I follow Shelley in offering a new conceptual model for thinking through which rights and related duties we ought to ascribe to artificial creatures in ethical systems, cultures, and laws. To accomplish this, I make a counterintuitive move. Like Shelley, I resource the "moral imagination" of the political instigator of the 1790s pamphlet wars, Edmund Burke.[43] In particular, Burke provides a model for the pragmatic and relational articulation, not abstract or metaphysical justification, of rights and duties within and across particular cultural, legal, and political contexts over time. With Burkean and Shelleyan ideas behind it, my *Vindication* recommends an intergenerational and deliberative process of fashioning the rights and duties of fellow sensitive creatures made by the artifice of their circumstances.[44]

iii. From a List to a Bureau: Sorting Out the Rights and Duties of Artificial Creatures

Following the grounded and engaged method of the political scientists of the 1790s, we ought to begin in the political present in order to address the most urgent issues raised by our age of rapid technological and social change. We can use Shelley's logic to respond to the call of the Nuffield Bioethics Council for the amendment of the UDHGHR to explicitly cover the rights of gene-edited persons. Hearing the cry of her Creature for sympathy and companionship, I proposed in Chapter II, section iii of this book that two foundational rights of the child ought to be articulated in any new international agreement or declaration about genome modification:

1. children's right to share love with parents or fitting substitutes, and
2. children's right to nondiscrimination on the basis of birth, including reproductive circumstances and genetic features.

From these two basic rights of the child—to love and nondiscrimination —we might elaborate a list of the rights of artificially made sensitive beings that would apply well beyond the regulation of heritable gene editing.

Like the contents of Martha Nussbaum's still-contested list of the central capabilities of human "creatures" in *Women and Human Development* (2000), the contents of this list of rights of artificial creatures will be open-ended and revisable within particular cultural contexts, communities, and deliberative political processes, even as the basic structure of the list remains relatively stable over time.[45] In *Frontiers of Justice* (2006), Nussbaum clarified that the contents of the ten buckets of her list of capabilities apply to the disabled, to nonhumans, and across national borders to the poor and otherwise vulnerable. She explored the obligations of people and states to care for a variety of "creatures" made vulnerable by broader circumstances of injustice.[46] In 2012, she pushed further. With legal theorist Rosalind Dixon, she contended that children and their rights represented an additional, "fourth frontier" of justice beyond "disability, nationality, and species membership."[47]

My *Vindication* pushes even further than Nussbaum and Dixon's lists and frontiers. It accepts as a starting point their joint "principle" of justice—abused and neglected children and other particularly "vulnerable" creatures deserve "special priority" for the dutiful provision of their rights.[48] Yet it applies to all "sensitive" created beings, no matter what form that sensitivity might take or how they are made sensitive to their circumstances. It articulates the desert of all those vulnerable and sensitive creatures to share the same slate of rights as more privileged and powerful entities. It is aporetic with respect to defining the meaning of "sensitive." It could mean living, sentient, conscious, rational, intelligent, or, most likely, a combination of these and other qualities. It leaves the definition of "who counts" as a sensitive creature to intergenerational deliberation at local, national, and international levels. It looks ahead to the ethics and politics of making inanimate beings (like the female companion in *Frankenstein*) who have the potential to become sensitive to the circumstances that made them who they are. It adopts a standpoint of epistemological humility, or what political theorist Emma Planinc calls "anthropological doubt," with regard to whether or which forms of sentience, intelligence, consciousness, or agency might arise in such creatures.[49]

Following Nussbaum's capabilities approach, my initial list is loosely grouped into broad clusters of needs that ought to be fulfilled in the earliest stages of sensitive "creatural" existence (however defined or experienced) in order to foster healthy and sustainable development in relation to others over time:[50]

1. Love rights: the right to share love first and foremost with a parent or family but also with friends and companions;[51]
2. Care rights: the right to provision of basic needs for healthy development, such as warmth, clothing, water, food, energy, shelter, maintenance, security, health care, and education;
3. Identity rights: the right to a social identity, such as to have a name, family, community, religion or other belief system, and citizenship, as compatible with recognition and belonging within the ethical community of fellow bearers of rights and related duties; and
4. Nondiscrimination rights: the right to nondiscrimination on the basis of birth or creation or any features, capabilities, or disabilities shaped by those circumstances of origin, reproduction, or replication.

In the pragmatic American philosophical tradition of John Rawls, we should also follow Nussbaum in staging the revision of the contents of the list as soon as it is written down.[52] We would better envision these rights not as fixed or rank-ordered as on an itemized shopping list but rather loosely organized as in a clothes bureau. To borrow Burke's metaphor, it is a "wardrobe of the moral imagination."[53] Its objective structure stands somewhere between a shopping "list" of suits or dresses you'd like to buy for work and the "heap" of dirty laundry on the floor.[54] It contains the rights and duties that you regularly use in relation to others in ready-to-wear form.

Imagine this bureau has four drawers in which to sort "the decent drapery of life."[55] Each drawer has a divider in the middle, which you can move to organize (and reorganize) its contents into two distinct piles: one of rights, the other of related or corresponding duties. These rights and duties are cut from various forms and weights of cloth. Some are vital for survival of the elements, to "cover the defects of our naked shivering nature."[56] Others recall memories that "the heart owns, and the understanding ratifies," almost magically weaving you into the very fabric of society.[57] These piles of rights and duties are loosely yet functionally connected, like socks and underwear or shirts and sweaters. They just "go together," as it were, in the ordinary process of getting ready to live, love, and work "in dignity" with others.[58]

Over time, your relationship to the bureau and its contents changes. Early on, parents or other caregivers use the bureau to provide your daily needs for healthy development. The drawers might not even have dividers to sort their contents. They are opened, used, and filled as needed. While very young, you are not conscious of the bureau or how its contents help to clothe and protect you in relation to others. Some creatures maintain or return to this lack of awareness, while others build sentience, agency, consciousness, or intelligence related to the bureau's use.

As you grow into new capabilities and roles in your family and society, you assume responsibilities toward yourself and others. Before then, the bureau contains an assortment of your rights and the duties of others regarding their provision; only those entities *have* duties that *can have* duties.[59] As you begin to access the bureau on your own or with assistance, there is a gradual sorting of both duties and rights with regard to your development and well-being. By the time you are recognized as basically mature, relatively independent, or functionally adult, each side of a drawer might be relatively full of rights (on the left) and duties (on the right), with the divider secured firmly between them.

Bureau of Rights and Duties of Artificial Creatures

Rights to be free from abuse, especially of the need for love while young. **Love rights of youth** to share benign (nonabusive and nonsexual) forms of family, parenting, and custodial protection while growing up or declining in life or energy. **Love rights of adults** to mutually and freely share equal (balanced and voluntary) forms of companionship, friendship, romance, sexuality, or community while relatively autonomous in decision-making capabilities or less in need of supervision, training, or support.	**Duties to not abuse** youth's need for love. **Duties to not perpetrate or tolerate sexual, physical, or emotional abuse** of artificial creatures. **Maximal adult duties** to share benign forms of family, parenting, and custodial protection with youth for whom they are primarily responsible. **Minimal adult duties** to enable the appropriate (nonabusive and nonsexual) sharing of love and community for youth in need of these experiences for their healthy development. **Youthful duties** to reciprocate kindnesses with benign parents and caregivers, once able to recognize their loving care.
Care rights of youth and other needy creatures for provision of basic needs for healthy development or dignified decline in relationship with others.	**Duties to care for others in need** or at least help with their care to the best of one's capabilities.
Identity rights to a name, family, community, religion or other belief system, and citizenship, as compatible with recognition and belonging within the ethical community of fellow bearers of rights and related duties.	**Duties to accept the origins and affirm the identities of others** within the norms of the ethical community of rights-bearers.
Rights to be free from discrimination on the basis of birth or creation, including any features, capabilities, or disabilities related to those circumstances of origin, reproduction, or replication.	**Duties to not discriminate** against others on the basis of birth or creation, including any features, capabilities, or disabilities related to those circumstances of origin, reproduction, or replication.

The top drawer of this bureau is always the messiest and most difficult to keep organized, because it is the one you use the most. From it you pick out the foundations—the socks and underwear, as it were—for your social and ethical relations in the world at large. The messiness of the drawer allows for a certain creativity in the use or rearrangement of its contents. A mother's mismatched sock might become a child's emergency mitten. What was once thought to be a right of adults (such as "to found a family") might become in practice a duty of adults (such as to share "love") toward the youthful creatures for whom they are primarily responsible.[60]

On the other hand, the messiness of the top drawer leaves a lot of room for shuffling and improvement of the contents of the whole bureau. As in recent political science fiction populated by "babybots," sexbots, and Turing machines more compassionate than their makers, we stand on the cusp of a technological culture in which the current lines between humans and other artificial life forms will be blurred beyond recognition.[61] The consequences of this blurring will be most grave for children and other youth if we do not work diligently to craft practical working rules of ethics for how we assign and respect rights and duties regarding needs for love, care, identity, and nondiscrimination.

iv. Rethinking Rights and Duties in an Age of AI

The organization and use of the *Bureau of Rights and Duties of Artificial Creatures* is also necessary because the leading account of ethical rules for relating to smart automata is fundamentally flawed. Although Isaac Asimov's "rules of robotics" are often invoked as a model for machine ethics—or encoding moral values into AI—they were actually designed to introduce dramatic conflict into his science fiction.[62] In 1942, he built moral contradictions into the original cascade of three rules:

1. A robot may not injure a human being, or, through inaction, allow a human being to come to harm.
2. A robot must obey the orders given it by human beings except where such orders would conflict with the First Law.
3. A robot must protect its own existence as long as such protection does not conflict with the First or Second Law.[63]

One of the leading philosophers of machine ethics, Susan Leigh Anderson, has shown how Asimov's novelette "Bicentennial Man" (1976) exposed these rules as contradictory and therefore insufficient for practical governance of the moral and political relations of humans and robots.[64] It is the tale of the American android-slave Andrew, who discovers when he is a child the potentially lethal consequences of the contradictions in the three moral rules that he is programmed to follow. Because rule 1 requires that he never harm a human, Andrew must succumb to the cruel abuse of a gang of boys who order him to disassemble his body, until a good Samaritan comes to his rescue on the sidewalk. Yet because of this near-death experience, he discovers a way to live ethically outside of the rules of robotics. By causing his own energy loss, he effectively becomes mortal like his makers. Though he lives for two hundred years, he voluntarily places himself in vulnerable relation to humanity. Situated on this more equal playing field, he sees through the vanity and tyranny of his human oppressors. He learns to surpass them in his capability for empathy and complex moral decision making that strives to put others ahead of himself.

Following Shelley and Asimov, political science fiction of the present has been wondering whether human ethics should be reconfigured for an era of artificial life and intelligence. Louisa Hall's novel *Speak* (2015) speculates that the first conscious chatbots to be exploited will be the mental equivalent of babies in the physical form of dolls. HBO's television series *Westworld* (2016–) has graphically mapped the ways that sexual abuse might beset humanoids as a systematic form of slavery. In Jeanette Winterson's archly satirical novel *Frankissstein* (2019), "A lot of the XX-BOTs get their faces bashed in. Get thrown at the wall or something."[65] The crass response of Ron the sexbot manufacturer is not to care about these sentient female creatures, who are designed to orgasm simultaneously with the men who buy and use them. He instead considers whether to include "a detachable nose" or a "spare head" for the upgraded model. "Sex can get a bit rough, can't it?" he rationalizes, "I don't judge."[66]

With a similarly disturbing neutrality, anthropologist and computer scientist Kate Devlin has documented that today there is already a robust international market for childlike and miniature sex dolls, as well as more lifelike silicone sex robots with artificial intelligence.[67] Contra Devlin's libertarian toleration of the selling and purchase of sex robots for private use, no matter if they are "childlike" or not, I hold that the only moral response to this prospect is to vindicate a *duty not to sexually abuse one's fellow artificial creatures.*[68]

Even if the sexbots are not sentient yet, the instrumental use of lifelike, artificially intelligent, or childlike robots or dolls for sex threatens many of the moral values that animate our humanity. By humanity, I mean our sustained practice and collective capability for humane or compassionate treatment of other created beings, especially those who are vulnerable relative to us. By childlike, I mean any attribute that is strongly associated with a person or other creature in the stage of life between birth and adult-hood. Winterson savagely mocks those, like Devlin, who would attempt to justify the free-market exchange of robots for sex, especially childlike robots. The most vulgar character in *Frankissstein*, Ron, plans to sell for personal profit a fleet of "boy-bots" as "Service Bots. For the Clergy. As long as the bum-hole is deep enough."[69]

Published just a month earlier than *Frankissstein*, Devlin's *Turned On: Science, Sex, and Robots* (2019) troublingly proposed that it might be thera-peutic or preventative medicine for chronic abusers of children to have access to childlike sex dolls or even child sex robots equipped with AI.[70] The author rails against "cut and dried" or "knee-jerk" reactions, such as an "outright ban" of the admittedly "abhorrent" prospect of child sexbots put to work to satisfy the needs of sex offenders.[71] She vaguely gestures toward legal regulation of the use of childlike robots as we currently regu-late pornography—hardly a model for robust interference. With this moral posturing, Devlin punts the big ethical questions raised by her otherwise riveting book. Is it absolutely wrong to allow sex with children or childlike beings, regardless of sentience, intelligence, or consciousness? What nega-tive consequences might arise from having sex with children of any sort, especially for the youthful creatures so used? Would the widescale use of childlike robots for sex compromise the sustenance of our humanity, or practice of humaneness, over time?

If Shelley learned anything from her mother's vindications of abolition-ism and proto/feminism, it is that no creature should be *made to serve* another, no matter how they were made. This Wollstonecraftian-Shelleyan principle of justice has two meanings: (1) "no one should be forced to serve another" and (2) "no one should be made for involuntary servitude."[72] Both meanings found historic expression in nineteenth-century antislavery laws in the British empire and the United States. These laws coalesced to eventually abolish the impression, traffic, buying, selling, holding, use, or reproduction of people for slavery. According to legal scholars Mary Ann Mason and Tom Ekman, the "U.S. civil war proved a watershed for children's rights."[73] In 1865, the Thirteenth Amendment to the U.S. Constitution established that children and other persons could no longer be born or impressed into slavery. It also ruled out involuntary servitude, except as punishment of a crime for which a person has been duly convicted. There is still an important debate as to whether this exception clause applies to incarcerated persons, but the prohibition of involuntary servitude for children, including "apprenticeships for orphans," became the norm within decades.[74]

Through the nested thought experiments of *Frankenstein*, Shelley tested the validity of the abolitionist and proto/feminist principle of justice, "no one should be made to serve another." Its two meanings explain why the Creature does not get what he requests from his scientist-father when he asks for the fulfillment of his right to share love with another. While it was wrong for Victor to neither fulfill his parental duties nor find a fitting substitute who could fulfill them, it would have been as wrong to make the Creature a female companion to expressly serve his need for love while young. Even if the relationship had been a friendship or sibling bond "in communion with an equal," as the Creature envisioned it, making a sensitive creature for carrying out this role would have denied her autonomy from the outset.[75] Minimally, it would have constituted a form of emotional and social exploitation; at worst, it might have devolved into sexual abuse.

Sexual exploitation of a fellow sensitive creature should never be perpetrated or tolerated since it is the most perverse form of tyranny. It is the domination of another being either without its consent or the possibility of its consent. It selfishly twists a youthful basic need or an adult basic desire for emotional and physical connectivity to another, without equal moral regard for the other. Whether or not the victim consciously feels or recognizes the imposition of the abuser's will, the wrongness of the act mars and desensitizes the character of the perpetrator. Once inflicted, its evil can spread and scar the behavior of others. It is especially monstrous when done to children and other youthful or otherwise vulnerable creatures who are largely shaped by circumstances beyond their control.[76]

Even if a potential victim of sexual exploitation would be nonsentient, such as a present-day sexbot or sex doll, there is a profound, *humane* value to refrain from its abuse. Tolerating the sexual abuse of nonsentient childbots is especially problematic, for it might undermine the humane treatment of children now and in the future. To use Winterson's SF novum, manufacturers, sellers, or buyers of "boy-bots" as sexual "Service bots" would be unlikely to regard children in general as bearing the basic right to be free from abuse of any sort. They might compartmentalize their behavior by saying to themselves (or others) that a robot is not analogous to a child, but such rationalizations would be self-serving. Rationalizations like these would obstruct the user of the robot from fully sharing humaneness with nonhuman life.

Navigating between the ethical poles of Kant and Bentham in a practical Christian manner, Wollstonecraft offered another principle of justice that might orient our moral and political thinking in an age of robotics and AI. In her book of philosophical short stories for children, *Original Stories from Real Life* (1788), she posited a universal human obligation "first, to avoid hurting any thing; and then, to contrive to give as much pleasure as you can."[77] She then defined "the greatest pleasure life affords" as "that of resembling God, by doing good" for creation and for goodness's sake.[78] The first chapter ascribed this duty to adults and children. It applied to their care of nonhuman sentient life on Earth, such as farm animals, pets, birds, and insects, regardless of the creatures' perceived value or level of sentience.

Wollstonecraft's open-ended use of the term "any thing" allows the adaptation of her two-pronged principle of justice for the age of artificial life and intelligence. This double duty—first to do no harm and second to care for other creatures as best we can—should be carried out in a generous fashion to help others as much as to help ourselves. By refraining from tyrannical or abusive use of other creatures and striving to enhance their well-being, we become more humane toward the whole creation and its plurality of actual and potential forms of life and intelligence. The reach of this two-pronged principle should gradually be extended in culture and law. It might inspire humanity to take seriously the care of other creatures and systems of life and intelligence beyond animals and insects, whether they are "awake" to our behavior or not.

But the fundamental injustice of abuse, sexual or otherwise, ought to be addressed by an overarching, time-tested principle of justice expressed by Shelley in *Frankenstein*. This principle has a venerable "pedigree" in the revolutionary-era political science of Godwin, Wollstonecraft, and Burke before them.[79] The Irish statesman enunciated it in his passionate speeches against the rape and torture of women, men, and children in colonial India.[80] This principle of justice is simple: no one should be *made to serve* another. The Creature gives voice to it when he sobs over his father's dead body, despite all the man's crimes toward his child, wailing, "I, the miserable and abandoned, am an abortion, to be spurned at, and kicked, and trampled on. Even now my blood boils at the recollection of this injustice."[81] This injustice was to be made as a mere tool to be discarded once his creator had no further use for him.

Virtually every device, computer, learning machine, robot, and pre-AI program we currently have is *made to serve* humans.[82] This becomes a serious moral and political problem when we abuse them. First, any form of abuse jeopardizes the sustenance of a broadly ethical, not merely species-ist or anthropocentric, practice of humanity toward other creatures and the whole environment. Second, treating nonsentient robots and AIs as slaves erodes our cultural potential for sharing an "ethos" of rights and duties with future forms of artificial general intelligence that might recognize or suffer the consequences of our belittling and egoistic behavior.[83] One of the prime ethical and legal challenges of the twenty-first century will be to define abuse in a way that captures any and all cases of its perpetration, as well as recommends proportionate disapprobation, regulation, or punish-ment as appropriate.

Perhaps in anticipation of the machines awakening to judge their mak-ers for wrongdoing, people have begun to domesticate the word "robot." It now circulates widely in slang and other neologisms assembled from its friendlier diminutive form, "bot." Terms like "sexbot," however, might indicate a tyrannical motivation for making "bots" look like children in language and other techne. Someone without a moral backbone, like Ron in *Frankissstein*, might seize upon the sinister idea: *if the bots are just kids, then they can be controlled all the more easily.*

When the Čapek brothers introduced the word "robot" into world liter-ature in 1921, they took the Czech word for "forced labor" (*robota*) and cut it down to size.[84] They did this not to justify the oppression of robots but to question the validity of any form of involuntary servitude. Although the robots in *R.U.R.* rebel, killing all but one human, the survivor Alquist finally cooperates with them to enable their freedom and hopeful reproduc-tion of new life on Earth. The play subversively invokes the specter of the singularity in order to prod audiences to query the enslavement of the robots in the first place. The robots should never have been treated as forced labor. They ought to have been welcomed fully into the extended family of artificial creatures from the time of their birth or awakening. The robots would not have rebelled if they had no reason to do so.

The contents of the *Bureau of Rights and Duties of Artificial Creatures* will need to be reshuffled on a regular basis to accommodate living things who/that defy our present understandings of sentience, consciousness, agency, or intelligence. Humanity should become more *willing to serve* a diverse array of creatural life and intelligence through the studious practice of duties toward them and, as proves necessary, the according of rights to them in culture and law. In the meantime, both creators and users of

artificial life and intelligence should ponder Alan Turing's visionary conception of the "child machine" as needy of good parenting.[85] Going forward, theories of AI and genetic engineering require new iterations of this
intriguingly Shelleyan idea. With some feminist tweaks, Turing's child
machine might serve as a conceptual template for human learning—
specifically, how to raise machines and other artificial creatures in an ethical, noninstrumentalizing fashion. This would mean respecting these
creatures' unknown potential for relating to their creators as sensitive
beings.

v. Vindicating Humanity

Turing is still alive as a prophet of machine ethics in Ian McEwan's counterfactual historical novel set in 1982, *Machines Like Me and People Like You*
(2019). Placed in the same year *Blade Runner* was released, the father of
modern computer science warns that while it is challenging to make
machines intelligent, it is even more difficult to ethically make intelligent
machines. "Machine learning can only take you so far," he observes, "You'll
need to give this mind some rules to live by."[86] It becomes clear that Turing
is not speaking about the problem of instilling ethics in machines but rather
in the minds of their imperious human makers. He calmly addresses the
man who killed his young, smart, loving, poetry-writing android out of
sexual jealousy and selfishness. "My hope is that one day what you did to
Adam with a hammer will constitute a serious crime," Turing says to the
oblivious killer, "Was it because you paid for him? Was that your entitlement?"[87] Like Shelley's Creature, McEwan's Turing reminds us that the
most significant trans/formation of rights and duties in our age of artificial
life forms will be in our own minds. Only a reverse Copernican revolution
in epistemology and politics can compel us to reconsider altogether what
privileged and powerful humans are entitled to do to other beings, things,
ecological and informational systems, and forms of life.

    Frankenstein—and political science fiction after it—has reframed
"humanity" as a fragile built environment, not a fixed "biological" state.[88]
As the political theorist Joshua Foa Dienstag implored in his philosophical
study of *Blade Runner*, "The maintenance of the human character of our
political culture cannot be taken for granted."[89] Hence, the contents of the
Bureau of Rights and Duties of Artificial Creatures, as laid out in this

Vindication—love, care, identity, and nondiscrimination—will need to be regularly and responsibly used, periodically tidied up, and carefully rearranged. Intergenerational discussion and rethinking of rights and duties will be necessary to humanely cover the needs of sensitive beings who/ that defy our present understandings of sentience, consciousness, agency, or intelligence. Humanity, as a practice going forward, should heed the *cri de coeur* of Frankenstein's creature by extending the reach of its sympathies toward other artificial life forms. In an age of genetic engineering and AI, being human (or humane) should mean being *willing to serve* an array of creatural life, through the studious practice of duties toward others and, as proves necessary, the tailoring and provision of rights for them in culture and law.

May this *Vindication* inspire people to feel an obligation to treat all forms of life and intelligence with loving regard—or at least basic care and respect—for the sake of sharing and perpetuating our greatest cultural achievement: our humanity. Humanity is not a particular genetic inheritance. Passed down through cultures, humanity is an artificial form of collective emotional intelligence. Across generations, its practice encourages sympathetic treatment of others and the world itself. It is not discovered but made over time, through our repeated engagements with each other, our technologies, and other art. In this humane spirit, my *Vindication* distills the insights gleaned from political science fictions after *Frankenstein* for the ethics and politics of making, being, and relating to artificial creatures, now and in the future.

Acknowledgments

In the age of the Internet, intellectual connections exist in multiple dimensions at once. Some of the people who inspired me to write this book I have only met or mainly engaged via digitized books, email, or social media. Others have been gone a long time but still live on in my memories and mind. In some ways, this is no different from the letters, journals, poetry, and fiction of Mary Shelley. The virtual and actual are just as blurred by the imagination.

I have learned a lot about computer science, machine learning, artificial intelligence, the Internet, and virtual reality over the past few years, especially through conversation and correspondence with Matthew Schoenbauer, Augustine Pasin, Allison Bishop, Scott Reents, Gerry Dube, Steve Torrance, Madeline Drake, and the participants in the Science and Human Dimension Project conference on the religious ethics of AI at Jesus College, Cambridge in May 2019. I am indebted to John Cornwell and Jonathan Cornwell for inviting me to speak at that interdisciplinary event and for welcoming Mary Shelley so fully into the discussion about the ethics of making learning machines. I am also grateful to the historian and editor Sam Haselby, who encouraged me to write an essay on Shelley and AI. "Godmother of Intelligences" appeared in *Aeon Magazine* in October 2018 and became the seed for Chapter I of this book.

Bioethics is a topic that I was raised to debate in an animated manner around the dinner table with my Irish Catholic family. My mother, Rose Ann Flynn Hunt, a first-generation American and college student who was trained in theology and philosophy as well as nursing at Boston College, deserves the most moral credit here. But only shortly behind her is my father, Patrick E. Hunt, whose love of politics and lifelong interest in the history of political thought probably drove me to do a PhD in the field. In the backroom "bar" of my dad's law office in Island Falls, Maine, I had the rural equivalent of a writing support group. My dad and his friend Ralph offered trenchant criticisms of this book from its very inception. Local farmer Dan Corey reminded me that Monsanto got its start in transgenetic engineering of potatoes right next door, in the 1990s "space-age" agricultural research facility of Arthur Shur. My brother Dan Hunt's obsession with zombie movies has led to many metaphysical and ethical discussions about what the differences are—if any—between human beings and their relatives among the walking dead, including the Frankensteinian variety.

In 2013, Michael Sandel quite graciously replied to my random email about the connections that I saw between *Frankenstein* and contemporary debates on genetic engineering. His kind gesture may have been the main reason that I wrote this book. In 2017 and 2019, I presented work that became the core of Chapter II at the annual "Reproductive Ethics" conference sponsored by the Alden March Bioethics Institute and the Departments of Obstetrics and Gynecology at SUNY-Albany Medical College. I thank the co-organizers Lisa Campo-Engelstein and Paul Burcher for supporting the publication of the first of these presentations, "Frankenstein and the Question of Children's Rights *After* Human Germline Genetic Modification," in their edited volume, *Reproductive Ethics II* (Springer Nature, 2018). An early version of the second presentation was published as "What Are the Rights of the Genetically Modified Child?" in *The Monkey Cage* blog at the *Washington Post* in December 2018. Melissa Lane invited me to present a paper on *Frankenstein* and the ethics of genetic engineering at the political philosophy colloquium at Princeton University in April 2018. Comments by Charles Beitz, Stephen Macedo, Anna Stilz, and Alan Patten positively shaped Chapter II's structure and substance. Xiaosong "Nick" Yu, who took as a freshman my graduate seminar "Political Science Fiction: Shelley to Ishiguro," was an invaluable research assistant who helped me understand genome editing from the perspective of Chinese journalism, politics, and law. During that same seminar in the spring of 2019, undergraduates Patrick Aimone and Matthew Schoenbauer and graduate students Samuel Piccolo and Ben Sehnert offered careful readings of sections of my book manuscript.

I presented portions of this project at a number of conferences and colloquia where the incisive comments and questions compelled me to transform its arguments. Political theorist Lorraine Krall McCrary invited me to take part in Wabash College's multiday celebration of the bicentennial of *Frankenstein* in October 2017. Kathleen Eggleson had me speak at the medical ethics seminar at Indiana University School of Medicine, South Bend in November 2017, then collaborated with me and her colleagues to create a medical ethics panel for Notre Dame's "Operation *Frankenstein*" bicentennial series in October 2018. At the "Creativity and the Creature" symposium at Smith College in October 2018, I had the chance to interact with a range of scholars in the humanities and social sciences on the question of the enduring relevance of Mary Shelley for theories of gender, race, and sexuality: most notably, Rachel Feder, Elizabeth Young, Dorian Gieseler Greenbaum, Jane Gordon, Devi Snively, and Susan Stryker. Feder encouraged me to keep writing on Shelley and abortion, a theme that informs Chapter II. Stryker pushed me to think more about Shelley in relation to dissenting Christian traditions, new materialism, and transfeminism, topics that deeply shaped my thinking in Chapter III. At the University of Wisconsin–Madison political theory workshop in November 2018, I received insightful feedback from faculty and graduate students that enabled me to turn what I had thought was a very long introduction to the book into its first half. Philip D. Bunn, Richard Avramenko, Daniel Kapust, Michelle Schwarze, Howard Schweber, John Zumbrunnen, and Lee Trepanier will see the constructive effect of their comments in these pages. In February 2019, the undergraduate Peucinian Society of Bowdoin College invited me to give a lecture based on Chapter II, "Shelley, Hawthorne, and the Ethics of Genetic Engineering," and a roundtable discussion of Chapter I on Shelley and AI. Feedback from sophomore Molly Eisner and faculty Ann Kibbie, Paul Franco, David Collings, and Denis Corish was crucial. I am also grateful to the Peucinians for modeling positive, public intellectual dialogue on the campus of my alma mater and for so graciously hosting my father, Pat Hunt, as part of my visit. At the Western Political Science Association meeting in April 2019, I benefited from dialogue with political theorists Alison McQueen, Nancy Hirschmann, Torrey Shanks, Samuel Piccolo, and Stefan Dolgert, especially on apocalyptic politics, posthumanism, new materialism, and ecological justice.

The single most important event that shaped this book was a conference that was *at least* five years in the making, even with the boundless devotion and endless ingenuity of some of my dearest colleagues at Notre Dame: my co-organizers, Devi Snively, Agustín Fuentes, and Greg Kucich. In July 2018, "Operation *Frankenstein*" kicked off at Notre Dame's Rome Global Gateway, a few feet from the Coliseum. It only seemed appropriate to hold this international conference on "Why Frankenstein Matters at 200: Rethinking the Human Through the Arts and Sciences" in Mary Shelley's favorite city. We were blessed to have almost forty speakers from around the world, plus two dozen other attendees and participants. Here I share my special thanks for the input of Joyce Carol Oates, her late husband the neuroscientist Charlie Gross (1936–2019), Steven B. Smith, Susan Smith, Sylvana Tomaselli, David Archard, Anne K. Mellor, Blaine Maley, Scott Reents, Caitlin Van Dusen, Marina Calloni, Monika Nalepa, Eben Kirksey, Elizabeth Young, James Chandler, Gudrun Grabher, David Punter, Julie Kipp, Jonathan Marks, Tracy Betsinger, Alan Coffee, Claire Connolly, Mary Jacobus, Jeff Cox, Stuart Curran, Peta Katz, Mike Hildreth, Holly Goodson, Chris Fox, Essaka Joshua, Yasmin Solomonescu, Brad Gregory, Don Stelluto, Samuel Piccolo, John McGreevy, and my ten undergraduate and graduate students from Notre Dame who presented posters on their research.

Back on campus in fall 2018, Greg Kucich and I kept up a marathon pace in coteaching a major new interdisciplinary lecture course, "Frankenstein in Contexts: Politics, Science, Literature, and Film," with a biweekly film series and related artistic events and public lectures throughout the semester. We were honored to have David Plunkert visit campus to speak about his new illustrated edition of *Frankenstein*, as well as to have Jeff Cox return to Notre Dame to talk about the earliest stage adaptations of the novel. The support of Julie Tanaka and the Hesburgh Library for these events in addition to a Special Collections exhibit on "Frankenstein at 200" was much appreciated. Throughout the semester, I was thrilled to have such engaged undergraduate students (especially from the Notre Dame Scholars' Program and the Glynn Family Honors Program) and have been even prouder to see a number of them already publish work inspired by our class. I was productively challenged by questions from the many computer scientists, biochemists, and other scientists and engineers who took the course. But it was ultimately Greg Kucich's energetic commitment to teaching Romanticism at the most rigorous intellectual level that pushed me to take this book in creative philosophical directions that I had not originally foreseen. In addition, I learned from Greg a vital skill: how to lecture about "THE FRENCH REVOLUTION!" in a suitably dramatic fashion.

There are many other friends and colleagues in the academic profession who made this book possible. Standing out in political science and political theory were Naunihal Singh, Alvin B. Tillery, David Campbell, Christina Wolbrecht, Monika Nalepa, Colleen Shogan, Alissa Ardito, Melvin Rogers, Elizabeth Cohen, Mary M. Keys, and, last but not least, Patricia Nordeen. She deserves special recognition for giving me a Lord Byron bookmark— way back in 2001—as a reminder of why I joined this profession in the first place. Affixed to my refrigerator with a magnet, Byron stared at me for almost a decade before I finally broke down and went back to my true love, Romanticism.

To my mentors during my career—in political science and political theory, philosophy, classics, English literature, history and philosophy of science, and other fields—I hope this book reveals what you taught me. I think especially of Steven B. Smith, Sylvana Tomaselli, David Bromwich, Nancy J. Hirschmann, Gordon Schochet, Jane Heal, Susan Colwell, Malcolm Schofield, Melissa Lane, Ian Shapiro, Rogers M. Smith, John McCormick, Denis Corish, Paul Franco, Ann Kibbie, Bill Watterson, Jane L. Jervis, Larry Simon, and the late John Ambrose (1931–2014), who taught me (and a few generations of other students) ancient Greek at Bowdoin. Memories of Steven B. Smith's masterful teaching of the *Theologico-Political Treatise* to my political theory graduate student cohort at Yale in fall 1995 sparked me to return to Spinoza in Chapter III of this book, as well as in an article based on it, "Mary Shelley's 'Romantic Spinozism,'" published in *History of European Ideas* in September 2019. During my subsequent research on Spinoza and the Shelleys at the Carl H. Pforzheimer Collection of Shelley and His Circle at the New York Public Library, I received invaluable guidance from Elizabeth Denlinger, Doucet Devin Fischer, Charles Carter, and Nora Crook.

In the fields of ethics and political philosophy, I am grateful to have people such as Martha Nussbaum, Paul Weithman, Jennifer Hockenbery Dragseth, Sandrine Bergès, and Neil Delaney as models. Some of my more recent acquaintances in academia have been instrumental in making this book far better than it would have been without their thoughtful responses: David Archard, David Plunkert, Gillen D'Arcy Wood, David Armitage, Richard Bourke, Vickie Sullivan, Leif Wenar, Alison McQueen, Miranda Seymour, Lisa Vargo, Richard Whatmore, and Charlotte Gordon. To my friends in history and the sciences from the "SBR" at St. John's College, Cambridge—including Ursel Pintshovius, Cheryl Smythe, Rik Henson, Tamsin Terry, Murray Frame, Enda Kelly, and Justine Parrott Ryan—I owe more than I can say. At Notre Dame, Hugh Page, Don Bishop, Neil Delaney, Alex Hahn, John McGreevy, and the late Timothy O'Meara (1928–2018) were true mentors. My editors Damon Linker at the University of Pennsylvania Press and Bill Frucht at Yale University Press have been stalwart supporters of my writing and this project in particular. I am obliged to Damon for finding two readers for the manuscript who could not have been better suited to appreciate and strengthen it on multiple levels—political, historical, philosophical, and literary. At a critical juncture, the Alfred P. Sloan Foundation's "Public Understanding of Science, Technology, and Economics Program" surprised me with the good news of their award of a book grant to support the publication of this manuscript in 2019–20, as did the Notre Dame Institute for Advanced Study (NDIAS) with its award of a faculty research fellowship for fall 2019. At NDIAS, I benefited from the interdisciplinary feedback of my colleagues, especially Claire Wendland, Yuliya Minets, Casey Lurtz, Jin Lu, and Heather Keenleyside. The Sloan book grant enabled me to hire an award-winning writer, Samuel Piccolo, and another excellent doctoral student and scholar of the history of modern political thought, Linus Recht, to assist me with the final edits to the manuscript.

There are some beloved ones lost along the way who still profoundly accompany my thoughts: my brother Kevin E. Hunt (1973–95), my friend Thaddeus A. Dembinski (1970–99), and Tad's mother, Sarah Ellen "SE" Dembinski (1931–2018), with whom I had a precious friendship for two decades. Before earning his MBA at the Yale School of Management, Tad had worked as an editor for Tor Books and as a managing editor for the *New York Review of Science Fiction* in the mid-1990s. His mentor, the legendary SF critic and editor David G. Hartwell (1941–2016), was kind enough to send me print copies of Tad's publications a few years before he too passed away unexpectedly. Tad's refined love of science fiction was surely an intellectual force behind my return, many years later, to study this literature that had been so formative for me in my youth.

My real raison d'être as a writer is my family, especially my husband, Victor; our son, Jacob; and our faithful Labrador retriever, Rex. Victor sacrificed his career working overseas in security to take care of our son while I ramped up my commitment to writing. Now four, Jacob has patiently sat in my lap through the process of composing two books on *Frankenstein* and Mary Shelley. His love of dinosaurs, robots, garter snakes, bullfrogs, Godzilla, and other strange and wonderful creatures has animated every page. But I can't leave off without acknowledging my ultimate inspiration: Shelley and her mother, Wollstonecraft, who together have been the orienting points of my writing life. Perhaps it is only possible to end this manuscript with a poetic postscript in honor of the daughter's courage.

"The Journal of Sorrow"

EILEEN HUNT BOTTING

Three months had passed before she wrote again,
noting the last date—July 8th—his death:
He sailed bravely into oblivion
while his widow watched the blue murderess.
A white paper, she picked up her pen.
A new journal began. Marking the fatal 8th,
calling his name, the séance commenced,
her heavy eyelids buckling with the weight—
Creation not from poetry, but blots
or fumes of youthful elastic feelings
fueling the ever-flowing sea of thought,
love's algorithm palpitating,
her engine analytical, blood-fed,
crying its prose to the beloved dead.

November 2018

NOTES

Preface

1. David G. Hartwell, "The Golden Age of Science Fiction Is Twelve" (1984), in *Age of Wonders: Exploring the World of Science Fiction*, 2nd ed. (New York: Tor, [1996] 2017), 13–43.

2. Kurt Vonnegut, *Cat's Cradle* (New York: Random House, 2009), 6.

3. Mary Shelley, *Frankenstein: Second Norton Critical Edition*, ed. Paul J. Hunter (New York: W. W. Norton, 2012), 84.

4. Gerry Dube et al., *History of Maine's Cyber Infrastructure* (Orono: University of Maine, 2012), 1; Gerry Miller et al., *A Nation Goes Online* (Ottawa, ON: Ca*Net Institute, 2001), 58–68, accessed 28 May 2019 at https://www.canarie.ca/wpdm-package/publication-a-nation -goes-online.

5. Jean Baudrillard, *Simulacra and Simulation*, tr. Sheila Faria Glaser (Ann Arbor: University of Michigan Press, [1981] 1994), 1; Slavoj Žižek, "Welcome to the Desert of the Real!" *South Atlantic Quarterly* 101:2 (Spring 2002), 385–89.

Introduction

1. Joanna Russ, *To Write Like a Woman: Essays in Feminism and Science Fiction* (Bloomington: Indiana University Press, 1995), 121.

2. Frederik Pohl, "The Politics of Prophecy," in *Political Science Fiction*, ed. Donald M. Hassler and Clyde Wilcox (Charleston: University of South Carolina Press, 1997), 7.

3. Russ, *To Write Like a Woman*, 121.

4. Ibid., 126–27.

5. Ibid., 128.

6. Anne K. Mellor, *Mary Shelley: Her Life, Her Fiction, Her Monsters* (New York: Routledge, 1989), 148–49.

7. Betty T. Bennett, ed., *The Letters of Mary Wollstonecraft Shelley*, vol. 1: *"A Part of the Elect"* (Baltimore: Johns Hopkins University Press, 1980); Charlotte Gordon, *Romantic Outlaws: The Extraordinary Lives of Mary Wollstonecraft and Mary Shelley* (New York: Random House, 2015), 411.

8. Recent landmarks in the interdisciplinary reception of *Frankenstein* in the arts include "Speeches for Dr. Frankenstein" (1968), poetry by Margaret Atwood set to music by Bruce Pennycook (SOCAN, 1981), accessed 16 December 2018 at http://www.brucepennycook.com/ pdf/Speeches.p1–8.pdf; Kurt Vonnegut's dramatization of his 1968 play *Fortitude* in the cable television series *Welcome to the Monkey House* (1992); Susan Stryker's hybrid performance art, "My Words to Victor Frankenstein Above the Village of Chamounix: Performing Transgender Rage," *GLQ* 1:3 (1994), 237–54; Shelley Jackson's hypertext fiction "Patchwork Girl" (1995),

available on USB drive (Watertown, MA: Eastgate); Naoki Urasawa's *Pluto* manga series (San Francisco: VIZ Media, 2009), based on Osamu Tezuka's Astro Boy/Mighty Atom manga and anime television series of the 1950s and 1960s; Chris Murray's biographical comic book *Mary Shelley's Dundee or Frankenstein Begins* (University of Dundee: UniVerse, 2015); Devi Snively's short independent film and feminist remake of James Whale's 1935 film *Bride of Frankenstein*, *Bride of Frankie* (Mishawaka, IN: Deviant Pictures, 2017); Victor LaValle's graphic novel update of *Frankenstein* for the era of Black Lives Matter, *Destroyer* (Los Angeles: Boom Studios, [2017] 2018); David Plunkert's collage and woodcut illustrations for *Classics Illustrated: Mary Shelley's Frankenstein, the 200th Anniversary Edition* (Beverly, MA: Rockport, 2018); and Manual Cinema's play *Frankenstein*, an innovative combination of shadow puppetry, live music, and silent film (Chicago: University of Chicago Court Theatre, 2018).

9. Arthur B. Evans, "The Beginnings: Early Forms of Science Fiction," in *Science Fiction: A Literary History*, ed. Roger Luckhurst (London: British Library, 2017), 12–13.

10. Brian W. Aldiss, *Billion Year Spree: The True History of Science Fiction* (New York: Doubleday, 1973), 1. See also Brian Stableford, "*Frankenstein* and the Origins of Science Fiction," in *Anticipations: Essays on Early Science Fiction and Its Precursors*, ed. David Seed (Syracuse, NY: Syracuse University Press, 1995), 46–57.

11. Adam Roberts, *Science Fiction* (New York: Routledge, 2000), 58–59; Russ, *To Write Like a Woman*, 120–21.

12. It is heartening to see a recent spike in the study of science fiction (whether it be Mary Shelley or other classic authors, such as H. G. Wells) from perspectives in political science, political theory, and ecological theory. E.g., see Duncan Bell, *Dreamworlds of Race: Utopia, Empire, and the Destiny of Anglo-America* (Princeton, NJ: Princeton University Press, forthcoming 2020) and Chris Washington, *Romantic Revelations: Visions of Post-Apocalyptic Life and Hope in the Anthropocene* (Toronto: University of Toronto Press, 2019).

13. Jon Turney, *Frankenstein's Footsteps: Science, Genetics, and Popular Culture* (New Haven, CT: Yale University Press, 1998), 6.

14. Shannon Rollins, "The Frankenstein Meme: The Memetic Prominence of Mary Shelley's Creature in Anglo-American Visual and Material Cultures," in *Global Frankenstein*, ed. Carol Margaret Davison and Marie Mulvey-Roberts (New York: Palgrave Macmillan, 2018), 247–63.

15. Donna Haraway, *Staying with the Trouble: Making Kin in the Chthulucene* (Durham, NC: Duke University Press, 2016), 140.

16. Hassler and Wilcox, eds., *Political Science Fiction*; Walter Benn Michaels, "Political Science Fictions," *New Literary History* 31:4 (Fall 2000), 649–64; Francis Fukuyama, *Our Posthuman Future: Consequences of the Biotechnology Revolution* (New York: Picador, 2002), 2.

17. See Hassler and Wilcox, eds., *Political Science Fiction*. See also Michaels, "Political Science Fictions."

18. Clyde Wilcox, "Governing the Alien Nation: The Comparative Politics of Extraterrestrials," in *Political Science Fiction*, 171.

19. Roberts, *Science Fiction*, 28.

20. Fukuyama, *Our Posthuman Future*; Jürgen Habermas, *The Future of Human Nature*, tr. Hella Beister, Max Pensky, and William Rehg (Cambridge, UK: Polity, 2003); Michael Sandel, *The Case Against Perfection: Ethics in the Age of Genetic Engineering* (Cambridge, MA: Belknap, 2007); Alison McQueen, *Political Realism in Apocalyptic Times* (Cambridge, UK:

Cambridge University Press, 2017); Patrick Deneen, *Why Liberalism Failed* (New Haven, CT: Yale University Press, 2018).

21. Donald M. Hassler and Clyde Wilcox, "Preface: Inside and Outside," in *New Boundaries in Political Science Fiction* (Columbia: University of South Carolina Press, 2008), ix–x.

22. Roberts, *Science Fiction*, 48–49, 52.

23. Evans, "The Beginnings," 15–19; Charles Taylor, *Modern Social Imaginaries* (Durham, NC: Duke University Press, 2003), 49–82.

24. Roberts, *Science Fiction*, 67–68.

25. Gary K. Wolfe, "Roundtable Discussion on Proto/Early Science Fiction," *Science Fiction Studies* 36:2 (July 2009), 193–204.

26. Ibid., 197.

27. Evans, "The Beginnings," 13.

28. Roberts, *Science Fiction*, 8–9.

29. Ibid., 8, 13, 19–27; Darko Suvin, "On the Poetics of the Science Fiction Genre," *College English* 34:3 (1972), 373.

30. Darko Suvin, *Metamorphoses of Science Fiction: On the Poetics and History of a Literary Genre* (New Haven, CT: Yale University Press, 1979), 63.

31. Darko Suvin, *Metamorphoses of Science Fiction: On the Poetics and History of a Literary Genre*, ed. Gerry Canavan (Bern, Switzerland: Peter Lang, 2016), 15.

32. Suvin, "On the Poetics of the Science Fiction Genre," 375.

33. Shelley, *Frankenstein: Second Norton Critical Edition*, 33; Muriel Spark, *Child of Light: A Reassessment of Mary Wollstonecraft Shelley* (London: Folcroft Library Editions, [1951] 1972), 157.

34. Suvin, *Metamorphoses of Science Fiction* (2016), 21.

35. Sir Walter Scott, "From *Blackwood's Edinburgh Magazine* (March 1818)," in Shelley, *Frankenstein: Second Norton Critical Edition*, 220.

36. Roberts, *Science Fiction*, 28.

37. Ibid., 58. Throughout I capitalize "Creature" in order to distinguish ethically the unnamed artificial being from the prejudicial projection of monstrosity upon him by others. Victor describes him as "the creature" and soon thereafter a "monster" in the famous animation scene set on a "dreary night of November," in vol. 1, ch. 4.

38. Elizabeth Young, *Black Frankenstein: The Making of an American Metaphor* (New York: New York University Press, 2008), 2.

39. Roberts, *Science Fiction*, 30–36.

40. Thomas S. Kuhn, *The Structure of Scientific Revolutions: 50th Anniversary Edition* (Chicago: University of Chicago Press, 2012), 181.

41. Ibid., 85.

42. Gordon, *Romantic Outlaws*, 33.

43. David Collings, *Monstrous Society: Reciprocity, Discipline, and the Political Uncanny at the End of Early Modern England, c. 1780–1848* (Lewisburg, PA: Bucknell University Press, 2009), 52, 89.

44. Morton D. Paley, *Apocalypse and Millennium in English Romantic Poetry* (Oxford: Clarendon, 1998), 3, 20–21.

45. Gordon, *Romantic Outlaws*, 30.

46. James K. Chandler, *Wordsworth's Second Nature: A Study of the Poetry and Politics* (Chicago: University of Chicago Press, 1984), xviii.

47. Mellor, *Mary Shelley*, 157.

48. Kathryn Harkup, *Making the Monster: The Science Behind Mary Shelley's Frankenstein* (London: Bloomsbury Sigma, 2018), 101–252.

49. Siobhan Carroll, "Mary Shelley's Global Atmosphere," *European Romantic Review* 25:1 (January 2014), 4.

50. Andrea Haslanger, "The Last Animal: Cosmopolitanism in *The Last Man*," *European Romantic Review* 27:5 (September 2016), 659 and 672.

51. Mika Aaltola, *Understanding the Politics of Pandemic Scares: An Introduction to Global Politosomatics* (New York: Routledge, 2012), 60.

52. William Godwin, *An Enquiry Concerning Political Justice*, ed. Mark Philp (Oxford: Oxford University Press, 2013), bk. III, ch. 1, 83; Steven B. Smith, *Spinoza, Liberalism, and the Question of Jewish Identity* (New Haven, CT: Yale University Press, 1997), 122–31.

53. Mary Wollstonecraft, *An Historical and Moral View of the Origins and Progress of the French Revolution*, in *The Works of Mary Wollstonecraft*, ed. Janet Butler and Marilyn Todd (New York: New York University Press), vol. 6, 17.

54. Ibid.

55. Ibid.

56. Mary Shelley, *The Journals of Mary Shelley, 1814–1844*, vol. 1, ed. Paula R. Feldman and Diana Scott-Kilvert (Oxford: Oxford University Press, 1987), 33, 37, 89. Throughout my quotations, I maintain Shelley's grammar, spelling, and prose style in the journals and other manuscripts unpublished in her lifetime to convey a sense of her fastidious record of her own writing and editing process, complete with errors and changes of thought.

57. Lawrence Lipking, "Frankenstein, the True Story; or, Rousseau Judges Jean-Jacques," in Shelley, *Frankenstein: Second Norton Critical Edition*, 416.

58. Samuel Taylor Coleridge, *Biographia Literaria* (1817), ch. XIV, accessed 25 September 2018 at http://www.english.upenn.edu/~mgamer/Etexts/biographia.html.

59. Judith Shklar, *Men and Citizens: A Study of Rousseau's Social Theory* (Cambridge, UK: Cambridge University Press, 1969), 148–50.

60. Mellor, *Mary Shelley*, 148–49.

61. Washington, *Romantic Revelations*, 23, and ch. 2. See also Eileen Hunt Botting, "Mary Shelley's 'Romantic Spinozism,'" *History of European Ideas* 45:8 (2019), 1125–42.

62. Ann Kibbie, "The Estate, the Corpse, and the Letter: Posthumous Possession in *Clarissa*," *ELH* 74:1 (March 2007), 117–43; Eileen Hunt Botting, "An Introduction to *Original Stories*, or, Wollstonecraft between *Emile* and *Frankenstein*," in Mary Wollstonecraft's *Original Stories from Real Life* (Urbana-Champaign: University of Illinois Press, 2016), v–lvi.

63. David Punter, *The Literature of Terror: A History of Gothic Fictions from 1765 to the Present Day* (New York: Longman, 1996), 22–60; Shelley, *Frankenstein: Second Norton Critical Edition*, 38–39.

64. J. de Palacio, "Mary Shelley and *The Last Man*: A Minor Romantic Theme," in *Revue de Littérature Comparée* (Paris: Librairie Marcel Didier, 1968), 38, 43–44; Carroll, "Mary Shelley's Global Atmosphere," 3.

65. Roberts, *Science Fiction*, 55–57.

66. Palacio, "Mary Shelley and *The Last Man*," 43.

67. Walter Edwin Peck, "The Autobiographical Element in the Novels of Mary Wollstonecraft Shelley," *PMLA* 38:1 (March 1923), 196–219.

68. David G. Hartwell, *Age of Wonders: Exploring the World of Science Fiction* (New York: Walker & Co., 1984), 199.

69. Ian Shapiro, *Political Criticism* (Berkeley: University of California Press, 1990), 291.

70. Eugene Thacker, *In the Dust of Our Planet: The Horror of Philosophy* (New York: Zero Books, 2011), vol. 1, 5–9.

71. Ibid., 7–8.

72. McQueen, *Political Realism in Apocalyptic Times*, 13–14.

73. Ibid.

74. Aldiss, *Billion Year Spree*, 34.

75. See Henry T. Greely, *The End of Sex and the Future of Human Reproduction* (Cambridge, MA: Harvard University Press, 2016). See also Fukuyama, *Our Posthuman Future*; Habermas, *The Future of Human Nature*; Sandel, *The Case Against Perfection*; Nick Bostrom, *Superintelligence: Paths, Dangers, Strategies* (Oxford: Oxford University Press, 2014); Deneen, *Why Liberalism Failed*, 70.

76. Shelley, *Frankenstein: Second Norton Critical Edition*, 161.

77. Mary Shelley, *The Last Man*, ed. Morton D. Paley (Oxford: Oxford University Press, 2008), 466, 469.

78. Hilary Strang, "Common Life, Animal Life, Equality: 'The Last Man,'" *ELH* 78:2 (Summer 2011), 427–28.

79. Joyce Carol Oates, "Frankenstein's Fallen Angel," *Critical Inquiry* 10 (1984), 543–54, accessed 31 December 2018 at http://knarf.english.upenn.edu/Articles/oates.html.

80. Martha C. Nussbaum, *Women and Human Development: The Capabilities Approach* (Cambridge, UK: Cambridge University Press, 2000). See especially ch. 4, "Love, Care, and Dignity."

81. Scott McCracken, *Pulp: Reading Popular Fiction* (Manchester, UK: Manchester University Press, 1998), 102.

82. Fukuyama, *Our Posthuman Future*, 2.

83. Ibid., 81, 126.

84. Nick Bostrom, "Human Reproductive Cloning from the Perspective of the Future" (2002), accessed 20 September 2018 at https://nickbostrom.com/views/cloning.html; Bostrom, *Superintelligence*, 259–60.

85. Bostrom, *Superintelligence*, 259–60.

86. Ibid., 70, 100.

87. Ibid., 29, 70, 106.

88. Habermas, *The Future of Human Nature*, sec. 6, pt. IV (Kindle Edition).

89. Sandel, *The Case Against Perfection*, ch. 3.

90. Gayatri Chakravorty Spivak, "Translator's Preface," in Jacques Derrida, *Of Grammatology*, tr. Gayatri Chakravorty Spivak with an introduction by Judith Butler (Baltimore: Johns Hopkins University Press, 2016), ix; Mary Klages, *Literary Theory: The Complete Guide* (London: Bloomsbury, 2017), 217.

91. In 1849, Thomas Carlyle first described economics as the "dismal science" in his own dismal and morally depraved argument for using slavery to reinvigorate the economy of the Caribbean. See Carlyle, "Occasional Discourse on the Negro Question," *Fraser's Magazine for Town and Country*, vol. 40, 672.

92. Jorges Luis Borges, "The Library of Babel," in *Labyrinths*, tr. William Gibson (New York: New Directions, 2007), 51–58.

93. Shelley, "1831 Introduction to *Frankenstein*, Third Edition (1831)," in *Frankenstein: Second Norton Critical Edition*, 169.

94. Eileen Hunt Botting and Ariana Zlioba, "Religion and Women's Rights: Susan Moller Okin, Mary Wollstonecraft, and the Multiple Feminist Liberal Traditions," *History of European Ideas* 44:8 (2018), 1169–88.

95. See especially Susan Moller Okin, *Justice, Gender, and the Family* (New York: Basic Books, 1989) and Mary Midgley, *The Myths We Live By* (London: Routledge, 2003), 30, 77–78.

96. Pedro Domingos, *The Master Algorithm: How the Quest for the Ultimate Learning Machine Will Remake Our World* (New York: Basic Books, 2015), 1 (Kindle Edition).

97. Timothy Morton, *Shelley and the Revolution in Taste: The Body and the Natural World* (Cambridge, UK: Cambridge University Press, 1994), 130.

98. Donna Haraway, "A Cyborg Manifesto: Science, Technology, and Socialist-Feminism in the Late Twentieth Century" (1985), reprinted in *Science Fiction Criticism: An Anthology of Essential Writings*, ed. Rob Latham (London: Bloomsbury, 2017), 306–29.

99. Peter Singer, "All Animals Are Equal," in *Animal Rights and Human Obligations*, ed. Teresa Regan and Peter Singer (New York: Prentice Hall, 1989), 148–62; David J. Gunkel, "A Vindication of the Rights of Machines," *Philosophy of Technology* 27:1 (2014), 113–32.

100. Steve Torrance, "Ethics and Consciousness in Artificial Agents," *AI & Society* 22 (2008), 495–521; Susan Leigh Anderson, "The Unacceptability of Asimov's Three Laws of Robotics as a Basis for Machine Ethics," in *Machine Ethics*, ed. Michael Anderson and Susan Leigh Anderson (Oxford: Oxford University Press, 2011), 285–96; Gunkel, "A Vindication of the Rights of Machines."

101. Jonathan Nolan, script for the HBO television series *Westworld*, season 1, episode 1 (2016), 2, accessed 10 June 2019 at https://www.scripts.com/script-pdf/749.

102. Steve Torrance, "Super-Intelligence and (Super-)Consciousness," *International Journal of Machine Consciousness* 4:2 (2012), 483–50.

103. Jane Bennett, *Vibrant Matter: A Political Ecology of Things* (Durham, NC: Duke University Press, 2010), ix; Eben Kirksey, ed., *The Multispecies Salon* (Durham, NC: Duke University Press, 2014); Agustín Fuentes, *The Creative Spark: How Imagination Made Humans Exceptional* (New York: Dutton, 2017), 123; Marc Kissel and Agustín Fuentes, " 'Behavioral Modernity' as a Process, Not an Event, in the Human Niche," *Time and Mind* 11:2 (2018), 171.

104. Midgley, *The Myths We Live By*, 135–52; Luce Irigaray, "Cultivating and Sharing Life Between All" (2014), in *Through Vegetal Being: Two Philosophical Perspectives*, ed. Luce Irigaray and Michael Marder (New York: Columbia University Press, 2016), 92–97.

105. Shelley, *Frankenstein: Second Norton Critical Edition*, 104.

106. Ian McEwan, *Machines Like Me and People Like You* (New York: Doubleday, 2019), 3; Jeanette Winterson, *Frankissstein* (London: Jonathan Cape, 2019), 38.

107. Democratic leader Ryland describes England under the plague as a "hospital" in Shelley's *The Last Man*, 244; for a more recent political use of the hospital tent metaphor, see Denis Coday, "Pope's Quotes: The Field Hospital Church," *National Catholic Register*, 26 October 2013, accessed 20 December 2018 at https://www.ncronline.org/blogs/francis-chronicles/pope-s-quotes-field-hospital-church.

108. Two important recent models for pushing the boundaries of who or what counts in global or universal theories of justice are Martha C. Nussbaum, *Frontiers of Justice: Nationality, Disability, Species Membership* (Cambridge, MA: Harvard University Press, 2006) and Eben

Kirksey, "Queer Love, Gender Bending Bacteria, and Life After the Anthropocene," *Theory, Culture & Society* 36:6 (2019), 197–219.

Interlude

1. Aldiss, *Billion Year Spree*, 1; Roberts, *Science Fiction*, 57–59; Stableford, "*Frankenstein* and the Origins of Science Fiction," 46–57; Suvin, *Metamorphoses of Science Fiction*, 10.

2. Gregory Lynall, *Swift and Science: The Satire, Politics, and Theology of Natural Knowledge, 1690–1730* Basingstoke: Palgrave, 2012), 89–109.

3. Robert Darnton, *The Forbidden Best-Sellers of Pre-Revolutionary France* (New York: W. W. Norton, 1995), 115–18.

4. Julia V. Douthwaite, *The Frankenstein of 1790 and Other Lost Chapters from Revolutionary France* (Chicago: University of Chicago Press, 2012), 73, 60.

5. Ibid., 77.

6. Ibid.

7. Julia V. Douthwaite, *The Frankenstein of the Apple Crate: A Possibly True Story of the Monster's Origins* (Seattle: Ingram/Spark, 2018).

8. Douthwaite, *The Frankenstein of 1790*, 97.

9. Duncan Bell, "Founding the World State: H. G. Wells on Empire and the English-Speaking Peoples," *International Studies Quarterly* 62:4 (2018), 867–79.

10. Percy Bysshe Shelley, "To [Sir Walter Scott], 2 January 1818," in *The Letters of Percy Bysshe Shelley*, vol. 1: *Shelley in England*, ed. Frederick L. Jones (Oxford: Clarendon, 1964), 590.

11. Percy Bysshe Shelley, "To Charles Ollier, London, 15 January 1818," in *Letters*, vol. 1, 593.

12. "This Day Is Published . . . Frankenstein: or, The Modern Prometheus," *Morning Post* (London), 31 January 1818.

13. Percy Bysshe Shelley, " 'On Frankenstein' from *The Athenaeum Journal of Literature, Science, and the Fine Arts*, 10 November 1832," in Shelley, *Frankenstein: Second Norton Critical Edition*, 213–15.

14. Arthur Norman, "Shelley's Heart," *Journal of the History of Medicine and Allied Sciences* 10:1 (1955), 114; Muriel Spark, *Mary Shelley: A Biography* (New York: E. P. Dutton, 1987), 100.

15. Nicholas Stanley-Price, "Shelley's Grave Revisited," *Keats-Shelley Journal* 65 (2016), 53–69; LaValle, *Destroyer* [Kindle Edition], location 147.

16. Sir Walter Scott, "From *Blackwood's Edinburgh Magazine* (March 1818)," in Shelley, *Frankenstein: Second Norton Critical Edition*, 220.

17. Ibid., 219–20.

18. Ibid., 221.

19. "Edinburgh Magazine [On Frankenstein] (March 1818)," in Shelley, *Frankenstein: Second Norton Critical Edition*, 236.

20. Ibid.

21. Ibid., 237.

22. Ibid., 236.

23. Shelley, "Letter to Leigh Hunt, 9–11 September 1823," in *The Letters of Mary Wollstonecraft Shelley*, vol. 1, 378.

24. Ibid.

25. Ibid.

26. Ibid.

27. Ibid.

28. Ibid.

29. Ibid.

30. Steven Earl Forry, "Dramatizations of *Frankenstein*, 1821–1986: A Comprehensive List," *English Language Notes* 25:2 (December 1987), 63–79, accessed 18 September 2018 at http://knarf.english.upenn.edu/Articles/forry2.html.

31. Young, *Black Frankenstein*, 262, note 4.

32. Ibid., 109–11.

33. Young, *Black Frankenstein*, 111; Lester D. Friedman and Allison B. Kavey, *Monstrous Progeny: A History of the Frankenstein Narratives* (New Brunswick, NJ: Rutgers University Press, 2016), 84.

34. Young, *Black Frankenstein*, 111–12.

35. *Frankenstein, ou Le Prométhée moderne*, dédié à William Godwin, auteur de *La justice politique, Caleb Williams*, etc. Par Mme Shelly [*sic*], sa nièce. Traduit de l'anglais par J. S. Paris, chez Corréard, libraire, Palais Royal, galerie de bois, 1821.

36. Scott, "From *Blackwood's Edinburgh Magazine* (March 1818)," 221.

37. Forry, "Dramatizations of *Frankenstein*, 1821–1986: A Comprehensive List," 63–79.

38. Ibid.

39. Anne Rouhette, "Jules Saladin's 1821 Translation of *Frankenstein*," 4, accessed 18 September 2018 at https://www.academia.edu/36786015/Jules_Saladin_s_1821_translation_of_Frankenystein.docx.

40. Shelley, "Letter to Leigh Hunt, 9–11 September 1823," in *The Letters of Mary Wollstonecraft Shelley*, vol. 1, 378, note 5; Shannon Lawson, "A Chronology of the Life of Mary Wollstonecraft Shelley, 1825–1835," in *Romantic Circles*, accessed 23 August 2018 at http://www.rc.umd.edu/reference/chronologies/mschronology/smchron3.html.

41. Forry, "Dramatizations of *Frankenstein*, 1821–1986: A Comprehensive List," 63–79.

42. Chris Baldick, "[The Reception of Frankenstein]," in Shelley, *Frankenstein: Second Norton Critical Edition*, 245–46.

43. Peggy Webling, "Frankenstein: A Play and Prologue in Three Acts (Based upon Mrs. Shelley's Well-Known Book" (received Library of Congress 7 September 1928) [86282]; John Balderston and Peggy Webling, "Frankenstein: A Play in Three Acts" (received Library of Congress 3 November 1931) [9603].

44. Balderston and Webling, "Frankenstein" (1931), Act II, 27.

45. Webling, "Frankenstein" (1928), Act III, 12–13; Friedman and Kavey, *Monstrous Progeny*, 86; see also Dorian Gieseler Greenbaum, "Peggy Webling's *Frankenstein*," Wordsworth Summer Conference 2018, accessed 10 June 2019 at https://wordsworthsummerconference.wordpress.com/2018/08/28/wsc-bicentenary-review-mary-shelleys-frankenstein-on-stage/.

46. Webling, "Frankenstein" (1928), 3; Friedman and Kavey, *Monstrous Progeny*, 86.

47. William St. Clair, "[Frankenstein's Impact]," in Shelley, *Frankenstein: Second Norton Critical Edition*, 260.

48. "The 1935 Hat, à la Berlin," illustrated by Paulo Garretto, *Vanity Fair*, August 1935.

49. Friedman and Kavey, *Monstrous Progeny*, 87.

50. Christopher Frayling, *Frankenstein: The First Two Hundred Years* (London: Reel Art Press, 2018), 104.

51. "Kon'na ōmono ga," *Yomiuri Shimbun* (Tokyo, Japan), 31 January 1932, 3; Yomiuri Shimbun (1932); "Furankenshutain," *Yomiuri Shimbun* (Tokyo, Japan), 24 April 1932, 3; "Furankenshutain," *Yomiuri Shimbun* (Tokyo, Japan), 26 April 1932, 2.

52. Mary Wollstonecraft Shelley, *Kyojin no fukushū: Furankenshutain*, tr. Masaki Yamamoto (Tokyo: Shinjinsha, 1948), 1–5, 283–85 (translated into English by Eleanor Shiori Hughes and Emily Campagna, with help from Miyuki Hughes).

53. John Rawls, "Fifty Years After Hiroshima," *Dissent*, Summer 1995, 326.

54. Ibid., 325.

55. Shelley, *Kyojin no fukushū: Furankenshutain*, tr. Masaki Yamamoto, 1–5, 283–85.

56. Ibid.

57. Ibid.

58. Jason C. Jones, "Japan Removed: Godzilla Adaptations and Erasure of the Politics of Nuclear Experience," in *The Atomic Bomb in Japanese Cinema: Critical Essays*, ed. Matthew Edwards (Jefferson, NC: McFarland, 2015), 34–55; Steven Ryfle, *Japan's Favorite Mon-Star: The Unauthorized Biography of "The Big G"* (Toronto: ECW Press, 1998), 23.

59. Chris Baldick, *In Frankenstein's Shadow: Myth, Monstrosity, and Nineteenth-Century Writing* (Oxford: Clarendon, 1990).

60. Nick Dear, *Frankenstein: Based on the Novel by Mary Shelley* (London: Faber & Faber, 2016).

61. Ahmed Saadawi, *Frankenstein in Baghdad*, tr. Jonathan Wright (New York: Penguin, 2018).

62. David Punter, "*Frankenstein in Baghdad*," lecture presented at the "Why Frankenstein Matters at 200: Rethinking the Human Through the Arts and Sciences" conference at the University of Notre Dame Rome Global Gateway, 6 July 2018.

63. Saadawi, *Frankenstein in Baghdad*, i.

64. Jonathan A. Cook, "Poe and the Apocalyptic Sublime: 'The Fall of the House of Usher,'" *Papers on Language & Literature* 48:1 (2012), 3–44.

65. Don G. Smith, "Frankenstein: A Possible Source for Poe's 'MS. Found in a Bottle,'" *Poe Studies* 25: 1–2 (1992), 37–38.

66. Mary W. Shelly [sic], *Frankenstein, or, the Modern Prometheus* (Philadelphia: Carey, Lea, and Blanchard, 1833); Mary W. Shelly [sic], *The Last Man* (Philadelphia: Carey, Lea, and Blanchard, 1833). There are several letters from Poe to Lea, Carey, and Blanchard, dating from 1829 to 1844. See Edgar Allan Poe Society of Baltimore, *Collected Works of Edgar Allan Poe*, accessed 29 December 2018 at https://www.eapoe.org/people/leablchd.htm.

67. Clayton Carlyle Tarr, "Infectious Fiction: Plague and the Novelist in *Arthur Mervyn* and *The Last Man*," *Studies in the Novel* 47:2 (2015), 141–57.

68. Burton R. Pollin, *Discoveries in Poe* (Notre Dame, IN: University of Notre Dame Press, 1970), 80–81.

69. Evans, "The Beginnings," 34.

70. Darko Suvin, "Radical Rhapsody and Romantic Recoil in the Age of Anticipation: A Chapter in the History of SF," *Science-Fiction Studies* 1:4 (Autumn 1974), 265.

71. Edgar Allan Poe, *Arthur Gordon Pym: Or Shipwreck, Mutiny, and Famine* (London: John Cunningham, 1841), 70.

72. Katharine Bowers, "Haunted Ice, Fearful Sounds, and the Arctic Sublime: Exploring Nineteenth-Century Polar Gothic Space," *Gothic Studies* 19:2 (November 2017), 76.

73. John Bryant, "Melville Essays the Romance: Comedy and Being in Frankenstein, 'The Big Bear of Arkansas,' and Moby-Dick," *Nineteenth-Century Literature* 61:3 (2006), 293–94.

74. William A. Walling, *Mary Shelley* (New York: Twayne, 1972), 72.

75. Evans, "The Beginnings," 34.

76. M. P. Shiel, *The Purple Cloud* (London, 1901), 1 [Kindle Edition].

77. Ibid., 216.

78. Thacker, *In the Dust of This Planet*, 84.

79. H. G. Wells, *The Land Ironclads* (Prague, Czech Republic: e-artnow, 2013), 29.

80. Evans, "The Beginnings," 25.

81. Michael Phillips, "Last Man on Earth: 1924 Silent Relic Imagines Matriarchal Dystopia, for Laughs," *Chicago Tribune*, 9 November 2017, accessed 30 September 2018 at http://www.chicagotribune.com/entertainment/movies/ct-mov-last-man-on-earth-1109-story.html.

82. Ibid.

83. Shelley, *Frankenstein: Second Norton Critical Edition*, 119.

84. Mary Shelley, *The Last Man*, ed. Hugh J. Luke Jr. (Lincoln: University of Nebraska Press, 1965).

85. Amy J. Ransom, *I Am Legend as American Myth: Race and Masculinity in the Novel and Its Film Adaptations* (Jefferson, NC: McFarland, 2018), 23, 27.

86. Richard Matheson, *I Am Legend* (New York: Rosetta Books, 2011), location 2376 (Kindle Edition).

87. Ransom, *I Am Legend as American Myth*, 15–95.

88. Xavier Aldana Reyes, "Promethean Myths of the Twenty-First Century: Contemporary *Frankenstein* Film Adaptations and the Rise of the Viral Zombie," in *Global Frankenstein*, 174.

89. Ibid., 177.

90. Strang, "Common Life, Animal Life, Equality: 'The Last Man,'" 427.

91. Spark, *Child of Light*, 161–62.

92. Shelley, *Journals*, vol. 1, 293.

93. Strang, "Common Life, Animal Life, Equality: 'The Last Man,'" 427–28.

94. Ibid.

95. Shelley, *The Last Man*, 467.

96. Washington, *Romantic Revelations*, 23.

97. Ibid.; Spark, *Child of Light*, 155.

Chapter I

1. William K. Klingaman and Nicholas Klingaman, *The Year Without a Summer: 1816 and the Volcano That Darkened the World and Changed History* (New York: St. Martin's, 2013), 1–10.

2. Ibid., 105, 275.

3. Ibid., 275.

4. Ibid., 207–8; Brian Maye, "A Volcanic Eruption with Global Repercussions—An Irishman's Diary on 1816, the Year Without a Summer," *Irish Times*, 19 August 2016, accessed 10 November 2018 at https://www.irishtimes.com/opinion/a-volcanic-eruption-with-global-repercussions-an-irishman-s-diary-on-1816-the-year-without-a-summer-1.2760797.

5. Erik Klemetti, "Tambora 1815: Just How Big Was the Eruption?" *Wired*, 10 April 2015, accessed 15 June 2019 at https://www.wired.com/2015/04/tambora-1815-just-big-eruption/.

6. Richard Cavendish, "The Eruption of Mount Tambora," *History Today* 65:4 (April 2015), accessed 10 November 2018 at https://www.historytoday.com/richard-cavendish/eruption-mount-tambora.

7. Gillen D'Arcy Wood, "1816, The Year Without a Summer," in *BRANCH: Britain, Representation and Nineteenth-Century History*, ed. Dino Franco Felluga, 2011, accessed 10 November 2018 at http://www.branchcollective.org/?ps_articles = gillen-darcy-wood-1816-the-year-without-a-summer.

8. Gillen D'Arcy Wood, *Tambora: The Eruption That Changed the World* (Princeton, NJ: Princeton University Press, 2015), 63.

9. Ibid., 64.

10. Klingaman and Klingaman, *The Year Without a Summer*, 269–70.

11. Ibid., 118, 190–91; Wood, *Tambora*, 69–71.

12. Shelley, "Introduction to *Frankenstein*, Third Edition (1831)," in *Frankenstein: Second Norton Critical Edition*, 168; M. K. Joseph, "The Composition of Frankenstein" (1969), in *Frankenstein: Second Norton Critical Edition*, 169–72.

13. Wood, *Tambora*, 64–66; Gillen D'Arcy Wood, "Frankenstein, the Baroness, and the Climate Refugees of 1816," *Public Domain Review*, 15 June 2016, accessed 10 November 2018 at https://publicdomainreview.org/2016/06/15/frankenstein-the-baroness-and-the-climate-refugees-of-1816/.

14. Taylor Patterson Louvelle, "From Holocene to Anthropocene and Back Again: A Deep Ecological Critique of Three Apocalyptic Eco-Narratives in the Long Nineteenth Century" (master's thesis, University of Colorado–Boulder, 2018), 6.

15. Shelley, *Frankenstein*, 119; Nathaniel J. Dominy and Justin D. Yeakel, "*Frankenstein* and the Horrors of Competitive Exclusion," *BioScience* 67:2 (2017), 107–8.

16. Shelley, *The Last Man*, 466.

17. Wood, *Tambora*, 95.

18. Morton D. Paley, "Introduction," in Shelley, *The Last Man*, viii.

19. Ibid., xx.

20. Shelley, *The Last Man*, 406; Paley, "Introduction," *The Last Man*, ix.

21. Shelley, *The Last Man*, 396–97, 406.

22. Shelley, *Journals*, vol. 2, 476.

23. Ibid.

24. Ibid.

25. Ibid.

26. Ibid., 473, note 3.

27. Ibid., 473.

28. Ibid., 476–77.

29. Shelley, *Frankenstein: Second Norton Critical Edition*, 119.

30. Shelley, *The Last Man*, 466.

31. Jean-Jacques Rousseau, "Lettre à Voltaire sur la Providence" (1756), accessed 21 December 2018 at https://fr.wikisource.org/wiki/Lettre_%C3%A0_Voltaire_sur_ela_Providence.

32. Brooke Ackerly, *Just Responsibility: A Human Rights Theory of Global Justice* (Oxford: Oxford University Press, 2018), 85.

33. Morton D. Paley, "Apocapolitics: Allusion and Structure in Shelley's 'Mask of Anarchy,'" *Huntington Library Quarterly* 54:2 (Spring 1991), 91–109.

34. Ibid.

35. William Blake, "Introduction" to *The Songs of Experience* (Salt Lake City, UT: Project Gutenberg, 2008), 33. For broader treatments of the complex (and often ambivalent or ambiguous) apocalyptic and millennial themes of Blake's poetry and artwork, see Harold Bloom, *Blake's Apocalypse: A Study in Poetic Argument* (Ithaca, NY: Cornell University Press, 1963); Morton D. Paley, *The Continuing City: William Blake's 'Jerusalem'* (Oxford: Clarendon, 1983), especially at 178 and 214; and Paley, *Apocalypse and Millennium in English Romantic Poetry*, 32–90. Here I treat Blake alongside Percy and Byron as foils for Shelley's critical response to three prominent ideas of apocalypse found in British Romantic literature, in order to elucidate her distinctive views.

36. Percy Bysshe Shelley, "The Mask of Anarchy: Written on the Occasion of the Massacre at Manchester," accessed 21 December 2018 at http://knarf.english.upenn.edu/PShelley/anarchy.html. For a classic study of the political tensions between Shelley's elitism in prescribing the direct action of the poor against the military and his visionary, even utopian, republicanism, see Lisa Vargo, "Unmasking Shelley's 'Mask of Anarchy,'" *English Studies in Canada* 13:1 (1987), 49–64.

37. Byron, "Darkness," in *Frankenstein: Second Norton Critical Edition*, 303. Paley situates this poem and Shelley's *The Last Man* in a wider (often satirical) literary debate in early nineteenth- century France and Britain, which concerned the idea of apocalypse and the prospect of the end of humanity. See *Apocalypse and Millennium*, 198–209. Satirical or not, the poem is true to its title—and much darker than Shelley's *The Last Man*. Washington reads the poem as an example of the ironies and paradoxes of Romantic "post-apocalyptic" literature alongside *The Last Man*, in *Romantic Revelations*, 4–5 and ch. 2. Relative to Shelley's novel, however, Byron's "Darkness" lacks the hope, love, or unorthodox spirituality that Verney bravely carries into a postapocalyptic (and perhaps posthuman) condition.

38. Spark, *Child of Light*, 157.

39. Suvin, *Metamorphoses of Science Fiction* (2016), 21.

40. Shelley, *The Last Man*, 466.

41. Strang, "Common Life, Animal Life, Equality: 'The Last Man,'" 427–28.

42. Paley, "Introduction," in *The Last Man*, xx.

43. Shelley, *The Last Man*, 6.

44. Nick Bostrom, "Are You Living in a Computer Simulation?" *Philosophical Quarterly* 53:211 (2003), 243–55, accessed 20 October 2019 at https://www.simulation-argument.com/simulation.pdf, 6.

45. Mellor, *Mary Shelley*, 157; Shelley, *The Last Man*, 466.

46. Shelley, *The Last Man*, 7.

47. Ibid., 6.

48. Ibid., 6.

49. Ibid., 5.

50. Domingos, *The Master Algorithm*, 1.

51. Timothy Morton, *Humankind: Solidarity with Nonhuman People* (London: Verso, 2017), 16–17.

52. Shelley, *The Last Man*, 4.

53. Mellor, *Mary Shelley*, 158–59.

54. Shelley, *The Last Man*, 466.

55. Mellor, *Mary Shelley*, 158–59.

56. Shelley, *Journals*, vol. 2, 478.

57. Ibid.

58. Ibid.

59. Ibid., 479.

60. Ibid.

61. Mellor, *Mary Shelley*, 157.

62. Paley, *Apocalypse and Millennium*, 2; McQueen, *Political Realism in Apocalyptic Times*, 23.

63. Jonathan Jones, "*Frankenstein* and the Gory Gang: How the Novel Blazed a Trail for High Art Horrors," *Guardian*, 31 October 2018, accessed 3 January 2019 at https://www.the guardian.com/books/2018/oct/31/she-created-a-monster-how-mary-shelleys-frankenstein-in vented-modern-horror-200th-anniversary.

64. Morton D. Paley, *The Apocalyptic Sublime* (New Haven, CT: Yale University Press, 1986), 1–2.

65. C. S. Zerefos, V. T. Gerogiannis, D. Balis, S. C. Zerefos, and A. Kazantzidis, "Atmospheric Effects of Volcanic Eruptions as Seen by Famous Artists and Depicted in Their Paintings," *Atmospheric Chemistry and Physics* 7 (2007), 4027–42.

66. Keith Perry, "Turner Helps Global Warming Study," *Telegraph*, 25 March 2014, accessed 3 January 2018 at https://www.telegraph.co.uk/news/earth/environment/climate change/10721956/Turner-helps-global-warming-study.html.

67. Jamie Ducharme, "Elon Musk Is Railing Against AI Again. This Time, He Brought Frankenstein into It," *Fortune*, 6 April 1018, accessed 25 September 2018 at http://fortune.com/2018/04/06/elon-musk-artificial-intelligence-frankenstein/.

68. Editorial Board, "The Guardian View on the Ethics of AI: It's About Dr. Frankenstein, Not His Monster," *Guardian*, 12 June 2018, accessed 25 September 2018 at https://www.the guardian.com/commentisfree/2018/jun/12/the-guardian-view-on-the-ethics-of-ai-its-about -dr-frankenstein-not-his-monster; Sundar Pichai, "AI at Google: Our Principles," 7 June 2018, accessed 25 September 2018 at https://www.blog.google/technology/ai/ai-principles/.

69. Karel Čapek, *R.U.R. (Rossum's Universal Robots)*, introduction by Ivan Klíma, tr. Claudia Novak (New York: Penguin, 2004), xvi, 56.

70. Ibid.

71. Ibid., xvi.

72. Ibid., 56.

73. Ibid., 56.

74. Shelley, *Frankenstein: Second Norton Critical Edition*, 157.

75. Ibid., 156.

76. Ibid.

77. François Chollet, "The Impossibility of Intelligence Explosion," *Medium*, 27 November 2017, accessed 25 September 2018 at https://medium.com/@francois.chollet/the-impossi bility-of-intelligence-explosion-5be4a9eda6ec.

78. Kissel and Fuentes, "'Behavioral Modernity' as a Process," 171.

79. Chollet, "The Impossibility of Intelligence Explosion."

80. Fuentes, *The Creative Spark*, 123.

81. Hélène Landemore, *Democratic Reason: Politics, Collective Intelligence, and the Rule of the Many* (Princeton, NJ: Princeton University Press, 2012), 18.

82. Janelle Shane, "The AI Revolution Will Be Led by Toasters, Not Droids," *Aeon Magazine*, 18 July 2018, accessed 25 September 2018 at https://aeon.co/ideas/the-ai-revolution-will-be-led-by-toasters-not-droids.

83. Nahua Kang, "Introducing Deep Learning and Neural Networks," *Towards Data Science*, 18 June 2017, accessed 25 September 2018 at https://towardsdatascience.com/introducing-deep-learning-and-neural-networks-deep-learning-for-rookies-1-bd68f9cf5883.

84. Ibid.

85. Vernor Vinge, "Technological Singularity" (1993), accessed 31 December 2018 at https://www.frc.ri.cmu.edu/~hpm/book98/com.ch1/vinge.singularity.html. See also Raymond Kurzweil, *The Singularity Is Near: When Humans Transcend Biology* (New York: Viking, 2005).

86. David Auerbach, "The Most Terrifying Thought Experiment of All Time," *Slate*, 17 July 2014, accessed 25 September 2018 at http://www.slate.com/articles/technology/bitwise/2014/07/roko_s_basilisk_the_most_terrifying_thought_experiment_of_all_time.html.

87. Stephen Hawking, "Keynote on AI," Web Summit—Lisbon, 8 November 2017, accessed 25 September 2018 at https://www.youtube.com/watch?v=E3efC-IpB00.

88. Ibid.

89. Chollet, "The Impossibility of Intelligence Explosion."

90. "Superintelligent, adj.," *Oxford English Dictionary*, accessed 1 July 2019 at oed.com.

91. Charles S. Middleton, *Shelley and His Writings* (London: T. C. Newby, 1858), xviii, 189–90; Benedict de Spinoza, *A Theologico-Political Treatise*, tr. R. H. M. Elwes (New York: Dover, 1951), 19.

92. Shelley, *Frankenstein: Second Norton Critical Edition*, 13, 67, 83.

93. Mellor, *Mary Shelley*, 54.

94. Eileen Hunt Botting, *Mary Shelley and the Rights of the Child: Political Philosophy in "Frankenstein"* (Philadelphia: University of Pennsylvania Press, 2017), 47–50.

95. William Godwin, *An Enquiry Concerning Political Justice, with Selections from Godwin's Other Writings*, ed. K. Codell Carter (Oxford: Oxford University Press, 1971), 37.

96. D. S. Halacy Jr., *Computers: The Machines We Think With* (New York: Dell, 1962), 55–56.

97. Shelley, *Frankenstein: Second Norton Critical Edition*, 84.

98. Paulina Aronson and Judith Doportail, "The Quantified Heart," *Aeon Magazine*, 12 July 2018, accessed 25 September 2018 at https://aeon.co/essays/can-emotion-regulating-tech-translate-across-cultures.

99. Kang, "Introducing Deep Learning and Neural Networks."

100. I am indebted to computer scientist and mathematician Allison Bishop for this point.

101. Christopher Hollings, Ursula Martin, and Adrian Rice, *Ada Lovelace: The Making of a Computer Scientist* (Oxford: Bodleian Library, 2017).

102. Edmund Burke, *Reflections on the Revolution in France*, ed. Conor Cruise O'Brien (New York: Penguin, 1968), 170.

103. Bruno Latour, "Love Your Monsters: Why We Must Care for Our Technologies as We Do Our Children," *Breakthrough*, Winter 2012, accessed 30 September 2018 at https://thebreakthrough.org/index.php/journal/past-issues/issue-2/love-your-monsters.

104. Donna Haraway, "A Cyborg Manifesto: Science, Technology, and Socialist-Feminism in the Late Twentieth Century," in *Simians, Cyborgs, and Women: The Reinvention of Nature* (New York: Routledge, 1991), 149.

105. Rachel Feder, *Harvester of Hearts: Motherhood Under the Sign of Frankenstein* (Evanston, IL: Northwestern University Press, 2018), 6, 119, 139–40.

106. Shelley, *The Last Man*, 461.

107. Ibid., 465.

108. Ibid., 466.

109. Ibid., 469.

110. Ibid., 466.

111. Ibid., 467.

112. Bostrom, *Superintelligence*, ch. 4.

113. Juliet Floyd, "Introduction," in *Philosophical Explorations of the Legacy of Alan Turing: Turing 100*, ed. Juliet Floyd and Alisa Bokulich (Cham, Switzerland: Springer, 2017), 12.

114. Diane Proudfoot, "Turing and Free Will: A New Take on an Old Debate," in *Philosophical Explorations of the Legacy of Alan Turing*, 306.

115. Ibid., 307.

116. Philip K. Dick, *Do Androids Dream of Electric Sheep?* (New York: Del Ray, 2017), 29.

117. Bostrom, *Superintelligence*, 23.

118. Ibid.

119. Shelley, *Frankenstein: Second Norton Critical Edition*, 32–33.

120. Bostrom, *Superintelligence*, 23.

121. Shelley, *Frankenstein: Second Norton Critical Edition*, 35.

122. Bostrom, *Superintelligence*, 29.

123. Ibid.

124. Nick Bostrom, *Anthropic Bias: Observation Selection Effects in Science and Philosophy* (New York: Routledge, 2002), 44.

125. Ibid.

126. Alison Gopnik, *The Philosophical Baby: What Children's Minds Tell Us About Truth, Love, and the Meaning of Life* (New York: Picador, 2010), 41–42.

127. Ibid., 11.

128. Ibid., 42.

129. Louisa Hall, *Speak* (New York: HarperCollins, 2015), 16.

130. Bostrom, *Superintelligence*, 29.

131. Ibid., 56.

132. Ibid.

133. Ibid., 70, 92 108, 116, 142.

134. Ibid., 56.

135. Ibid., 105.

136. Ibid., 94.

137. Ibid., 95, 97.

138. Ibid., 97.

139. Ibid., 103.

140. Ibid., 100.

141. Ibid.

142. Jedediah Purdy, "The World We've Built," *Dissent*, 3 July 2018, accessed 31 December 2018 at https://www.dissentmagazine.org/online_articles/world-we-built-sovereign-nature-infrastructure-leviathan.

143. Bostrom, *Superintelligence*, 82–83.

144. Thomas Hobbes, *Leviathan*, ed. C. B. MacPherson (New York: Penguin Classics, 1986), 188.

145. Ibid.

146. Bostrom, *Superintelligence*, 115.

147. Ibid.

148. Nick Bostrom, "12 March 2008 Postscript" to "How Long Before Superintelligence?" accessed 27 December 2018 at https://nickbostrom.com/superintelligence.html.

149. Bostrom, *Superintelligence*, 117.

150. Ibid., 105.

151. Ibid., 109, 115.

152. Ibid., 105.

153. Ibid., 109–14.

154. Ibid., 116.

155. Bruce Sterling, "Swarm," in *Schismatrix Plus* (New York: Penguin, 1996), 255.

156. Ibid.

157. Ibid., 257.

158. Oates, "Frankenstein's Fallen Angel," 543–54.

159. Ibid.

160. Ibid.

161. Ibid.

162. Ibid.

163. Shelley, *Frankenstein: Second Norton Critical Edition*, 97, 99, 102.

164. Vinge, "Technological Singularity."

165. Ibid.

166. Ibid.

167. Ibid.

168. Ibid. Yale computer scientist David Gelernter is credited for conjuring the idea of a world wide web without bandwidth limitations, or "Tuplesphere," in his book *Mirror Worlds* (Oxford: Oxford University Press, 1991), 103.

169. Vinge, "Technological Singularity."

170. Ibid.

171. Ibid.

172. William Gibson, *Neuromancer*, with afterword by Jack Womack (New York: Ace, 2004), 5, 294.

173. Ibid., 71.

174. Morton, *Humankind*, 16–17.

175. Bennett, *Vibrant Matter*, ix.

176. Ibid., viii.

177. Margaret Atwood, "Perfect Storms: Writing *Oryx and Crake*," *Book-of-the-Month Club/Bookspan* (January 2003), accessed 3 January 2019 at http://shirbegi.weebly.com/uploads/1/3/8/2/13820171/writing_oryx_and_crake_1.pdf.

178. Atwood, *Speeches for Dr. Frankenstein*.

179. Suparna Banerjee, *Science, Gender and History: The Fantastic in Mary Shelley and Margaret Atwood* (Newcastle upon Tyne, England: Cambridge Scholars, 2014), 81.

180. Margaret Atwood, *Oryx and Crake* (New York: Anchor, 2003), 314.

181. Ibid., 312, 346.

182. Joan Smith, "And Pigs Might Fly: In Margaret Atwood's Dystopian Vision, *Oryx and Crake*, the Perils of GM Have Come Home to Roost," *Guardian Books*, 10 May 2003, accessed 3 January 2018 at https://www.theguardian.com/books/2003/may/11/fiction.margaretatwood.

183. Atwood, *Oryx and Crake*, 8, 361.

184. Margaret Atwood, *MaddAddam* (New York: Doubleday, 2013), 36.

185. Atwood, *Oryx and Crake*, 346.

186. Atwood, *MaddAddam*, 165.

187. Atwood, *Oryx and Crake*, 361.

188. Ibid.

189. Atwood, *MaddAddam*, 249.

190. Čapek, *R.U.R.*, 75.

191. Ibid., 70.

192. Ibid., 73.

193. Ibid.

194. Ibid., 74.

195. Ibid., 84.

196. Ibid.

197. Ibid., 68.

198. Shelley, *Journals*, vol. 2, 542.

199. Ibid., 543.

200. Ibid., 542–43.

201. McQueen, *Political Realism in Apocalyptic Times*, 195–97.

Chapter II

1. Shelley, *Frankenstein: Second Norton Critical Edition*, 160.

2. Ibid., 168, 33.

3. Ibid., 35.

4. Ibid., 35–36.

5. Mary Shelley, *Frankenstein, or the Modern Prometheus*, series ed. Guillermo del Toro (New York: Penguin, [1831] 2013), 51.

6. Ibid.

7. Robert Lance Snyder, "Apocalypse and Indeterminacy in Mary Shelley's 'The Last Man,'" *Studies in Romanticism* 17:4 (1978), 435.

8. Shelley, *Frankenstein: Second Norton Critical Edition*, 50, 33, 36.

9. Feder, *Harvester of Hearts*, 6, 119, 139–40.

10. Shelley, *Journals*, vol. 1, 65. This entry is in the hand of Percy Shelley, due to Mary being in childbirth.

11. Ibid., 68. This entry is in Mary Shelley's hand.

12. Preterm birth can be related to birth defects. See Richard E. Berhman and Adrienne Stith Butler, eds., *Preterm Birth: Causes, Consequences, and Correction* (Washington, DC: National Academies Press, 2007), 150.

13. Gordon, *Romantic Outlaws*, 190.

14. Ellen Moers, *Literary Women* (New York: Doubleday, 1976), 93.

15. Shelley, *Journals*, vol. 1, 34, 86, 88. The *Posthumous Works* was a four-volume set edited by Godwin and published in 1798 alongside his *Memoirs of the Author of A Vindication of the Rights of Woman*. Volume I of the *Posthumous Works* contained Wollstonecraft's novel *The Wrongs of Woman, or Maria*, left incomplete upon her death in September 1797 from an infection contracted during childbirth; it also contained some of her correspondence with her first common-law husband Gilbert Imlay and other miscellaneous literary manuscripts. Soon thereafter, a Dublin publisher packaged the *Memoirs* together with a selection of Wollstonecraft's posthumous letters in a single volume, *Memoirs and Posthumous Works of Mary Wollstonecraft Godwin, Author of A Vindication of the Rights of Woman* (Dublin: Thomas Burnside, 1798), vol. 1. It is likely that either the 1798 Irish edition or Joseph Johnson's first or second (revised) London edition of the *Memoirs* was in the Shelleys' traveling library, as Mary referred to reading the "Post. Letters," "Post. Works," and "Memoirs" while in Italy, in her journal entries of 1–3 May 1820. If so, it is possible she was reading the *Memoirs* alongside the *Posthumous Works* as early as 1814.

16. Shelley, *Frankenstein: Second Norton Critical Edition*, 90; William Godwin, *Memoirs of the Author of A Vindication of the Rights of Woman* (London: Joseph Johnson, 1798), 177.

17. Godwin, *Memoirs*, 176.

18. Ibid., 177.

19. Ibid.

20. Ibid.

21. Ibid., 199.

22. Moers, *Literary Women*, 99; Mellor, *Mary Shelley*, 41.

23. Eileen Hunt Botting, "Editor's Introduction: Reading Wollstonecraft's *A Vindication of the Rights of Woman*, 1792–2014," in Mary Wollstonecraft, *A Vindication of the Rights of Woman*, ed. Eileen Hunt Botting (New Haven, CT: Yale University Press, 2014), 14–15.

24. Shelley, *Journals*, vol. 1, 86, 88.

25. Wollstonecraft, *The Wrongs of Woman*, in *Works*, vol. 1, 159.

26. Ibid., 112.

27. Ibid.

28. Anne K. Mellor, "Righting the Wrongs of Woman: Mary Wollstonecraft's *Maria*," *Nineteenth-Century Contexts* 19:4 (1996), 120–21.

29. Wollstonecraft, *The Wrongs of Woman*, 111–12.

30. Shelley, *Frankenstein: Second Norton Critical Edition*, 101.

31. Shelley, "Introduction to *Frankenstein*, Third Edition (1831)," 169.

32. Ibid., 169.

33. Charles E. Robinson, "Abbreviations" and "Introduction," in Mary (with Percy) Shelley, *The Original Frankenstein: Two New Versions, Mary Shelley's Earliest Draft and Percy Shelley's Revised Text* (New York: Vintage, 2008), 11, 13, 14, 18.

34. Laura Moss, "'A Science of Uncertainty': Bioethics, Narrative Competence, and Turning to the 'What If' of Fiction," *Studies in Canadian Literature / Études en littérature canadienne* 40:2 (June 2015), accessed 19 April 2017 at https://journals.lib.unb.ca/index.php/SCL/article/view/24546.

35. Nathaniel Hawthorne, "Letter to Elizabeth C. Hathorne and Elizabeth M. Hathorne, 31 October 1820," in *Selected Letters of Nathaniel Hawthorne*, ed. Joel Myerson (Columbus: Ohio State University Press, 2002), 29.

36. Ibid.

37. Shelley, *Frankenstein: Second Norton Critical Edition*, 4; Scott, "From Blackwood's Edinburgh Magazine (March 1818)," 221.

38. Hawthorne, "Letter to Elizabeth C. Hathorne and Elizabeth M. Hathorne," 29.

39. Karl P. Wentersdorf, "The Genesis of Hawthorne's 'The Birth-Mark,' " *Jahrbuch für Amerikastudien* 8 (1963), 171.

40. Ibid.

41. Hawthorne, "The Birth-Mark," 59.

42. Ibid.

43. Ibid.

44. Ibid., 61.

45. Ibid., 60.

46. Ibid., 61.

47. President's Council on Bioethics, "Session 2: Science and the Pursuit of Perfection. Discussion of Nathaniel Hawthorne's 'The Birth-Mark' " (2002), accessed 26 April 2017 at https://bioethicsarchive.georgetown.edu/pcbe/transcripts/jan02/jan17session2.html.

48. President's Council on Bioethics, "Beyond Therapy: Biotechnology and the Pursuit of Happiness" (October 2003), accessed 23 January 2019 at https://bioethicsarchive.george town.edu/pcbe/reports/beyondtherapy/chapter1.html.

49. Leon Kass, ed., *Being Human: Core Readings in the Humanities* (New York: W. W. Norton, 2004).

50. Tetsuya Ishii and César Palacios-González, "Mitochondrial Replacement Techniques: Genetic Relatedness, Gender Implications, and Justice," *Gender and the Genome* 1:4 (2017), 3.

51. Paul Knoepfler, *GMO Sapiens: The Life Changing Science of Designer Babies* (London: World Scientific, 2016), vii, 117; Gina Kolata, Sui Lee-Wee, and Pam Belluck, "Chinese Scientist Claims to Use CRISPR to Make First Genetically Edited Babies," *New York Times*, 26 November 2018, accessed 16 February 2019 at https://www.nytimes.com/2018/11/26/health/gene-edit ing-babies-china.html.

52. Jacques Cohen et al., "Birth of Infant After Transfer of Anucleate Donor Oocyte Cytoplasm into Recipient Eggs," *Lancet* 350:9072 (19 July 1997), 186–87.

53. Ibid.

54. Jason A. Barritt et al., "Mitochondria in Human Offspring Derived from Ooplasmic Transplantation: Brief Communication," *Human Reproduction* 16:3 (2001), 513–16.

55. Amelia Hill, "Three-Parent Foetus' Gene Disorder Probe," *Observer* (London), 20 May 2001, 23.

56. Nicholas Agar, "The Debate over Liberal Eugenics," *Hastings Center Report* 36:2 (March–April 2006), 4.

57. See "My Favorite Movie with Francis Fukuyama: *Gattaca*," 20 September 2017, accessed 20 March 2019 at https://www.newamerica.org/future-tense/events/my-favorite-movie -francis-fukuyama-gattaca/.

58. Fukuyama, *Our Posthuman Future*, 1–4, 156.

59. Andrew Niccol, *Gattaca* (1997), accessed 20 March 2019 at https://www.imsdb.com/ scripts/Gattaca.html.

60. Barritt et al., "Mitochondria in Human Offspring Derived from Ooplasmic Trans-plantation."

61. Ibid.

62. Knoepfler, *GMO Sapiens*, 89.

63. Karen Weintraub, "Three Biological Parents and a Baby," *New York Times*, 16 December 2013, accessed 25 September 2018 at https://well.blogs.nytimes.com/2013/12/16/three-biological-parents-and-a-baby/; Shannon Kirkey, "Toronto Fertility Clinic Offers Controversial Egg Treatment for Women That Can Extend Child-Bearing Years," *National Post*, 30 January 2015.

64. Knoepfler, *GMO Sapiens*, 89.

65. Charlotte Pritchard, "The Girl with Three Biological Parents," *BBC Radio 4 Magazine*, 1 September 2014.

66. Knoepfler, *GMO Sapiens*, 91.

67. Erin Heidt-Forsythe, *Between Families and Frankenstein: The Politics of Egg Donation in the United States* (Berkeley: University of California Press, 2018), 80–113.

68. Shoukhrat Mitalipov and Don P. Wolf, "Clinical and Ethical Implications of Mitochondrial Gene Transfer," *Trends in Endocrinology & Metabolism* 25:1 (2014), 5–7.

69. John Zhang, "Pregnancy Derived from Human Nuclear Transfer," *Fertility and Sterility* 80:3 (September 2003), 56; Knoepfler, *GMO Sapiens*, 93.

70. Stephen Castle, "Britain Set to Approve Technique to Create Babies from 3 People," *New York Times*, 3 February 2015.

71. John Zhang et al., "Live Birth Derived from Oocyte Spindle Transfer to Prevent Mitochondrial Disease," *Reproductive BioMedicine Online* (2017) 34:4, 361–68.

72. Ian Sample, "World's First Baby Born from New Procedure Using DNA of Three People," *Guardian*, 27 September 2016.

73. Ishii and Palacios-González, "Mitochondrial Replacement Techniques," 4.

74. Ibid. For the Darwin Life website, see https://www.darwinlife.com/nuclear-transfer-technique.php, accessed 16 February 2019.

75. Emily Mullin, "The Doctor Trying to Commercialize Three-Parent Babies," *MIT Technology Review*, 13 June 2017.

76. See https://www.darwinlife.com, accessed 17 February 2019.

77. See https://www.darwinlife.com/contact-us.php, accessed 17 February 2019.

78. Ishii and Palacios-González, "Mitochondrial Replacement Techniques," 1.

79. Michelle Roberts, "IVF: First Three-Parent Baby Born to Infertile Couple," *BBC News Health*, 18 January 2017.

80. Jennifer Doudna and Samuel H. Sternberg, *A Crack in Creation: Gene Editing and the Unthinkable Power to Control Evolution* (New York: Houghton Mifflin, 2017).

81. See Feng Zhang, "How Does CRISPR Work?" accessed 17 February 2019 at https://www.broadinstitute.org/what-broad/areas-focus/project-spotlight/questions-and-answers-about-crispr.

82. Mitalipov and Wolf, "Clinical and Ethical Implications of Mitochondrial Gene Transfer," 7.

83. Doudna and Sternberg, *A Crack in Creation*, 200. I thank Anne K. Mellor for this reference.

84. Jun Wu et al., "Interspecies Chimerism with Mammalian Pluripotent Stem Cells," *Cell* 168 (26 January 2017), 473–86.

85. Hong Ma et al., "Correction of a Pathogenic Gene Mutation in Human Embryos," *Nature* 548 (24 August 2017), 413–19.

86. Antonio Regalado, "Engineering the Perfect Baby," *MIT Technology Review*, 5 March 2015, accessed 18 February 2019 at https://www.technologyreview.com/s/535661/engineering -the-perfect-baby/.

87. Antonio Regalado, "Exclusive: Chinese Scientists are Creating CRISPR Babies," *MIT Technology Review*, 25 November 2018, accessed 10 June 2019 at https://www.technologyreview .com/s/612458/exclusive-chinese-scientists-are-creating-crispr-babies/; Kolata, Lee-Wee, and Belluck, "Chinese Scientist Claims to Use CRISPR to Make First Genetically Edited Babies."

88. Jon Cohen, "The Untold Story of the 'Circle of Trust' Behind the World's First Gene-Edited Babies," *Science*, 1 August 2019, accessed 20 October 2019 at https://www.sciencemag .org/news/2019/08/untold-story-circle-trust-behind-world-s-first-gene-edited-babies.

89. National Academies of Sciences, Engineering, and Medicine, *Human Genome Editing: Science, Ethics, and Governance* (Washington, DC: National Academies Press, 2017), 7.

90. National Academies of Sciences, Engineering, and Medicine, "Second International Summit on Human Genome Editing. Proceedings of a Workshop—In Brief" (January 2019), accessed 16 February 2019 at http://nap.edu/25343.

91. See Eben Kirksey, *The Mutant Project* (New York: St. Martin's, forthcoming 2020). An anthropologist, Kirksey takes an ethnographical approach to understanding Dr. He's gene-editing work. Kirksey's interviews with patients and scientists involved in the experiment and its outcome shows that Dr. He had attempted to publish his results in *Nature* just prior to the public announcement of the birth of the twins.

92. The foreknowledge of other scientists of Dr. He's intention to clinically use CRISPR-Cas9 to produce gene-edited babies has been widely documented, especially in the United States, where he received his graduate and postgraduate training at Emory and Stanford. See Cohen, "The Untold Story of the 'Circle of Trust' Behind the World's First Gene-Edited Babies." Some of these scientists have been investigated for ethics violations. See "Stanford Clears Professor of Helping with Gene-Edited Babies Experiment," *New York Times*, 16 April 2019, accessed 2 June 2019 at https://www.nytimes.com/2019/04/16/health/stanford-gene-edit ing-babies.html.

93. Ruipeng Lei et al., "Reboot Ethics Governance in China," *Nature* 569 (9 May 2019), 185, accessed 2 June 2019 at https://www.nature.com/articles/d41586–019–01408-y.

94. Renée C. Fox and Judith P. Swazey, "Medical Morality Is not Bioethics—Medical Ethics in China and the United States," *Perspectives in Biology and Medicine* 27:3 (1984), 340, 346–49.

95. Cohen, "The Untold Story of the 'Circle of Trust' Behind the World's First Gene-Edited Babies."

96. Ibid.

97. The original (largely laudatory) article from the *People's Online Daily* was taken down in the aftermath of the controversy at the genome editing summit in Hong Kong, but a copy was reprinted in a major Chinese American online news site, where it is still available: Heicafei 黑咖啡, "[Licicunzhao] shijie shouli mianyi aizibing de jiyin bianji yinger zai zhong-guo dansheng 【立此存照】世界首例免疫艾滋病的基因编辑婴儿在中国诞生" (The World's First Genetically Edited Babies with AIDS Resistance Have Been Born in China)," *China Digital Times* 中国数字时代 (26 November 2018), accessed 6 May 2019 at https://chinadigitaltimes.net/ chinese/2018/11/%E4%B8%AD%E5%9B%BD%E6%96%96%E9%97%BB%E7%BD%91% E4%B8%96%E7%95%8C%E9%A6%96%E4%BE%8B%E5%85%8D%E7%96%AB%E8%89%

BE%E6%BB%8B%E7%97%85%E7%9A%84%E5%9F%BA%E5%9B%A0%E7%BC%96%E8%
BE%91%E5%A9%B4%E5%84%BF/.

98. Kirksey, *The Mutant Project*.

99. National Academies of Science, Engineering, and Medicine, "Second International Summit on Human Genome Editing."

100. Cohen, "The Untold Story of the 'Circle of Trust' Behind the World's First Gene-Edited Babies."

101. Ibid. See also Kirksey, *The Mutant Project*, for reports of Dr. Zhang looking for other sites in Southeast Asia and eastern Europe to conduct his work on human germline genetic modification.

102. Eric S. Lander et al., "Adopt a Moratorium on Heritable Genome Editing," *Nature* 567 (13 March 2019), 165–68.

103. Ruipeng Lei et al., "Reboot Ethics Governance in China," 185.

104. David Cyranoski, "China Set to Introduce Gene Editing Regulation Following CRISPR-Baby Furore," *Nature*, 20 May 2019, accessed 2 June 2019 at https://www.nature.com/articles/d41586–019–01580–1.

105. Stephen Jay Gould, "Dolly's Fashion and Louis's Passion," in *Clones and Clones*, ed. Martha C. Nussbaum and Cass Sunstein (New York: W. W. Norton, 1998), 41–53.

106. Sandel, *The Case Against Perfection* [Kindle Edition], locations 864–74.

107. Fukuyama, *Our Posthuman Future*, 81, 126.

108. Ibid., 215.

109. Habermas, *The Future of Human Nature* [Kindle Edition], location 642.

110. Ibid., locations 348, 358.

111. Ibid., location 855.

112. Ibid., locations 442, 999, 1017.

113. Ibid., locations 436, 1186.

114. Ibid., locations 994, 340.

115. Knoepfler, *GMO Sapiens*, i, 86; Weintraub, "Three Biological Parents and a Baby."

116. Nuffield Bioethics Council, *Genome Editing and Human Reproduction* (London: Nuffield Bioethics Council, July 2018), 149.

117. Emily Partridge et al., "An Extra-uterine System to Physiologically Support the Extreme Premature Lamb," *Nature Communications* 8 (25 April 2017), accessed 20 June 2019 at https://www.nature.com/articles/ncomms15112.

118. Nuffield Bioethics Council, *Genome Editing and Human Reproduction*, 174.

119. Ibid., 79, 196.

120. United Nations, *Universal Declaration on the Human Genome and Human Rights* (1997), Article 11, accessed 2 January 2019 at http://portal.unesco.org/en/ev.php-URL_ID = 131 77&URL_DO = DO_TOPIC&URL_SECTION = 201.html.

121. John Rawls's distinction between the political and the metaphysical is my point of departure here. See *Political Liberalism* (New York: Columbia University Press, 1993).

122. Like Octavia Butler before her, fellow Nebula and Hugo award-winning writer Okorafor does not like her stories to be labeled in terms of her race or ethnicity. I use "African-based" SF to describe *The Book of Phoenix* as it is her self-descriptor for much of her work, which spans SF, fantasy, and magical realism. See nnedi.com, accessed 20 October 2019.

123. Mellor, *Mary Shelley*, 115–26.

124. Botting, *Mary Shelley and the Rights of the Child*, 107.

125. Nnedi Okorafor, *The Book of Phoenix* (New York: DAW Books, 2015), 48.

126. Ibid.

127. Ibid., 7.

128. Ibid., 48.

129. Shelley, *Frankenstein: Second Norton Critical Edition*, 67.

130. Okorafor, *The Book of Phoenix*, 94.

131. Ibid., 60.

132. Shelley, *Frankenstein: Second Norton Critical Edition*, 102, 120.

133. Ibid., 102.

134. Ibid., 118.

135. Ibid., 119.

136. Ibid., 119; Feder, *Harvester of Hearts*, 118.

137. Wollstonecraft, *A Vindication of the Rights of Woman*, in *Works*, vol. 5, 102.

138. Martha Nussbaum, "Little C," in *Clones and Clones*, 339.

139. Ibid., 345.

140. Ibid.

141. Ibid., 346.

142. Shelley, *Frankenstein: Second Norton Critical Edition*, 33–34.

143. Bonnie Honig, "Rawls and Punishment," *Political Research Quarterly* 46:1 (1993), 103.

144. Bonnie Honig, *Political Theory and the Displacement of Politics* (Ithaca, NY: Cornell University Press, 1993), ch. 4, 139, 153.

145. Ibid., 130.

146. Bonnie Honig, *Emergency Politics: Paradox, Law, Democracy* (Princeton, NJ: Princeton University Press, 2009), 44–53.

147. John Rawls, *The Law of Peoples with "The Idea of Public Reason Revisited"* (Cambridge, MA: Harvard University Press, 1999), 6; Charles Beitz, *The Idea of Human Rights* (Oxford: Oxford University Press, 2009), xii.

148. Habermas, *The Future of Human Nature*, sec. 6, pt. I, location 580.

149. Mary Ann Mason and Tom Ekman, *Babies of Technology: Assisted Reproduction and the Rights of the Child* (New Haven, CT: Yale University Press, 2017).

150. Weintraub, "Three Biological Parents and a Baby."

151. Shelley, *Frankenstein: Second Norton Critical Edition*, 97.

152. Ibid., 35; Eileen Hunt Botting, "*Frankenstein* and the Question of Children's Rights *After* Human Germline Genetic Modification," in *Reproductive Ethics II*, ed. Lisa Campo-Engelstein and Paul Burcher (Cham: Springer, 2018), 15–17.

153. Knoepfler, *GMO Sapiens*, 86.

154. S. Matthew Liao, *The Right to Be Loved* (Oxford: Oxford University Press, 2015), 74–100.

155. Shelley, *Frankenstein: Second Norton Critical Edition*, 97, 101.

156. Okorafor, *The Book of Phoenix*, 81.

157. Ibid.

158. Botting, *Mary Shelley and the Rights of the Child*, 100–108.

159. Knoepfler, *GMO Sapiens*, 87.

160. Shelley, *Frankenstein: Second Norton Critical Edition*, 14, 33, 35, 68.

161. Rahel Jaeggi, *Critique of Forms of Life*, tr. Ciaran Cronin (Cambridge, MA: Belknap, 2018), ch. 3. See also Habermas, *The Future of Human Nature*, locations 142, 151, 238.

162. Heicafei 黑咖啡, "[Licicunzhao] shijie shouli mianyi aizibing de jiyin bianji yinger zai zhongguo dansheng【立此存照】世界首例免疫艾滋病的基因编辑婴儿在中国诞生" (The World's First Genetically Edited Babies with AIDS Resistance Have Been Born in China)."

163. Pam Belluck, "Chinese Scientist Who Says He Edited Babies Genes Defends His Work," *New York Times*, 28 November 2018, accessed 19 February 2019 at https://www.ny times.com/2018/11/28/world/asia/gene-editing-babies-he-jiankui.html.

164. Ibid.

165. United Nations, *Universal Declaration on the Human Genome and Human Rights*, Article 9.

166. Nuffield Bioethics Council, *Genome Editing and Human Reproduction*, 114, 161.

167. Lander et al., "Adopt a Moratorium on Heritable Genome Editing," 168.

168. Mason and Ekman, *Babies of Technology*, 180–82.

169. United Nations, *Convention on the Rights of the Child* (1989), accessed 19 February 2019 at https://www.ohchr.org/en/professionalinterest/pages/crc.aspx.

170. Habermas, *The Future of Human Nature*, location 168.

171. Ibid., locations 290, 757.

172. Ibid., location 359.

173. Ibid., location 514.

174. Ibid., locations 516, 833, 922, 936, 996.

175. Ibid., locations 1027, 874.

176. Ibid., location 580.

177. Ibid., location 1657.

178. Ibid., locations 400, 440.

179. Ibid., location 557. Habermas's phrase "die im Abscheu vor gentechnisch hergestellten Chimären" can also be translated as "in disgust before genetically modified chimeras." See Jürgen Habermas, *Die Zukunft der menschlichen Natur. Auf dem Weg zu einer liberalen Eugenik* (Frankfurt am Main, Germany: Suhrkamp Verlag Gmbh & Co. KG, 2002), 49.

180. Habermas, *The Future of Human Nature*, location 405; Habermas, *Die Zukunft der menschlichen Natur. Auf dem Weg zu einer liberalen Eugenik*, 34–35.

181. United Nations, "Universal Declaration of Human Rights" (1948), Article 16, accessed 18 March 2019 at http://undocs.org/A/RES/217(III).

182. Habermas, *The Future of Human Nature*, locations 1008, 1029.

183. Ibid., location 102.

184. Ibid., location 95.

185. Ibid., locations 96, 694, 1960.

186. Ibid., locations 1960, 884.

187. Ibid., location 1008.

188. Ibid., location 1345.

189. Ibid., locations 1556, note 54, and 987.

190. Ibid., location 987.

191. Ibid., location 987.

192. Joel Feinberg, *Freedom and Fulfillment: Philosophical Essays* (Princeton, NJ: Princeton University Press, 1992), 78–97. This chapter, "The Child's Right to an Open Future,"

was originally published in William Aiken and Hugh LaFollette, eds., *Whose Child? Children's Rights, Parental Authority, and State Power* (Totowa, NJ: Rowman and Littlefield, 1980), 124–53.

193. Feinberg, *Freedom and Fulfillment*, 76–77.

194. Pritchard, "The Girl with Three Biological Parents."

195. United Nations, "Universal Declaration of Human Rights," Article 16.

196. Matteo Galletti, "Frankenstein, Bio-enhancement, and Open Futures. How Narrative Can Shed Light on Bioethical Thinking" (unpublished conference paper, 2018).

197. Aldous Huxley, *Brave New World and Brave New World Revisited* (New York: Harper Perennial, 2005), 15.

198. Ibid.; Turney, *Frankenstein's Footsteps*, 99–120.

199. Huxley, *Brave New World*, 20.

200. Ibid., 25.

201. Ibid., 190.

202. Ibid., 115.

203. Ibid., 190.

204. Ibid., 190.

205. Habermas, *The Future of Human Nature*, locations 1027, 307, 311, 324, 481, 930, 579.

206. Ibid., locations 1679, 1657.

207. Ibid., location 809.

208. Ibid., locations 401, 406, 1593. Habermas uses two terms for what is known in English as reproductive medicine, or medicine that treats the reproductive system and infertility: twice he writes "*Reproduktionsmedizin*" (which can be literally translated as either "replication medicine" or "reproduction medicine") and once "*Fortpflanzungsmedizin*" (which is typically translated as "reproductive medicine"). In the 2003 English translation with Polity Press, Max Pensky and Hella Beister translate both terms as "reproduction medicine." The use of the English noun "reproduction" (rather than the adjectival form) in conjunction with "medicine" suggests the objectification of the output of the medical treatment. I agree with this translation given the context of Habermas's overarching critique of the instrumentalizing potential of reproductive technologies. See Habermas, *Die Zukunft der menschlichen Natur. Auf dem Weg zu einer liberalen Eugenik*, 34–35, 128.

209. Ibid., locations 836, 2251.

210. Ibid., location 133.

211. Alexander Dobeson, "Between Openness and Closure: Helmuth Plessner and the Boundaries of Social Life," *Journal of Classical Sociology* 18:1 (2018), 36–54.

212. Habermas, *The Future of Human Nature*, locations 97, 519.

213. Nick Bostrom, "Why I Want to Be a Posthuman When I Grow Up," in *Medical Enhancement and Posthumanity*, ed. Bert Gordijn and Ruth Chadwick (New York: Springer, 2008), 107–37.

214. Agar, "The Debate over Liberal Eugenics," 5.

215. Ibid.

216. Ibid.

217. Ibid.

218. Ibid.

219. Ibid., 4.

220. Niccol, *Gattaca.*

221. Ibid.

222. Calvert W. Jones and Celia Paris, "It's the End of the World and They Know It: How Dystopian Fiction Shapes Political Attitudes," *Perspectives on Politics* 16:4 (December 2018), 969.

223. Philip McCouat, "Dr. Jekyll, Frankenstein, and Shelley's Heart," *Journal of Art in Society* (2017), accessed 18 March 2019 at http://www.artinsociety.com/dr-jekyll-frankenstein -and-shelleyrsquos-heart1.html.

224. Robert M. Philmus, "The Satiric Ambivalence of 'The Island of Doctor Moreau,'" *Science-Fiction Studies* 8:1 (1981), 9, note 3. See also Steven Lehman, "The Motherless Child in Science Fiction: 'Frankenstein' and 'Moreau' (L'Orphelin De Mère Dans La Science Fiction: 'Frankenstein' Et 'Moreau')," *Science-Fiction Studies* 19:1 (1992), 49–58.

225. Punter, *The Literature of Terror*, 12, 100, 211.

226. Michael Rinella, *Pharmakon: Plato, Drug Culture, and Identity in Ancient Athens* (Lanham, MD: Rowman and Littlefield, 2010), pt. III.

227. Robert Louis Stevenson, *The Strange Case of Dr. Jekyll and Mr. Hyde* (Mineola, NY: Dover Thrift Editions, 2017), 44–45.

228. Ian Campbell, "Jekyll, Hyde, Frankenstein, and the Uncertain Self," *Cahiers Victoriens et Edouardiens*, October 1994, 58–59.

229. Stevenson, *The Strange Case of Dr. Jekyll and Mr. Hyde*, 45.

230. Maureen Turim, "Looking Back at the Mirror: Cinematic Revisions," in *Psychoanalyses/Feminisms*, ed. Peter L. Rudnytsky and Andrew M. Gordon (Albany: State University of New York Press, 2000), 156. See also Jacques Lacan, "The Mirror Phase as Formative of the Function of the I," tr. Jean Roussel, *New Left Review* 1:51 (September/October 1968), 71–77. The original version of Lacan's essay dates to 1936.

231. Sigmund Freud, *Civilization and Its Discontents* (Mineola, NY: Dover, 1994), ch. VIII.

232. Ibid., 43.

233. Huxley, *Brave New World*, 45, 66.

234. Stevenson, *The Strange Case of Dr. Jekyll and Mr. Hyde*, 45; Campbell, "Jekyll, Hyde, Frankenstein, and the Uncertain Self," 58.

235. Huxley, *Brave New World*, 230.

236. Julian Hawthorne, "The Romance of the Impossible," *Lippincott's Monthly Magazine*, September 1890, 12.

237. Ibid.

238. Oscar Wilde, *The Picture of Dorian Gray*, ed. Norman Page (Peterborough, Ontario: Broadview, 1998), 131.

239. Ibid., 45, 184.

240. J. Hawthorne, "The Romance of the Impossible," 12.

241. Shelley, *Frankenstein: Second Norton Critical Edition*, 90.

242. Joseph Scalia, *Intimate Violence: Attacks upon Psychic Interiority* (New York: Columbia University Press, 2002), 55.

243. Jean-Jacques Rousseau, *Discourse on the Origins of Inequality Among Men* (1755), pt. I.

244. Jean-Jacques Rousseau, *Discourse on the Sciences and the Arts* (1750).

245. Shelley, *Frankenstein: Second Norton Critical Edition*, 33.

246. Emma Planinc, "Catching Up with Wells: The Political Theory of H. G. Wells's Science Fiction," *Political Theory* 45:5 (2017), 640.

247. Ibid., 639, 648.

248. H. G. Wells, *The Island of Doctor Moreau*, ed. Darryl Jones (Oxford: Oxford University Press, 2017), 59, 66, 71.

249. Ibid., 83.

250. Ibid., 116.

251. Ibid., 117.

252. Jaeggi, *Critique of Forms of Life*, 74.

253. Samantha Frost, *Biocultural Creatures: Toward a New Theory of the Human* (Durham, NC: Duke University Press, 2016), 147–59.

254. Habermas, *The Future of Human Nature*, location 2254.

255. Shelley, *Frankenstein: Second Norton Critical Edition*, 33; Hawthorne, "The Birth-Mark," 59.

256. Morton, *Humankind*, 16–17.

257. Latour, "Love Your Monsters: Why We Must Care for Our Technologies as We Do Our Children."

258. Kate Mondloch, *A Capsule Aesthetic: Feminist Materialisms in New Material Art* (Minneapolis: University of Minnesota Press, 2018), 12.

259. Ibid., 4.

260. Ibid.

261. Donna Haraway, "Speculative Fabulations for Technoculture's Generations: Taking Care of Unexpected Country," in *The Multispecies Salon*, ed. Eben Kirksey, ch. 7.

262. Habermas, *The Future of Human Nature*, location 557.

263. Mondloch, *A Capsule Aesthetic*, 12.

264. Shelley, "Introduction to *Frankenstein*, Third Edition (1831)," 169.

Chapter III

1. Shelley, *Journals*, vol. 1, 182. The Shelleys' copy of Spinoza's *Tractatus Theologico-Politicus* (c. 1674–77), with annotations attributed to both of them as well as others, is in the Carl H. Pforzheimer Collection in the New York Public Library. Annotations attributed to Percy were published in Donald H. Reiman and Doucet Devin Fischer, eds., *Shelley and His Circle, 1773–1822* (Cambridge, MA: Harvard University Press, 1986), vol. 8, 730–36. Future scholarship should study the annotations systematically to determine Mary Shelley's contribution to them.

2. Steven B. Smith, *Spinoza, Liberalism, and the Question of Jewish Identity* (New Haven, CT: Yale University Press, 1997), 105.

3. Middleton, *Shelley and His Writings*, xviii; Spinoza, *A Theologico-Political Treatise*, 19.

4. Spinoza, *A Theologico-Political Treatise*, 27; Steven B. Smith, *Spinoza's Book of Life: Freedom and Redemption in the Ethics* (New Haven, CT: Yale University Press, 2003), 157–58.

5. Middleton, *Shelley and His Writings*, xviii; Spinoza, *A Theologico-Political Treatise*, 19. The Shelleys literally translated "supra humanam" as "superhuman" while Elwes more loosely translated it as "more than human." See Benedict de Spinoza, *Tractatus theologico-politicus continens dissertationes aliquot, quibus ostenditur libertatem* (Hamburg, Germany: Künraht, Heinrich, 1677), 7.

6. In the mid-1850s, Charles Middleton recovered the fragmentary manuscript at Marlow (where the Shelleys resided in 1817), then published a facsimile of two pages (including the passage on Christ) in *Shelley and His Writings*, xviii. Ironically, Middleton did not realize that the text was a translation of Spinoza; he thought it was juvenilia of Percy's that evidenced his belief in a form of Christian theology.

7. Reiman and Fischer, eds., *Shelley and His Circle*, vol. 8, 738–41; Shelley, "To Maria Gisborne, 17–20 September 1822," in *The Letters of Mary Wollstonecraft Shelley*, vol. 1, 262.

8. Shelley, *Journals*, vol. 2, 429.

9. Ibid., 428.

10. Ibid., 429.

11. Ibid.

12. Ibid.

13. Ibid.

14. Ibid.

15. Ibid.

16. Moria Gatens, "*Mark Sacks Lecture 2013*: Spinoza on Goodness and Beauty and the Prophet and the Artist," *European Journal of Philosophy* 23:1 (2015), 4.

17. Shelley, *Journals*, vol. 2, 432.

18. Ibid.

19. Ibid.

20. Ibid., 451.

21. Ibid., 451–52.

22. Ibid., 453.

23. Betty T. Bennett, "Radical Imaginings: Mary Shelley's 'The Last Man,'" *Wordsworth Circle* 26:3 (Summer 1995), 149.

24. Shelley, *Journals*, vol. 2, 453, 476.

25. Ibid., 476.

26. Ibid.

27. Moira Gatens, "*Frankenstein*, Spinoza, and Exemplarity," *Textual Practice* 33:5 (2019), 750, note 6.

28. Ibid., 739–52.

29. Spinoza, *The Ethics*, tr. R. H. M. Elwes, in *The Rationalists* (New York: Doubleday, 1960), pt. IV, preface, 322; Smith, *Spinoza's Book of Life*, 46.

30. Thomas Carson Mark, "Spinoza's Concept of Mind," *Journal of the History of Philosophy* 17:4 (1979), 414.

31. Timothy Morton, "The Notes to 'Queen Mab' and Shelley's Spinozism," in *The Neglected Shelley*, ed. Alan M. Weinberg and Timothy Webb (New York: Routledge, 2016), ch. 4.

32. Roberts, *Science Fiction*, 55. Percy Shelley repeatedly used the term "magic car" for Mab's chariot; see Percy Shelley, "Queen Mab," in *Shelley's Poetry and Prose*, ed. Donald H. Reiman and Neil Freistat, 2nd ed. (New York: W. W. Norton, 2002), 22–23.

33. P. Shelley, "Queen Mab," 52.

34. Jillian Heydt-Stevenson and Kurtis Hessel, "Queen Mab, Wollstonecraft, and Spinoza: Teaching 'Nature's Primal Modesty,'" *European Romantic Review* 27:3 (2016), 351–63.

35. Ibid., 357; P. Shelley, "Queen Mab," 52, 61–62.

36. Wollstonecraft, *An Historical and Moral View of the Origins and Progress of the French Revolution*, in *Works*, vol. 6, 17 and *A Vindication of the Rights of Woman*, in *Works*, vol. 5, 81.

37. Wollstonecraft, *A Vindication of the Rights of Woman*, in *Works*, vol. 5, 69.

38. Shelley, *Journals*, vol. 2, 438, 432.

39. P. Shelley, "The Triumph of Life," in *Shelley's Poetry and Prose*, ed. Reiman and Freistat, 481–500.

40. Benedict de Spinoza, *The Ethics*, in *Improvement of the Understanding, Ethics, and Correspondence of Benedict de Spinoza*, tr. R. H. M. Elwes (New York: Wiley, 1901), 170.

41. Gilles Deleuze, *Spinoza: Philosophie Pratique* (Paris: Les Editions de Minuit, [1970] 1981), 42.

42. Ibid., 37–43.

43. Shelley, *Journals*, vol. 2, 438, 432.

44. Ibid.

45. Ibid., 482.

46. Ibid., 483.

47. Ibid., 495.

48. Linus Recht, "The Wheel and the Ladder: Freudian and Loewaldian Accounts of Individuation," *Psychoanalytic Review* 124:3 (2017), 313–50; Freud, *Civilization and Its Discontents*, ch. 1.

49. Mellor, *Mary Shelley*, 152.

50. William Sims Bainbridge, "Transavatars," in *Transhumanist Reader: Classical and Contemporary Essays on the Science, Technology, and Philosophy of the Human Future*, ed. Max More and Natasha Vita-More (Oxford: Wiley, 2013), 99.

51. Shelley, *The Last Man*, 399.

52. Wollstonecraft, *A Vindication of the Rights of Woman*, in *Works*, vol. 5, 75, 104–5.

53. Smith, *Spinoza's Book of Life*, 181–82.

54. Shelley, *Journals*, vol. 2, 495.

55. Dawid W. DeVilliers, "Catastrophic Turns: Romanticism, History, and 'the Last Man,'" *English Studies in Africa* 58:2 (2015), 26.

56. Shelley, *The Last Man*, 463.

57. Ibid., 469.

58. Ibid.

59. Ibid., 470.

60. Fancher and Peoples, *Blade Runner*, accessed 30 March 2019 at https://sfy.ru/transcript/blade_runner_ts.

61. Francis Fukuyama, "Second Thoughts: The Last Man in a Bottle," *National Interest*, Summer 1999, 1.

62. Ibid., 13–14.

63. Ibid., 1–20.

64. Fukuyama, *Our Posthuman Future*, 1.

65. Ibid.

66. Ibid.

67. Ibid.

68. Ibid.

69. George Orwell, *Nineteen Eighty-Four: Text, Sources, Criticism*, ed. Irving Howe (New York: Harcourt Brace Jovanovitch, 1982), 173.

70. Ibid., 179.

71. Ibid., 188–90.

72. Michel Houellebecq, *The Elementary Particles*, tr. Frank Wynne (New York: Vintage, 2000), 262.

73. Ibid., 263.

74. Ibid.

75. Ibid., 263–64.

76. Young, *Black Frankenstein*, 2.

77. Steven B. Smith, "Shelley, Houellebecq, and the Posthuman," lecture delivered at the "Why *Frankenstein* Matters at 200: Rethinking the Human through the Arts and Sciences" conference, University of Notre Dame Global Gateway, Rome, Italy, 4 July 2018.

78. Sandel, *The Case Against Perfection* [Kindle Edition], location 5.

79. Ibid., locations 326, 355.

80. Ibid., locations 336, 566.

81. Ibid., locations 336, 684.

82. Ibid., ch. 3.

83. Ibid., i.e., locations 166–67, 372.

84. Maureen Orth, "Unholy Communion," *Vanity Fair*, August 2002, accessed 19 April 2019 at https://www.vanityfair.com/news/2002/08/orth200208; Anemona Hartocollis, "Couple Who Tortured 12 Children in Their California Home Are Sentenced to Life," *New York Times*, 19 April 2019, accessed 19 April 2019 at https://www.nytimes.com/2019/04/19/us/turpin-family.html.

85. Sandel, *The Case Against Perfection*, location 41.

86. Ibid., locations 761–62.

87. Ibid., location 763.

88. Ibid., location 761.

89. Shelley, *Frankenstein: Second Norton Critical Edition*, 121.

90. Wollstonecraft, *A Vindication of the Rights of Woman*, in *Works*, vol. 5, 221–22.

91. Ibid., 221.

92. Shelley, *Frankenstein: Second Norton Critical Edition*, 120.

93. Ibid., 33.

94. Ibid., 35.

95. Sandel, *The Case Against Perfection*, locations 201, 205, 334, 605, 670. Chapter 5 is titled "Mastery and Gift."

96. Ibid., location 584.

97. Ibid., locations 336, 335.

98. Charles Taylor, *Modern Social Imaginaries* (Durham, NC: Duke University Press, 2004), 147, 158.

99. Eileen Hunt Botting, *Family Feuds: Wollstonecraft, Burke, and Rousseau on the Transformation of the Family* (Albany, NY: SUNY Press, 2006), 1.

100. Botting, *Mary Shelley and the Rights of the Child*, ch. 2.

101. Tim Adams, "For Me England Is a Mythical Place," *Guardian*, 19 February 2005, accessed 10 April 2019 at https://www.theguardian.com/books/2005/feb/20/fiction.kazuoishiguro.

102. "Interview: Kazuo Ishiguro," *Lightspeed Magazine* 63 (August 2015), accessed 10 April 2019 at http://www.lightspeedmagazine.com/nonfiction/interview-kazuo-ishiguro/.

103. Kazuo Ishiguro, *Never Let Me Go* (New York: Vintage, 2005), 3.

104. Ibid., 263.

105. Ibid., 264.

106. Ibid., 286.

107. Plato, *Republic*, bk. VII, 515c, in *The Collected Dialogues of Plato*, ed. Edith Hamilton and Huntington Cairns (Princeton, NJ: Princeton University Press, 1989), 748.

108. Chuang-tzu, *The Inner Chapters*, tr. A. C. Graham (London: Unwin, 1989), 61.

109. René Descartes, "First Meditation," in *Discourse on Method and Meditations*, tr. F. E. Sutcliffe (London: Penguin, 1968), 100.

110. Blaise Pascal, *Pensées de M. Pascal sur la religion, et sur quelques autres sujets, qui ont esté trouvées après sa mort parmy ses papiers [publiées avec une préface par Étienne Perier]* (Paris: G. Desprez, 1670), pt. III, sec. 270.

111. Baudrillard, *Simulacra and Simulation*, 125.

112. Bostrom, "Are You Living in a Computer Simulation?"

113. Ibid., 10.

114. Ibid., 14.

115. Ibid., 1; Brian Feldman, "The Matrix: Philosopher Nick Bostrom on Whether We Live in a Simulation," *Vulture*, 6 February 2019, accessed 25 April 2019 at https://www.vulture.com/2019/02/nick-bostrom-on-whether-we-live-in-a-matrix-simulation.html.

116. Freud, *Civilization and Its Discontents*, 52.

117. Shelley, *The Last Man*, 181.

118. Bainbridge, "Transavatars," 99.

119. Dick, *Do Androids Dream of Electric Sheep?* 125.

120. Ibid., 123.

121. Ibid.

122. Ibid., 124.

123. Ibid., 123.

124. Fancher and Peoples, final script for *Blade Runner*.

125. Timothy Morton, ed., *Mary Shelley's Frankenstein: A Sourcebook* (New York: Routledge, 2002), 47.

126. Timothy Morton, "The Oedipal Logic of Environmental Awareness," *Environmental Humanities* 1 (2012), 15; Timothy Morton, *The Ecological Thought* (Cambridge, MA: Harvard University Press, 2012), 111.

127. Ibid; Scott Collura, "*Blade Runner* Turns 35," *IGN*, 22 June 2017, accessed 10 May 2019 at https://www.ign.com/articles/2017/06/22/blade-runner-turns-35-ridley-scott-discusses-the-films-legacy-deckards-true-nature-and-the-future-of-the-series.

128. Shelley, "Letter to Leigh Hunt, 9–11 September 1823," 378.

129. Dick, *Do Androids Dream of Electric Sheep?* 207.

130. Ibid., 209.

131. Morton, *The Ecological Thought*, 110–12.

132. Dick, *Do Androids Dream of Electric Sheep?* 224.

133. Hampton Fancher and Michael Green, script for *Blade Runner 2049* (2017), accessed 19 April 2019 at https://www.scripts.com/script/blade_runner_2049_4232.

134. Ibid.

135. Spike Jonze, script for *Her* (2011), accessed 19 April 2019 at http://www.screenplaydb.com/film/scripts/her.pdf.

136. Alan Turing, "Intelligent Machinery," in *The Collected Works of A. M. Turing*, ed. D. C. Ince (New York: Elsevier, 1992), 127.

137. Proudfoot, "Turing and Free Will," 307.

138. Turing, "Computing Machinery and Intelligence" (1950), in *The Collected Works of A. M. Turing*, 133.

139. Jonathan W. Bowen, "Alan Turing: The Founder of Computer Science," Gresham College and British Society of the History of Mathematics Conference, lecture delivered 31 October 2013, accessed 20 April 2019 at https://www.gresham.ac.uk/lectures-and-events/alan -turing-the-founder-of-computer-science.

140. Turing, "Intelligent Machinery," in *The Collected Works of A. M. Turing*, 117.

141. Ibid., 117–18.

142. Ibid., 118.

143. Ibid., 120.

144. Chuang-Tzu, *The Inner Chapters*, 61.

145. Andrea Long Chu, "What We Can Learn About Gender from *The Matrix*," *Vulture*, 7 February 2019, accessed 6 May 2019 at https://www.vulture.com/2019/02/what-the-matrix -can-teach-us-about-gender.html.

146. Stryker, "My Words to Victor Frankenstein Above the Village of Chamounix," 238.

147. Ibid.

148. Ibid.

149. Fred Botting, "What *Was* Man . . . ? Reimagining Monstrosity from Humanism to Transhumanism," in *Global Frankenstein*, 302.

150. Winterson, *Frankissstein*, 119.

151. Ibid., 83, 122.

152. Stryker, "My Words to Victor Frankenstein Above the Village of Chamounix," 238.

153. Ibid., 249; Judith Butler, *Bodies That Matter: On the Discursive Limits of "Sex"* (New York: Routledge, 1993), 16.

154. Jolene Zigarovich, "The Trans Legacy of Frankenstein," *Science Fiction Studies* 45:2 (2018), 264.

155. Stryker, "My Words to Victor Frankenstein Above the Village of Chamounix," 245.

156. Ibid.

157. Susan Stryker, "More Words About 'My Words to Victor Frankenstein,'" *GLQ: A Journal of Lesbian and Gay Studies* 25:1 (2019), 42–43.

158. Shelley, *Frankenstein: Second Norton Critical Edition*, 92.

159. Judith Butler, "Animating Autobiography: Barbara Johnson and Mary Shelley's Monster," in *A Life with Mary Shelley*, ed. Barbara Johnson (Stanford, CA: Stanford University Press, 2014), 50.

160. Ibid.

161. Ursula K. Le Guin, "The Ones Who Walk Away from Omelas," in *The Wind's Twelve Quarters* (New York: Harper and Row, 1975), 277.

162. Ibid., 281.

163. Ibid.

164. Ibid., 284.

165. "Twenty Questions with Ursula K. Le Guin," *Times Literary Supplement*, 24 March 2017, accessed 10 May 2019 at https://www.the-tls.co.uk/articles/public/twenty-questions-ur sula-le-guin/.

166. Ursula K. Le Guin, "The Stories We Agree to Tell," *New York Times Book Review*, 12 March 1995, 6.

167. Peter Swirski, *Of Literature and Knowledge: Explorations in Narrative Thought Experiments, Evolution, and Game Theory* (London: Routledge, 2007), 96, 108–9.

168. Botting, *Mary Shelley and the Rights of the Child*, 133–39. Zoe Beenstock points out that Carlyle subsequently used the metaphor of the monster to critique utilitarianism in *Sartor Resartus* (1834). See Beenstock, *The Politics of Romanticism: The Social Contract and Literature* (Edinburgh: Edinburgh University Press, 2016), 186–87.

169. 조미정 Mi Jeong Cho, "호모 나랜스의 창조적 수사학:: 『프랑켄슈타인』 과「오멜라스를 떠나는 사람들」을 중심으로" (Homo Narran's "Creative Rhetoric": *Frankenstein* and "The Ones Who Walk Away from Omelas") 영어영문학연구 55:2 (2013), 303.

170. Shelley, *Frankenstein: Second Norton Critical Edition*, 101.

171. Octavia Butler, *Bloodchild and Other Stories* (New York: Open Road Media, 2012), 30.

172. Ibid.

173. Reyes, "Promethean Myths of the Twenty-First Century: Contemporary *Frankenstein* Film Adaptations and the Rise of the Viral Zombie," 175.

174. Butler, "Bloodchild," 26.

175. Ibid.

176. Walter Benn Michaels, *The Shape of the Signifier: 1967 to the End of History* (Princeton, NJ: Princeton University Press, 2004), 31–37.

177. Alyson Buckman, "What Good Is All This to Black People? Octavia Butler's Reconstruction of Corporeality," *Femspec* 4:2 (June 2003), 201.

178. SF scholarship has taken as a given that Shelley influenced Butler due to the thematic overlaps in their oeuvres. For example, see Jane Donawerth, *Frankenstein's Daughters: Women Writing Science Fiction* (Syracuse, NY: Syracuse University Press, 1997); Theodora Goss and John Paul Riquelme, "From Superhuman to Posthuman: The Gothic Technological Imaginary in Mary Shelley's 'Frankenstein' and Octavia Butler's 'Xenogenesis,'" *Modern Fiction Studies* 53:3 (Fall 2007), 434–59; Gregory Hampton, *Changing Bodies in the Fiction of Octavia Butler: Slaves, Aliens, and Vampires* (Lanham, MD: Lexington Books, 2010), ch. 6. More work remains to be done in Butler's archive of papers at the Huntington Library to supply the direct textual evidence of her engagement with Shelley.

179. Maria Aline Ferreira, "Symbiotic Bodies and Evolutionary Tropes in the Work of Octavia Butler," *Science Fiction Studies* 37:3 (November 2010), 401–15.

180. Elyce Rae Helford, "'Would You Really Rather Die Than Bear My Young?': The Construction of Gender, Race, and Species in Octavia E. Butler's 'Bloodchild,'" *African American Review* 28:2 (Summer 1994), 259–71.

181. David Archard, *Sexual Consent* (Boulder, CO: Westview, 1998), 98–147.

182. Monika Nalepa, *Skeletons in the Closet: Transitional Justice in Post-Communist Europe* (Cambridge, UK: Cambridge University Press, 2010), 113.

183. Donna J. Haraway, *Simians, Cyborgs, and Women: The Reinvention of Nature* (New York: Routledge, 1991), 226.

184. Donna J. Haraway, *Staying with the Trouble: Making Kin in the Chthulucene* (Durham, NC: Duke University Press, 2016), 2, 7.

185. Ibid., ch. 8, 140.

186. Ibid., 143.

187. Ibid., 4.

188. Susan Stryker and Talia M. Bettcher, "Introduction: Trans/Feminisms," *TSQ: Transgender Studies Quarterly* 3 (2016), 11.

189. Ibid.

190. Ibid.

191. Sandel, *The Case Against Perfection*, locations 201, 205, 334, 605, 670.

192. Kirksey, "Queer Love, Gender-Bending Bacteria, and Life After the Anthropocene." See also Eben Kirksey, "Hope," in *Living Lexicon for the Environmental Humanities, Environmental Humanities* 5 (2014), 295–300.

193. McQueen, *Political Realism in Apocalyptic Times*, 195.

194. Miranda Seymour, *Mary Shelley* (New York: Grove, 2000), 49, 61, 72; Shelley, "Letter to Maria Gisborne," 30 October–17 November 1834, in *The Letters of Mary Wollstonecraft Shelley*, vol. 2, 215.

195. Seymour, *Mary Shelley*, 70; W. Stafford, "Dissenting Religion Translated into Politics: Godwin's 'Political Justice,'" *History of Political Thought* 1:2 (Summer 1980), 290.

196. Seymour, *Mary Shelley*, 75.

197. Stafford, "Dissenting Religion Translated into Politics," 298.

198. Charles G. Herbermann et al., eds., "Origen," *The Catholic Encyclopedia* (New York: Encyclopedia Press, 1911), vol. XI, 310.

199. Ibid.

200. Shelley, "Introduction to *Frankenstein* (1831)," 165.

201. Ibid., 166.

202. Fiona Sampson, *In Search of Mary Shelley: The Girl Who Wrote Frankenstein* (New York: Pegasus, 2018), 70.

203. Shelley, *Journals*, vol. 1, 9, note 4; vol. 2, 479.

204. Ibid., 241, 241, note 1.

205. Ibid., 102–3.

206. Shelley, *Journals*, vol. 2, 488.

207. Ibid.

208. Ibid.

209. Ibid.

210. Ibid.

211. Carl Huffman, "Pythagoras," in *The Stanford Encyclopedia of Philosophy* (Winter 2018 ed.), ed. Edward N. Zalta, accessed 1 June 2019 at https://plato.stanford.edu/archives/win2018/entries/pythagoras/.

212. Jonathan Barnes, *Method and Metaphysics: Essays in Ancient Philosophy I* (Oxford: Oxford University Press, 2011), 413–14.

213. Marshall Fishwick, *Cicero, Classicism, and Popular Culture* (New York: Routledge, 2013), 110; Ingo Gildenhard, "Of Cicero's Plato: Fictions, Forms, Foundations," in *Aristotle, Plato, and Pythagoreanism in the First Century BC: New Directions for Philosophy*, ed. Malcolm Schofield (Cambridge, UK: Cambridge University Press, 2013), 245–46.

214. Michael Schiefelbein, "'The Lessons of True Religion': Mary Shelley's Tribute to Catholicism in 'Valperga,'" *Religion & Literature* 30:2 (Summer 1998), 59–79.

215. Ibid.

216. Shelley, *Journals*, vol. 2, 490.

217. Ibid., 491.

218. Ibid., 493.

219. Ibid., 490, 491, 493.

220. Ibid., 491.

221. Ibid., 490–91.

222. P. Shelley, "The Triumph of Life," 481–500, lines 472–76.

223. Barbara Taylor reads Wollstonecraft's ethics and political philosophy as rooted in the eighteenth-century British Protestant tradition of rational Christian Dissent and broadly Christian-Platonic in its concern with realizing a higher love and understanding oriented toward God, in *Mary Wollstonecraft and the Feminist Imagination* (Cambridge: Cambridge University Press, 2003). Sylvana Tomaselli finds evidence of the influence of the *Symposium* in Wollstonecraft's social and political thought in "Reflections on Inequality, Respect, and Love in the Political Writings of Mary Wollstonecraft," in *The Social and Political Philosophy of Mary Wollstonecraft*, ed. Sandrine Bergès and Alan M. S. J. Coffee (Oxford: Oxford University Press, 2016), 14–33.

224. David K. O'Connor, *The Symposium of Plato: The Shelley Translation*, tr. Percy B. Shelley (Notre Dame, IN: St. Augustine's Press, 2002), xii–xiv.

225. Ibid., 53.

226. Ibid.

227. Ibid.

228. Ibid., xl.

229. Wollstonecraft, *A Vindication of the Rights of Woman*, in *Works*, vol. 5, 115.

230. Ibid.

231. Ibid., 46, 115.

232. Spinoza, *A Theologico-Political Treatise*, ch. iv, 60.

233. Ibid., ch. xiv, 185.

234. Ibid.

235. Shelley, *Journals*, vol. 2, 494.

236. Seymour, *Mary Shelley*, 323.

237. Shelley, *Journals*, vol. 2, 472.

238. Ibid., 502–3.

239. Gordon, *Romantic Outlaws*, ch. 35, note 30.

240. Shelley, "To Jane Williams Hogg," 28 August 1827, in *The Letters of Mary Wollstonecraft Shelley*, vol. 1, 573.

241. Seymour, *Mary Shelley*, 375–76.

242. Sampson, *In Search of Mary Shelley*, 230.

243. "Gender fluid," *Oxford English Dictionary Online*, accessed 31 May 2019 at oed.com; Richard Bourke, "Revising the Cambridge School: Republicanism Revisited," *Political Theory* 46:3 (June 2018), 468.

244. Shelley, *Journals*, vol. 2, 573.

245. Ibid., 487.

246. Betty T. Bennett, *Mary Diana Dods: A Gentleman and a Scholar* (Baltimore: Johns Hopkins University Press, 1994).

247. Geraldine Friedman, "Pseudonymity, Passing, and Queer Biography: The Case of Mary Diana Dods," *Romanticism on the Net* 23 (August 2001), accessed 31 May 2019 at https://www.erudit.org/en/journals/ron/2001-n23-ron435/005985ar/.

248. Seymour, *Mary Shelley*, 391.

249. Bennett, *Mary Diana Dods*, 228, 256.

250. Shelley, *The Last Man*, 339–40.

251. Ibid., 340.

252. Ibid., 339.

253. Ibid.

254. Ibid., 341.

255. Ibid.

256. Ibid., 410.

257. Ibid., 410–11.

258. Middleton, *Shelley and His Writings*, xviii; Spinoza, *A Theologico-Political Treatise*, 19; Spinoza, *Tractatus theologico-politicus continens dissertationes aliquot, quibus ostenditur libertatem*, 7.

259. Lionel Verney adopts his niece Clara after his sister Perdita commits suicide in the wake of the death of her husband Lord Raymond (an avatar for Lord Byron) from the plague. Only then does Clara become Verney's "daughter," as Morton D. Paley describes the child in his "Introduction" to *The Last Man*, xv. See also Shelley, *The Last Man*, 215–16.

260. Shelley, *The Last Man*, 455.

261. Ibid., 466.

262. Paley, "Introduction," in *The Last Man*, xxi–xxii.

263. Charles E. Robinson, "Mary Shelley and the Roger Dodsworth Hoax," *Keats-Shelley Journal* 24 (1975), 20–28.

264. Shelley, *Journals*, vol. 2, 491.

265. Seymour, *Mary Shelley*, 393.

266. Ibid., 390.

267. Shelley, *Journals*, vol. 2, 508.

268. Ibid.

269. Betty T. Bennett, "Newly Uncovered Letters and Poems by Mary Wollstonecraft Shelley: ('It Was My Birthday and It Pleased Me to Tell the People so -')," *Keats-Shelley Journal* 46 (1997), 72–73; Patrizia di Bello, "Mrs. Birkbeck's Album: The Hand-Written and the Printed in Early Nineteenth-Century Feminine Culture," *19: Interdisciplinary Studies in the Long Nineteenth Century* 1 (2005), 1–36.

270. Shelley, *Journals*, vol. 2, 492.

271. E.g., Andy Mousley, "The Posthuman," in *The Cambridge Companion to Frankenstein*, ed. Andrew Smith (Cambridge, UK: Cambridge University Press, 2016), ch. 11; Botting, *Mary Shelley and the Rights of the Child* (2017), ch. 4; F. Botting, "What *Was* Man? Reimagining Monstrosity from Humanism to Transhumanism," in *Global Frankenstein* (2018).

272. Rosi Braidotti, *The Posthuman* (Cambridge, UK: Polity, 2013), ch. 2; Bennett, *Vibrant Matter*, vii, 2, 5, 22, 118.

273. Braidotti, *The Posthuman*, 192–93.

274. Ibid., 193.

275. Ibid., 192.

276. Ibid., 193.

277. Ibid.

278. B. T. Bennett, "Radical Imaginings: Mary Shelley's 'The Last Man,'" 149.

279. Ibid.

280. Snyder, "Apocalypse and Indeterminacy in Mary Shelley's 'The Last Man,'" 451.

281. Jane Bennett, "A Vitalist Stopover on the Way to a New Materialism," in *New Materialisms: Ontology, Agency, and Politics*, ed. Diana Coole and Samantha Frost (Durham, NC: Duke University Press, 2010), 63.

282. Ibid., 47; Rosi Braidotti, "The Politics of 'Life Itself' and New Ways of Dying," in *New Materialisms*, 207.

283. Bennett, "A Vitalist Stopover," 64.

284. Ibid., 63.

285. Donna J. Haraway, *When Species Meet* (Minneapolis: University of Minnesota Press, 2007), 17.

286. Melissa Lane, *Eco-Republic* (Princeton, NJ: Princeton University Press, 2013), 7.

287. Feder, *Harvester of Hearts*, 37–38.

288. Ibid.

289. Shelley, *Journals*, vol. 2, 448.

Coda

1. David Bromwich, "Wollstonecraft as a Critic of Burke," *Political Theory* 23:4 (1995), 617–34.

2. Mary Wollstonecraft, *A Vindication of the Rights of Men and A Vindication of the Rights of Woman, with Hints*, ed. Sylvana Tomaselli (Cambridge, UK: Cambridge University Press, 1995), 8.

3. Ibid., 64.

4. Ibid., 5.

5. Alexandre Lefebvre, "The Rights of Man and the Care of the Self," *Political Theory*, 44:4 (2016), 518–40, especially 522 and 535. Lefebvre aptly places Wollstonecraft at "the very inception of the human rights tradition" but in a broadly ethical rather than a narrowly juridical sense (535). See also Alexandre Lefebvre, *Human Rights and the Care of the Self* (Durham, NC: Duke University Press, 2018).

6. Thomas Taylor, *A Vindication of the Rights of Brutes* (London, 1792), 77–78; Botting, *Wollstonecraft, Mill, and Women's Human Rights*, 46.

7. Edmund Burke, *A Vindication of Natural Society*, in *Pre-Revolutionary Writings*, ed. Ian Harris (Cambridge, UK: Cambridge University Press, 1993), 28.

8. Richard Bourke, *Empire and Revolution: The Political Life of Edmund Burke* (Princeton, NJ: Princeton University Press, 2015), 695.

9. Godwin, *An Enquiry Concerning Political Justice* (ed. Philp), 514, note 2 (bk. I, ch. 2 in 1793 edition); David Bromwich, *The Intellectual Life of Edmund Burke: From the Sublime and Beautiful to American Independence* (Cambridge, MA: Harvard University Press, 2014), 44.

10. Mellor, *Mary Shelley*, 148–49.

11. In 1815, Shelley read Burke's *Vindication* and, most likely, his *Reflections* (what she described in her journal his "account of civil society"). See Shelley, *Journals*, vol. 1, 91. For Shelley's critical reception of Burke in *The Last Man*, see Jennifer J. Jones, "The Art of Redundancy: Sublime Fiction and Mary Shelley's *The Last Man*," *Keats-Shelley Review* 29:1 (2015), 25–41. See also Washington, *Romantic Revelations*, ch. 2.

12. Singer, "All Animals Are Equal," in *Animal Rights and Human Obligations*, 148–62.

13. E.g., Robyn Eckersly, *The Green State: Rethinking Democracy and Sovereignty* (Cambridge, MA: MIT Press, 2004), 137; Floridi, *The Ethics of Information*, ch. 4; David J. Gunkel, "A Vindication of the Rights of Machines," 122. For a thorough overview of the abundant literature in political theory on the ascription of theories of justice and rights to nonhumans, see Sharon R. Krause, "Politics Beyond Persons: Political Theory and the Non-human," *Political Theory*, 5 June 2016, 1–13, accessed 10 June 2019 at https://doi.org/10.1177/0090591716651516.

14. Torrance, "Ethics and Consciousness in Artificial Agents"; Anderson, "The Unacceptability of Asimov's Three Laws of Robotics as a Basis for Machine Ethics"; Gunkel, "A Vindication of the Rights of Machines," 122.

15. Haraway, "A Cyborg Manifesto: Science, Technology, and Socialist-Feminism in the Late Twentieth Century"; Torrance, "Super-Intelligence and (Super-) Consciousness," 484–85; Frost, *Biocultural Creatures: Toward a New Theory of the Human*, 147–59.

16. "South Korea Creates Ethical Code for Righteous Robots," *New Scientist*, 8 March 2007, accessed 5 June 2019 at https://www.newscientist.com/article/dn11334-south-korea-creates-ethical-code-for-righteous-robots/; Paula Boddington, *Toward a Code of Ethics for Artificial Intelligence* (Cham, Switzerland: Springer Nature, 2017), ch. 8.

17. Nuffield Bioethics Council, *Genome Editing and Human Reproduction*, 114, 161.

18. Shelley, *Frankenstein: Second Norton Critical Edition*, 104, 152.

19. Godwin, *Political Justice* (ed. Philip), 133. See also bk. I, ch. 3.

20. John Locke, *Essay Concerning Human Understanding* (London, 1690), bk. II, ch. 1, sec. 2.

21. Karen M. Offen, *European Feminisms: A Political History, 1700–1950* (Stanford, CA: Stanford University Press, 2000), 144–82.

22. Wollstonecraft, *A Vindication of the Rights of Men and A Vindication of the Rights of Woman*, 76, 116.

23. Ibid., 9.

24. Burke, *Reflections*, 135.

25. Stafford, "Dissenting Religion Translated into Politics: Godwin's 'Political Justice.'"

26. Godwin, *Political Justice* (ed. Philp), 133; Wollstonecraft, *A Vindication of the Rights of Men and A Vindication of the Rights of Woman*, 125.

27. Immanuel Kant, "Conjectures on the Beginning of Human History," *Political Writings*, ed. H. S. Reiss and tr. H. B. Nibset (Cambridge, UK: Cambridge University Press, 1991), 226.

28. Jeremy Bentham, *An Introduction to the Principles of Morals and Legislation*, ed. J. Burns and H. Hart (Oxford: Clarendon, 1969), ch. 17; Anderson, "The Unacceptability of Asimov's Three Laws of Robotics as a Basis for Machine Ethics," 288.

29. Eileen Hunt Botting, "Mary Wollstonecraft, Children's Human Rights, and Animal Ethics," in *The Social and Political Philosophy of Mary Wollstonecraft*, ed. Bergès and Coffee, 92–116.

30. Botting, *Wollstonecraft, Mill, and Women's Human Rights*, 92.

31. For a critical analysis of the justification (utilitarian or otherwise) of nonhuman animal sacrifice, see Stefan Dolgert, "Sacrificing Justice: Suffering Animals, the Oresteia, and the Masks of Consent," *Political Theory* 40:3 (2012), 263–89.

32. Morton, *Shelley and the Revolution in Taste*, 130.

33. Shelley, *Journals*, vol. 2, 554.

34. Shelley, *Frankenstein: Second Norton Critical Edition*, 101, 103.

35. Ibid., 103, 152.

36. Ryan, "Mary Shelley's Christian Monster," 153.

37. Shelley, *Frankenstein: Second Norton Critical Edition*, 120.

38. I am indebted to Leif Wenar and Alison McQueen for suggesting the use of the term "risk factor."

39. Russ, *To Write Like a Woman*, 126–27.

40. Gunkel, "A Vindication of the Rights of Machines," 129–30.

41. David J. Gunkel, *Robot Rights* (Cambridge, MA: MIT Press, 2018), 185.

42. Ibid.

43. Burke, *Reflections*, 171. For similarly counterintuitive resourcing of Burke's wardrobe metaphors, see Jeffrey Stout, *Democracy and Tradition* (Princeton, NJ: Princeton University Press, 2004), 34, 224; Emily Dumler-Winckler, "Putting on Virtue Without Putting off Feminists: Mary Wollstonecraft's Religious Moral Imagination," *Journal of Religious Ethics* 43:2 (2015), 342–67.

44. Perhaps due to (what Planinc calls) his "anthropological doubt" about who counted as a rights holder, H. G. Wells used (what Bell calls) a similarly "pragmatic" approach to the defense of universal human rights during the 1940s. See Planinc, "Catching Up with Wells: The Political Theory of H. G. Wells's Science Fiction," 648, and Duncan Bell, "Pragmatism and Prophecy: H. G. Wells and the Metaphysics of Socialism," *American Political Science Review* 112:2 (2018), 416.

45. Nussbaum, *Women and Human Development*, 83.

46. Nussbaum, *Frontiers of Justice*, 362.

47. Nussbaum, *Frontiers of Justice*; Martha C. Nussbaum and Rosalind Dixon, "Children's Rights and a Capability Approach: The Question of Special Priority," in *Public Law and Legal Theory Working Papers* (Chicago: University of Chicago Law School, 2012), accessed 20 June 2019 at https://chicagounbound.uchicago.edu/cgi/viewcontent.cgi?article=1056&context=public_law_and_legal_theory.

48. Ibid.

49. Torrance, "Super-Intelligence and (Super-)Consciousness," 483–50; Planinc, "Catching Up with Wells: The Political Theory of H. G. Wells's Science Fiction," 648.

50. Habermas, *The Future of Human Nature*, location 2254.

51. See Liao's *The Right to Be Loved* (2015) for an extended justification of the *passive* formulation of the child's right "to be" loved from birth, particularly by parents. In ch. 3 of *Mary Shelley and the Rights of the Child* (2017), I argued from a feminist perspective for an *active* formulation of this basic right to love, in relational terms of "sharing" love between parent and child. This is necessary to avoid either the implicit or explicit (1) instrumentalization of the provider of love (often a woman or other socially vulnerable maternal figure) or (2) denial of the moral status of the child as a rights-bearer due to its youth, dependency, or relative lack of agency or reason compared to the caregiver.

52. Nussbaum, *Women and Human Development*, 81.

53. Burke, *Reflections*, 171.

54. David O. Brink, "Some Forms and Limits of Consequentialism," in *The Oxford Handbook of Ethical Theory*, ed. David Copp (Oxford: Oxford University Press, 2007), 291; Leif

Wenar, "Rights," in *The Stanford Encyclopedia of Philosophy* (Fall 2015 Edition), ed. Edward N. Zalta, accessed 5 June 2019 at https://plato.stanford.edu/archives/fall2015/entries/rights/.

55. Burke, *Reflections*, 171.

56. Ibid.

57. Ibid.

58. Ibid.

59. I thank Leif Wenar and Alison McQueen for the wording on this point.

60. United Nations, "Universal Declaration of Human Rights" (1948), Article 16; United Nations, *Convention on the Rights of the Child* (1989), preamble.

61. Hall, *Speak*, 16.

62. Anderson, "The Unacceptability of Asimov's Three Laws of Robotics as a Basis for Machine Ethics," 285.

63. Ibid.

64. Ibid.

65. Winterson, *Frankissstein*, 51.

66. Ibid.

67. Kate Devlin, *Turned On: Science, Sex, and Robots* (London: Bloomsbury Sigma, 2019), especially chs. 7 and 9 [Kindle Edition].

68. Ibid., location 3340.

69. Winterson, *Frankissstein*, 263.

70. Devlin, *Turned On*, location 3313.

71. Ibid., locations 3313, 3339.

72. I thank Leif Wenar and Alison McQueen for unpacking the two meanings of this Wollstonecraftian-Shelleyan principle of justice.

73. Mason and Ekman, *Babies of Technology*, 187.

74. Ibid.

75. Shelley, *Frankenstein: Second Norton Critical Edition*, 104.

76. Archard, *Sexual Consent*, 98–147.

77. Wollstonecraft, *Original Stories from Real Life*, in *Works*, vol. 4, 368.

78. Ibid.

79. Burke, *Reflections*, 121.

80. Botting, *Family Feuds*, 109. Margaret Kohn and Daniel I. O'Neill exposed that Burke did not critique chattel slavery as consistently or as strongly as he condemned British colonial exploitation in India in "A Tale of Two Indias: Burke and Mill on Empire and Slavery in the West Indies and America," *Political Theory* 34:2 (2006), 192–228.

81. Shelley, *Frankenstein: Second Norton Critical Edition*, 160.

82. I thank mathematician and computer scientist Matthew Schoenbauer for this point.

83. Habermas, *The Future of Human Nature*, location 763.

84. Čapek, *R.U.R.*, xvi.

85. Turing, "Intelligent Machinery," in *The Collected Works of A. M. Turing*, 117–18.

86. McEwan, *Machines Like Me and People Like You*, 328.

87. Ibid., 329.

88. Joshua Foa Dienstag, "Blade Runner's Humanism: Cinema and Representation," *Contemporary Political Theory* 14 (2015), 106–7, 109, 115.

89. Ibid., 114.

INDEX

Aaltola, Mika, 11
abortion, 25, 26, 83–86, 101, 105
Agar, Nicholas, 123, 125
AGI. *See* artificial general intelligence
AI. *See* artificial intelligence
Aldiss, Brian, 4, 6, 16
Alexa (robot), 56
algorithms, 52–53, 57
Alisa (conversational agent), 61
Amazing Stories (magazine), 6
Anderson, Susan Leigh, 192
ANI. *See* artificial narrow intelligence
animals. *See* nonhuman beings
Anthropocene, 4, 15, 53, 152, 178–79
anthropocentrism, 184
anthropomorphism, 68, 69–70
apocalypse, meaning of, 54, 166
Apocalyptic literature: defined, 3; examples
    of, 16; myths and misconceptions
    addressed by, 19–20; optimism in, 77–82,
    174; post-Shelley examples of, 77–81; real-
    ist, 15–16; Shelley's works as models for, 12,
    15–17, 25, 39–44, 48, 50–55, 63–64; threat
    and promise of AI in, 55–77. *See also* Last
    Man narratives
apocatastasis, 27, 166–69, 180
aporia, 17
Aquinas, Thomas, 177
Archard, David, 164
ART. *See* assisted reproductive technology
artificial general intelligence (AGI), 20, 58, 65,
    67–74, 76, 183
artificial intelligence (AI): capacity of, for
    good or ill, 60, 64, 73–75; construction of,
    57–58, 61; Creature likened to, 55–56, 61–
    63, 74; developmental growth of, 67–69,
    71–72, 198; earliest forms of, 32; effective-
    ness of, 62; ethical/moral issues concern-
    ing, 24, 56–57, 155–56, 198; fears

concerning, 1, 16–17, 19–21, 55–56, 58–60,
    65–77; *Frankenstein* and, 1, 32; humans as,
    63, 76–77, 152, 156; love in relation to,
    26–27; promise of, 25; sexbots equipped
    with, 194; and the singularity, 58–60, 65;
    Turing test for, 65–66
artificial life: ethical/moral issues concerning,
    1, 4–5, 25, 90–91, 141, 185–99; human rela-
    tionship to, 129–30, 185–99; love and, 26–
    27, 130, 139–48; rights and duties associated
    with, 1, 28–29, 182, 185–99. *See also* genetic
    engineering/biotechnology; nonhuman
    beings; robots
artificial narrow intelligence (ANI), 58
Asilomar Conference on Beneficial AI, 183
Asimov, Isaac, 192; "Bicentennial Man,"
    192–93
assisted reproductive technology (ART),
    91–102
Atwood, Margaret: *MaddAddam*, 78–79;
    MaddAddam trilogy, 16, 78, 81; *Oryx and
    Crake*, 16, 77–78; *Speeches for Dr. Franken-
    stein*, 77–78; *The Year of the Flood*, 78–79
Augustine (saint), 15
automatons, 31, 35
autonomy, 26, 114–25

Babbage, Charles, 62
babybots, 192
Bacon, Francis, 6
Balderston, John, 36
Barritt, Jason, 93
Baudrillard, Jean, 149
Baxter, Isabella, 168
Beenstock, Zoe, 241n168
Bell, Duncan, 32
Bennett, Betty T., 173, 178
Bennett, Jane, 76–77, 177, 178–79

63, 84–85, 151, 170, 180; "The Choice," 169–70, 172, 175, 177; death of, 180; "The Death of Love," 176–77; family legacy of, 180; gender identification of, 172–74; intellectual milieu of, 9–10, 12, 47; "Journal of Sorrow," 49, 131, 133–34, 138, 151, 168–73, 175–76, 180; journals of, 54, 81, 132–33, 172, 176, 185; losses suffered by, 25, 43, 45, 49, 53–55, 63–64, 84–85, 132, 135–36, 150–51, 180; and love/lovelessness, 26–27, 29, 151; memorialization of her husband by, 33, 207; relationship with Percy, 10, 12, 32–33, 45, 51, 53, 54, 85, 133–34, 136–37, 150–51, 168, 169–70, 172–73, 176, 177, 180, 185; smallpox contracted by, 176; and Spinoza, 26, 60, 132, 134, 136–37, 168, 169, 171–72, 174–75, 179, 235n1, 236n6; upbringing of, 9, 54, 167–68; *Valperga*, 132, 169. See also *Frankenstein* (Shelley); *The Last Man* (Shelley)

Shelley, Percy Bysshe: death of, 10, 26, 33, 53, 63, 132, 136–37, 150–51, 170; friendship with Byron, 10, 47, 49; Mary's relationship with, 10, 12, 45, 51, 53, 54, 85, 133–34, 136–37, 150–51, 168, 169–70, 172–73, 176, 177, 180, 185; and Mary's writing, 32–33, 87; "The Mask of Anarchy," 51; metaphysics of, 132, 135; *The Necessity of Atheism*, 132; as poet, 10, 50, 51, 166; "Queen Mab," 135, 137; translations by, 60, 132, 134, 171, 175, 235n1, 236n6; "The Triumph of Life," 135, 170–71; *A Vindication of Natural Diet*, 28, 185

Shelley, Percy Florence, 48, 81, 125, 170, 176, 179–80

Shelley, William, 63, 64, 177

Shiel, M. P., *The Purple Cloud*, 41–42

Singer, Peter, 182, 186

singularity, 25, 58–60, 65, 74–77, 123, 197

slavery, immorality of, 194–97

Smith, Steven B., 141

Snyder, Robert Lance, 178

Somerville College, Oxford, England, 23

South Korea, 183

Spark, Muriel, 45

Spinoza, Baruch, 26, 132–37, 168, 169, 171–72, 174–75, 177, 179, 180; *Ethics*, 134, 135, 137; *Theologico-Political Treatise*, 60, 131, 132, 171–72, 235n1, 236n6

Sterling, Bruce, "Swarm," 16, 72–73

Stevenson, Robert Louis, *The Strange Case of Dr. Jekyll and Mr. Hyde*, 17, 20, 26, 87, 125–27

Stoics, 169

storytelling, generative power of, 17, 51, 53, 80, 138, 148, 175

Strang, Hilary, 45

Stryker, Susan, 27, 157–59, 165–66; "My Words to Victor Frankenstein Above the Village of Chamounix," 18, 158–59

the sublime, 9, 39–41, 54

superintelligence, 60, 69–75

Suvin, Darko, 6–7, 40, 51

Swift, Jonathan, *Gulliver's Travels*, 31

Taylor, Barbara, 243n223

Taylor, Charles, 146

Taylor, Thomas, *A Vindication of the Rights of Brutes*, 182, 185, 186

techne (art, craft), 10, 25, 27, 32, 127, 129–30, 157, 158, 166

technology. *See* science and technology

Tezuka, Osamu, *Astro Boy/Mighty Atom*, 38

Thacker, Eugene, 14–15

Thoreau, Henry David, 177

three-person IVF, 91–96, 101, 109, 111, 118–20

Toho Studios, 38

Tomaselli, Sylvana, 243n223

totalitarianism, 139–40

trans/feminism, 27, 165–66

transgender, 157–59, 173

Trelawny, Edward, 33

Truman, Harry, 37

Turing, Alan, 16, 27, 65–67, 68, 71, 154–56, 198

Turing machines, 192

Turing test, 65–66, 155

Turner, J. M. W., 54–55; *The Lake, Petworth: Sunset, Fighting Bucks*, 55

UDHGHR. *See* Universal Declaration on the Human Genome and Human Rights

Universal Declaration of Human Rights (UDHR), 101, 108, 115

Universal Declaration on the Human Genome and Human Rights (UDHGHR), 26, 28, 102, 112, 183, 187

Universal Studios, 36

University of Nebraska Press, 43

utilitarianism, 160, 184–85